At last the guns had fallen silent, and like millions of Europeans these citizens of Cologne in 1946 resume the daily business of peacetime living in what remains of their beloved city. For most, the routine was simple and harsh: a constant search for warm clothing, shelter and the next meal.

THE AFTERMATH: EUROPE

THE POLITICAL FACE OF POSTWAR EUROPE

The redrawn map of Europe that emerged from World War II reflected one immense change: the westward spread of Communism through both the expansion of the Soviet Union and the imposition of Communist governments upon lands the Red Army had occupied.

   With modest adjustments, Western Europe reverted to its prewar boundaries. Not so the East. From Finland to Rumania, the Soviet border was extended westward. On the Baltic Sea, Estonia, Latvia and Lithuania no longer existed, except as provincial "republics" within the U.S.S.R. East Prussia—a former German territory just southwest of Lithuania—was divided between Poland and the Soviet Union. Poland, which had been carved in two by Germany and the Soviet Union at the beginning of the War, found itself gaining territory in the West from Germany while losing land in the East to the U.S.S.R. And truncated Germany was divided, east from west, into two eventually independent states. All nations in Eastern Europe except Greece and Turkey had Communist governments dominated by the Soviet Union. Yugoslavia and Albania, although not occupied by the Red Army, had established their own Communist regimes.

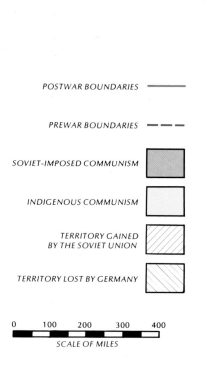

POSTWAR BOUNDARIES ———

PREWAR BOUNDARIES - - - -

SOVIET-IMPOSED COMMUNISM

INDIGENOUS COMMUNISM

TERRITORY GAINED
BY THE SOVIET UNION

TERRITORY LOST BY GERMANY

0   100   200   300   400

SCALE OF MILES

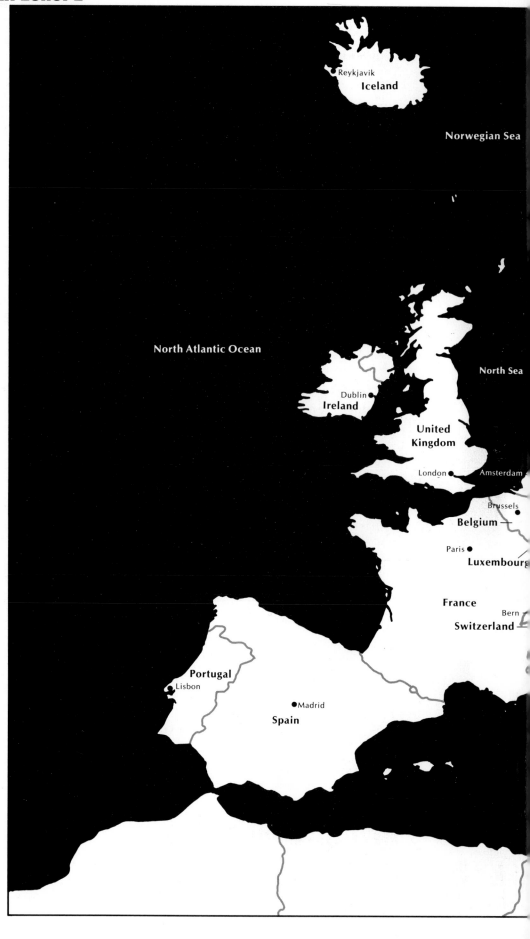

Norway

Sweden

Finland

Oslo

Stockholm

Helsinki

Denmark

Estonia

Baltic Sea

Latvia

Lithuania

Copenhagen

Netherlands

Berlin

Warsaw

East Germany

Bonn

Poland

West
Germany

Prague

Czechoslovakia

Vienna

Austria

Budapest

Hungary

Rumania

Belgrade

Bucharest

Yugoslavia

Italy

Bulgaria

Sofia

Rome

Adriatic Sea

Albania

Tirana

Greece

Aegean
Sea

Athens

Mediterranean Sea

Moscow

Soviet Union

Black Sea

Ankara

Turkey

This volume is one of a series that chronicles in full
the events of the Second World War. Previous books in
the series include:

WORLD WAR II · TIME-LIFE BOOKS · ALEXANDRIA, VIRGINIA

BY DOUGLAS BOTTING
AND THE EDITORS OF TIME-LIFE BOOKS

THE AFTERMATH: EUROPE

Time-Life Books Inc.
is a wholly owned subsidiary of
TIME INCORPORATED

Founder: Henry R. Luce 1898-1967

Editor-in-Chief: Henry Anatole Grunwald
President: J. Richard Munro
Chairman of the Board: Ralph P. Davidson
Executive Vice President: Clifford J. Grum
Editorial Director: Ralph Graves
Group Vice President, Books: Joan D. Manley
Vice Chairman: Arthur Temple

TIME-LIFE BOOKS INC.

Editor: George Constable
Executive Editor: George Daniels
Director of Design: Louis Klein
Board of Editors: Dale M. Brown, Thomas H. Flaherty Jr.,
Thomas A. Lewis, Martin Mann, Robert G. Mason,
John Paul Porter, Gerry Schremp, Gerald Simons,
Rosalind Stubenberg, Kit van Tulleken
Director of Administration: David L. Harrison
Director of Research: Carolyn L. Sackett
Director of Photography: John Conrad Weiser

President: Reginald K. Brack Jr.
Executive Vice Presidents: John Steven Maxwell,
David J. Walsh
Vice Presidents: George Artandi, Stephen L. Bair,
Peter G. Barnes, Nicholas Benton, John L. Canova,
Beatrice T. Dobie, James L. Mercer, Paul R. Stewart

WORLD WAR II

Editor: Thomas H. Flaherty Jr.
Designer: Van W. Carney
Chief Researcher: Philip Brandt George

Editorial Staff for *The Aftermath: Europe*
Associate Editors: Marion F. Briggs,
Peggy Sawyer Seagrave (pictures)
Text Editors: Richard D. Kovar, Paul N. Mathless,
Robert Menaker, Richard Murphy
Staff Writer: Donald Davison Cantlay
Researchers: Loretta Britten, Scarlet Cheng,
Ann Dusel Corson, Sara Mark, Jane A. Martin, Trudy
W. Pearson, Paula York-Soderlund
Copy Coordinators: Ann Bartunek, Elizabeth Graham,
Barbara F. Quarmby
Art Assistant: Mikio Togashi
Picture Coordinator: Renée DeSandies
Editorial Assistant: Myrna E. Traylor

Editorial Operations
Design: Arnold C. Holeywell (assistant director);
Anne B. Landry (art coordinator); James J. Cox (quality control)
Research: Jane Edwin (assistant director),
Louise D. Forstall
Copy Room: Susan Galloway Goldberg (director),
Celia Beattie
Production: Feliciano Madrid (director),
Gordon E. Buck, Peter Inchauteguiz

Correspondents: Elisabeth Kraemer (Bonn); Margot
Hapgood, Dorothy Bacon (London); Miriam Hsia,
Lucy T. Voulgaris (New York); Maria Vincenza Aloisi,
Josephine du Brusle (Paris); Ann Natanson (Rome).
Valuable assistance was also provided by: Wibo
van de Linde (Amsterdam); Mirka Gondicas
(Athens); Pavle Svabic (Belgrade); Helga Kohl,
Angelika Lemmer (Bonn); Ellen Keir (Boston);
Sandy Jacobi, Lois Lorimer (Copenhagen); Lance
Keyworth (Helsinki); Lesley Coleman, Millicent
Trowbridge (London); Christina Lieberman, Cornelis
Verwaal (New York); Mimi Murphy, June Taboroff,
Ann Wise (Rome); Traudl Lessing (Vienna); Bogdan
Turek (Warsaw).

The Author: Born in London, DOUGLAS BOTTING was educated at Oxford University, served as an infantry subaltern in the King's African Rifles and became an ardent traveler. While he was still an undergraduate, he wrote his first book—about a summer's journey through Arabia. He has written since about places as disparate as Amazonia and Arctic Siberia and is the author of six previous volumes for Time-Life Books. Among them: *The U-Boats* in The Seafarers series, *The Giant Airships* in The Epic of Flight series, *Wilderness Europe* in The World's Wild Places series and *The Second Front* in the World War II series.

The Consultants: COLONEL JOHN R. ELTING, USA (Ret.), served as an intelligence officer with the 8th Armored Division in Germany and Czechoslovakia during World War II and its aftermath. A former Associate Professor of Military Art and Engineering at West Point, he was associate editor of *The West Point Atlas of American Wars*, co-author of *Military History and Atlas of the Napoleonic Wars* and is the author of *The Battle of Bunker's Hill, The Battles of Saratoga, American Army Life* and—for the Time-Life Books World War II series—*Battles for Scandinavia*.

MICHAEL M. HARRISON is Associate Professor of European Studies at The Johns Hopkins University School of Advanced International Studies in Washington, D.C. An expert on French politics and U.S.-European relations, he is the author of *The Reluctant Ally: France and Atlantic Security* and co-author of *A Socialist France and Western Security*.

Library of Congress Cataloguing in Publication Data

Botting, Douglas.
      The aftermath: Europe.

      (World War II; 38)
      Bibliography: p.
      Includes index.
      1. Europe—History—1945-   . 2. Reconstruction
(1939-1951)—Europe. 3. Economic assistance, American—
Europe. 4. World politics—1945-   .
I. Time-Life Books.   II. Title.   III. Series.
D1053.B68   1983   940.55   82-10324
ISBN 0-8094-3411-3
ISBN 0-8094-3412-1 (lib. bdg.)
ISBN 0-8094-3413-X (retail ed.)

For information about any Time-Life book, please write:

Reader Information
Time-Life Books
541 North Fairbanks Court
Chicago, Illinois 60611

CHAPTERS

1: New Rivalries amid the Ashes   20

2: Germany's Bitter Harvest   36

3: Armies of Wanderers   80

4: Politics of Confrontation   128

5: An Iron Curtain Descends   164

PICTURE ESSAYS

The Price of War   8

Justice at Nuremberg   64

Voyage into Adversity   100

A Nation Born in Violence   112

The Miracle of Recovery   152

The Berlin Airlift   192

Bibliography   204

Picture Credits   205

Acknowledgments   205

Index   206

CONTENTS

THE PRICE OF WAR

AN ALL-CONSUMING STRUGGLE TO SURVIVE

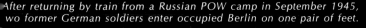

After returning by train from a Russian POW camp in September 1945, two former German soldiers enter occupied Berlin on one pair of feet.

Shortly after the shooting stopped in Europe, a British journalist in Bavaria interviewed two refugees from the Sudetenland. "I asked where they were going," she wrote, "and they shrugged their shoulders. I asked them how they lived and they said on anyone who would feed them." The relentless, elementary problems that plagued those postwar drifters—ethnic Germans displaced from their homes in Czechoslovakia—were shared by millions of others across the prostrate Continent. The struggle to survive in peace had become as total and consuming as the War itself had been.

Fields in much of Europe lay fallow or were sown only with mines, or—with no one to tend them—grew crops destined to rot unharvested. Battered transportation systems could not distribute what was grown, and the consequence was almost universal hunger. In Germany, people competed with the flies for edible garbage at GI dumps. In Paris, a visitor wrote, "you don't throw apple cores in the wastebasket. You fling them out the window" to be eaten. In England, one village raffled off a single fresh egg.

People everywhere were cold. They combed bombed-out buildings for kindling and stripped city parks of trees. Britons scavenged for bits of coal like gleaners cleaning up the remains of a bad harvest. Swiss families were allotted only enough winter fuel to warm one room for a month.

Some cities, like Warsaw, had to be rebuilt virtually from scratch, and celebrated their rebirth with a touching series of very basic "firsts"—the first bridge, the first street light, the first running water. The builders themselves lived in cellars and earthen dugouts or claimed squatters' rights to damaged and deserted buildings.

For some, the peace brought joyous reunion with lost loved ones. But for most, the struggle went unrelieved. British writer Angela Thirkell underscored her bitterness by writing always of the "blight" or "outbreak" of peace, as though it were a disease—or a new kind of war. Another observer reported a general hardening of hearts. "All the affections and loyalties of ordinary human relationships have fled," he wrote, "before the struggle for mere survival."

Eyes raised to the hand that cups the bowl, two barefooted young Sicilians hungrily watch a man finish a meal of gruel in a Palermo doorway.

Bone-weary, a mother and her daughter share a wicker trunk in a Frankfurt am Main railway station, waiting for a train that seemed never to come.

Heading westward on foot, a former Wehrmacht soldier carries his entire collection of worldly goods through the streets of Berlin in October of 1945.

Warmed by a soldier's castoff coat, a homeless orphan comforts her sister on a street in Rome.

Weeping with joy, a Viennese mother is reunited with

her son in 1945. Thousands of such meetings took place across Europe as soldiers and prisoners returned home, and refugees sought out their lost families.

Outside her makeshift home in Nuremberg, a woman boils a meal of potatoes, apples and greens.

In bombed-out Hamburg, a couple in 1945 hang their

laundry to dry in an apartment without walls. Hamburg's already desperate housing shortage was made worse by a flood of German refugees from the East.

1

Two views of victory in Moscow
Cracks in the Grand Alliance
A continent in ruins
The collaborators' harsh fate
Redrawing the map of Europe
Britain's grim cycle of shortages and austerity
Vengeance and disillusionment in France
A road built by hand in Yugoslavia
A purge of nationalists in Poland
A 200-year-old blueprint for restoring Warsaw
Prodigious recovery in a "hero city"
Electricity to light the holes in the rubble

From Moscow on the evening of May 9, 1945, Josef Stalin broadcast a message to his people. "Comrades, fellow countrymen and women," he began, "the great day of victory over Germany has come. Fascist Germany has been forced to her knees by the Red Army and the troops of our Allies. The great patriotic war has ended with our complete victory. Glory to our heroic Red Army and our great people. Eternal glory to the heroes who fell in the struggle."

As Stalin spoke, one of the heroes he extolled so fulsomely was observing Moscow's celebration of V-E Day from an unpleasant vantage point. Former Artillery Captain Alexander Solzhenitsyn watched the skies over the city light up from the tiny deep-set window at the top of his cell in the infamous Lubyanka Prison. "Above the muzzle of our window, and from all the other cells of the Lubyanka, and from all the windows of all the Moscow prisons," he wrote, "we, too, former prisoners of war and former frontline soldiers, watched the Moscow heavens, patterned with fireworks and crisscrossed by the beams of searchlights. That victory was not for us."

Solzhenitsyn, who would become a world-renowned writer, had been thrown into prison for criticizing Stalin in a personal letter to a friend. He was one of millions of innocent Russians, among tens of millions of European survivors of World War II, whose suffering, on this day of peace, was far from over. Whole populations celebrated V-E Day as the end of Nazi tyranny and the dawn, they believed, of a new era of hope and peace. But in the months and years that immediately followed the War, hope gave way to a new despair. Wholesale displacement, mass starvation and outright slaughter of helpless people continued, and peace itself became uncertain as the nations that fought the War groped inexorably toward new alliances and new rivalries.

Even in the flush of victory, the Allies felt a resurgence of the tensions that had been the hallmark of prewar Europe. To survive Hitler's onslaught, and then destroy him, nations had been thrust together in alliances that required them to distort grossly their real feelings; they were nations that were at least philosophical rivals, if not deadly enemies. The state of things in the early years of the War was perhaps best symbolized by Winston Churchill's remark in mid-June of 1941 about what Britain would do if Germany invaded the Soviet Union: "I have only one purpose, the destruction

NEW RIVALRIES AMID THE ASHES

of Hitler, and my life is much simplified thereby," he said. "If Hitler invaded Hell I would make at least a favorable reference to the Devil in the House of Commons."

That Churchill intended a perfect parallel to be drawn between the Devil and Stalin is beyond proof, but likely. Certainly the defeat of Nazi Germany meant that the straightforward course of Allied leaders was fast ending. Ethnic and ideological antagonisms, Europe's eternal plague, were rapidly tearing apart the expedient wartime association between the Western Allies and the Soviet Union.

Even the German surrender was an occasion for bad feelings among the victors. The Nazi government, headed by Grand Admiral Karl Dönitz after Hitler killed himself on April 30, had approached the Anglo-American high command on May 3 to seek armistice terms. Told that the only terms were immediate unconditional surrender, the Germans proceeded to stall as long as they could to allow hundreds of thousands of their troops and civilian refugees on the collapsing Russian front to escape westward. To a man, they feared the Russians more than the British, French and Americans. When the Western Allies threatened to close their lines to Wehrmacht troops fleeing from the east, the Germans capitulated at Rheims, France, on May 7, with the surrender to take effect the next day.

From its inception, the surrender was fraught with conflict. The suspicious Russians saw the event as a cleverly disguised Anglo-American separate peace with Germany. They believed, and justly so, that German troops in the East would refuse to surrender to the Russians and would fight desperately to reach American or British lines before giving up. And the Soviets were driven to paranoia when they learned that the surrender document was a substitute. It was not the one painstakingly drafted by a joint Allied commission, but an ad hoc version hastily written on the orders of General Dwight D. Eisenhower's chief of staff, Lieut. General Walter Bedell Smith. Smith had filed the "authorized" version weeks earlier and had forgotten about it in the last-minute commotion of dealing with the Germans.

Stalin flatly rejected the May 8 surrender. At his insistence, the signing had to be reenacted, this time with the original document, on May 9 in Soviet-controlled Berlin. That date thus became V-E Day for the Russians, even though most of the world had already exploded in jubilation over Germany's capitulation the previous day. The difference between the two V-E Days, which was never resolved, symbolized the growing number of disagreements—both trivial and momentous—that were shaping postwar Europe.

Europe in mid-1945 could ill afford the burden of a new international rivalry. From London to the gates of Moscow, from Norway to Greece, much of the Continent lay in ruins. Its people were numbed by death on a scale that beggared ordinary grief. Tens of millions of the survivors were malnourished, diseased and homeless or far from home. The Continent's industry and transportation systems were devastated, its agricultural output greatly reduced, its political structures collapsed.

At least 33 million Europeans are known to have lost their lives in World War II. The killing, especially of civilians, was so widespread and casual that estimates of the toll vary by many millions, and some historians have stated that well over 40 million people perished. By comparison, the 1914-1918 "Great War" had caused a combined total of about 20 million military and civilian deaths.

Eastern Europe had suffered the most, in both actual numbers and percentage of the population killed. Partly in combat, but mostly through cold-blooded murder, Poland lost more than one sixth of its prewar population of 32 million. In the month of fighting that began on September 1, 1939, an estimated 66,000 Polish soldiers and airmen lost their lives; in the subsequent five and one half years under the Germans and the Russians, almost 5.5 million Polish civilians perished. The Soviet Union lost 20 million soldiers and civilians—more than 10 per cent of its prewar population.

Germany, too, paid a dreadful human price for the devastation it unleashed. More than three million fighting men were killed, as well as immense numbers of civilians. In addition, approximately two million German-speaking civilians died during forced emigrations from the Slavic lands of Eastern Europe after the War.

The worst casualty ratios of all were suffered by ethnic groups who fell victim to Nazi racial-extermination programs. The gypsies of Eastern Europe were virtually wiped out—nearly half a million died in German death camps. Almost six million Jews died out of about 10 million estimated to have been living in Europe before the War. Most

Jewish victims were from Poland and the Soviet Union.

Compared with these awful figures, casualties among the Western Allies were relatively low in proportion to their populations. France, Great Britain, the United States and Canada each lost 1 per cent or less of its population. Italy, the Germans' major European Axis partner, also suffered a casualty rate of less than 1 per cent. The death toll of soldiers and civilians in these countries nevertheless added up to more than 1.5 million.

The sharp increase in the World War II casualty rate over that of World War I was due partly to the wider extent of the conflict, which ebbed and flowed across virtually the entire European continent, involving the populations of 21 major nations. It was due, as well, to more deadly weaponry, especially in the air. But in the main the responsibility lay with a shift both unconscious and deliberate in the moral view of those who waged the War—on both sides, though in different degrees. Civilian casualties in World War II not only

were considered acceptable—as, for example, in air raids on cities—they were even encouraged as an important means of achieving strategic military objectives. For the Germans, this attitude also included using terror as a means of subjugating occupied countries.

In the War and its aftermath, between 50 and 60 million European civilians—about 10 per cent of the total population—were uprooted from their homes under unimaginably cruel conditions. Many of these displaced persons were murdered by hostile soldiers or civilians; many died of starvation and exposure. For years after V-E Day, bedraggled bands of DPs wandered throughout the Continent or wasted away in camps set up for them by the Allies.

The material destruction of the Continent was as thorough as the human slaughter. Few cities of any size escaped damage from air raids, shellfire, street fighting and the scorched-earth tactics of the Russians and the Germans. Of the belligerent capitals, Warsaw and Berlin were nearly wiped out. To many Poles it seemed that Warsaw might never be rebuilt; in Berlin people were estimating that it might take 15 years just to clear the rubble. Capitals such as London, Vienna, Budapest and Belgrade were severely damaged, as were scores of other large cities that provided Europe with much of its culture and character.

Whole towns and villages were utterly destroyed. The Czechoslovakian town of Lidice, like Warsaw, met its doom not in the toils of war but on direct orders from Hitler that it be systematically razed. Wiener Neustadt, near Vienna, became a ghost town, emerging from Allied air raids and street battles with only 18 houses intact and the population reduced from 45,000 to 860.

Nor was the War's physical devastation limited to housing, industry and transportation. Such material losses could always be made good, at whatever cost in human effort and however long it might take. An even greater tragedy was that much of the heritage of European civilization had been wiped out as well.

A large part of what was missing—paintings, sculptures, goldwork and jewelry—had been looted by the Nazis and eventually would be returned. But much more had perished in the blast and fire of battle. Centuries-old buildings, architectural masterpieces of the Middle Ages and the Renaissance, whole quarters of ancient towns lay in ruin along

A poster that was typical of many adorning the walls of France in 1945 proclaims victory over Germany, with the Nazi eagle plummeting in flames. But the War had reduced victor and vanquished to almost the same plight: Two million of France's homes had been damaged or destroyed, half its trains wrecked and many of its key bridges ruined.

with their precious contents—especially great libraries, historic archives and irreplaceable records. The medieval center of Rouen, the waterfront of the old harbor at Marseilles, the 13th Century Medici Palace at Pisa, the Roman temple at Pula, the Royal Palace and 14th Century Market Square of Warsaw, the Royal Palace in Budapest, the 15th Century kremlin walls of Novgorod, the palace of Peter the Great at Peterhof, the 16th Century Abbey of Monte Cassino in Italy, the Frauenkirche in Dresden, the cathedrals of Exeter and Coventry—a forlorn guidebook could be, and was, compiled of such losses.

The ravages in the material substance of Europe's cultural legacy were matched by the spiritual injury sustained by European men and women—a psychological shock that produced a wasteland of the mind. The trauma of Nazi occupation and terrorism, of saturation bombing and the holocaust of the death camps produced a general paralysis of Europe's human resources. The War's horrors left a sickness not only in the minds of individuals but in the collective psyche of Europe as well, requiring a radical reassessment of the nature of the society that would be reshaped in the ruins. Pessimists doubted whether Europe had a future at all, whether the ruins would ever be rebuilt. Others, as a consequence of the worst excesses of the War, were plagued by a guilt about the nature of man. Many others believed that neither mankind, nor Europeans in general, but the German people in particular—or at least a large Nazi element—were alone to blame.

After the euphoria of liberation and victory, doubt, guilt and a desire for revenge and expiation had taken over. "What is Europe now?" Winston Churchill wrote in 1947. "A rubble heap, a charnel house, a breeding ground of pestilence and hate."

The purge of Nazi collaborators began with each country's liberation and continued after V-E Day. Its intensity varied from nation to nation. In Austria, which had been deeply permeated with Nazism, only 9,000 cases were brought to court and 35 death sentences were carried out. Italy was similarly lenient with its Fascists, although there were cases of individuals administering their own private justice. In Belgium, on the other hand, 634,000 cases were examined, 87,000 people brought to trial and sentences passed on 77,000. In the Netherlands, 150,000 to 200,000 suspected collaborators were detained after the War and 66,000 of them were tried and convicted.

The issue was bitterest in France. Summary wartime executions of accused collaborators by the Resistance gave way after V-E Day to a more systematic and legal purge. French courts sentenced 120,000 collaborators and executed 2,000, notable among them Pierre Laval, the Premier of the Vichy government. Marshal Henri Philippe Pétain, the elderly Vichy head of state, received a death sentence that was commuted to life imprisonment out of respect for his service to the country in World War I.

Other notorious targets of official retribution included the Norwegian Nazi, Vidkun Quisling, who was executed in October 1945. Drazha Mihailovich, the Yugoslavian royalist guerrilla leader, was hunted down as a collaborator, found living in a hole in the ground like an animal, and tried and executed by the Tito government in 1946. William Joyce, the American-born British turncoat known to the British as Lord Haw-Haw for his propaganda broadcasts from Berlin during the War, was brought to London, tried and executed in 1946. John Amery, the son of a top British government official and leader of the Legion of St. George—an SS auxiliary unit of defected Allied prisoners of war in Germany—was hanged for high treason in late 1945. The American poet Ezra Pound was indicted for treason by the U.S. government for pro-Fascist broadcasts he made on Italian radio during the War and was held for 12 years after the War in an American mental hospital.

Such official acts of vengeance were no doubt inevitable—in many cases they were the workings of simple justice, and in all cases they were a necessary outlet for the pent-up grief and rage of the surviving victims of the Nazi plague. But once the guilty heads had rolled and the passions of retribution were spent, Europeans had to face the future—a seemingly hopeless one in a continent half graveyard and half junkyard.

Above the lunar landscape of craters and rubble, the specter of famine and pestilence hovered everywhere. Huge areas of arable land had been devastated by flooding and by scorched-earth tactics. Severe shortages of labor, machinery, fertilizer, seed and livestock combined with a summer drought in 1945 to produce a disastrous grain harvest—al-

most 50 per cent lower than the prewar average outside the Soviet Union. Throughout Europe there was strict food rationing—100 million people were eating 1,500 calories a day or less. Clothes, shoes, medicines and fuel were in desperately short supply.

The cost of the War was one thing, the effect of it another. Europe had changed irreversibly. Its political map was redrawn. Some nations had ceased to exist: Lithuania, Latvia and Estonia never reemerged from their forcible 1940 absorption into the Soviet Union. East Prussia was divided between Poland and Russia. Other nations reappeared: Austria, Poland, Czechoslovakia and Yugoslavia were restored as separate states.

The boundaries of many countries were irrevocably altered, mainly as a result of substantial bites taken out of them by the Soviet Union. The Soviets took parts of Finland, Czechoslovakia and Rumania and held on to an immense stretch of eastern Poland that the Red Army had occupied in connivance with the Nazis in September 1939. By way of compensation, Poland was given a huge part of the ancient eastern provinces of Germany as far west as the line formed by the Oder and Neisse Rivers. The change in effect moved the nation of Poland 200 miles westward and was to lead to immense suffering for the German occupants of these territories, who were, as a result, forcibly displaced.

Other European territorial changes, though less drastic, echoed centuries of violent dispute between ethnic groups and nations over the ownership of pieces of land. France retook Alsace and Lorraine from Germany. Yugoslavia took from Italy a section of Venezia Giulia, the area surrounding the contested port of Trieste—once, like Yugoslavia, part of the Austro-Hungarian Empire. Bulgaria was allowed to keep the southern part of the Dobruja region that had been regained from Rumania in 1940; Czechoslovakia gained northern borderlands from Hungary.

Germany itself was placed under the military rule of its conquerors, the United States, Britain, France and the Soviet Union. The Americans and the French occupied southern Germany; the British had the Ruhr, northern Germany and part of the Rhineland; the Russians settled into the eastern provinces. In accordance with wartime agreements, the British and American armies withdrew from advanced posi-

Two years after the War, Hamburg still presents a panorama of almost unrelieved destruction. But the row of Quonset huts in the foreground— supplied by the Allies—provided temporary shelter for some of the city's homeless, and the stacks of wooden barrels adjacent to the huts stored such food as sauerkraut, potatoes and salted herring.

tions they held at the time of the German surrender and allowed the Russians to move up to the agreed zonal frontiers—to the intense dismay of those Germans who thus fell under Soviet domination. Austria was similarly divided among the victors, although it was regarded more as a liberated than an occupied state.

The end of the War brought about changes not only in the political map of Europe but also in the balance of power among the nations. The old order of 1939 had been swept aside. In effect the War in Europe had been a civil war among nation-states, the culmination of hundreds of years of savage internecine violence. It had been resolved by the intervention of two outside powers—the United States and the Soviet Union. Victory elevated both of those nations to the status of superpowers—the United States by virtue of its wealth and its newfound sense of global power, the Soviet Union by virtue of its conquests.

Although the United States had suffered nearly 300,000 casualties abroad, it had sustained no damage at home. Even as its war production had grown to gigantic size, its domestic economy had been maintained at a high level. The United States was thus the only nation in the world with the capital resources to solve the problems of postwar reconstruction, and this capital could be used to direct the form that the reconstruction would take and to extend American influence abroad. Moreover, America had the atomic bomb, which was regarded as the supreme weapon.

The Soviets, with their armies on the Elbe in the west and the Danube in the south, had made immense territorial gains. Victory saw the Russians deep in the heart of Europe, suzerain over Eastern Europe and much of the Balkans. The Red Army was ensconced in Poland, Czechoslovakia, Hungary, Rumania, Bulgaria and eastern Germany; Communist governments controlled Yugoslavia and Albania; and the political process of turning all these countries into satellite states had already begun.

Western Europe, on the other hand, was entirely dependent on the United States for survival. The leading European powers of 1939 were leaders no more. Germany was smashed, Italy defeated, France morally exhausted and politically divided, and Britain, though a victor, was as debilitated as its erstwhile rivals—though tragically it was unable to perceive the fact. The fate of Europe was to be decided in Moscow and Washington, and the old European balance of power, which had once been the fulcrum of the world, was replaced by a global balance between the United States and the Soviet Union.

Among most of the nations of Europe, the end of the War brought a profound alteration in political orientation. Throughout the Continent there was a marked swing to the left, a massive rejection of the oligarchic order of the privileged and powerful—whether respectable conservatism or aggressive fascism—that had led the world into the abyss. Communism was stronger than it had ever been—not merely in Soviet-occupied Eastern Europe, but in Western European countries as well.

The Communists had been extremely active in resistance to Nazi and Fascist occupation, and in several countries—Italy, France, Belgium, Bulgaria, Czechoslovakia, Greece, Yugoslavia and Albania—they emerged from the War with considerable popular support. In Brussels, Rome and Paris, Communists staged massive demonstrations in an attempt

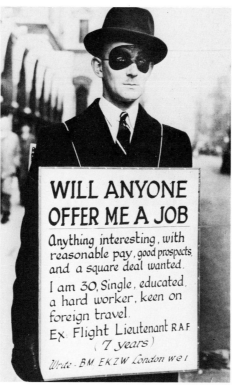

Returning veterans on both sides frequently had trouble finding jobs in Europe's collapsed economy. At far left, a German wears a sign that declares "I am looking for work. I will do anything!" At left, a chagrined RAF pilot, hiding his identity behind a mask, advertises for work in the streets of London.

to disrupt economic recovery. In Greece they waged civil war to win control of the country. Only in the Soviet Union was there a dramatic return to conservatism. Stalin tightened his grip on the reins of totalitarian power by purging a number of victorious generals who had become too popular and opinionated at the front and party politicians who had grown too liberal in the laxer climate at home.

It was against this background of ruin, uncertainty and change that the administrators of the newly liberated nations and the Anglo-American military governments and relief agencies had to operate. The destructiveness of the conflict had been so general that there was little to choose from between the winners and the losers. The Soviet Union's agricultural output was far below that of the last peacetime year of czarist Russia 32 years earlier, its industrial performance much less than that of 1940.

For Great Britain, the hollowness of victory was starkly epitomized in a column in *The Saturday Evening Post*. The British author, reporting to American readers from London three years after the end of the War, used the entire column to beg, in effect, for food packages from the United States, making it clear that once-mighty Britain was reduced to the mendicancy normally associated with the starving millions of China. Well-meaning donations of a variety of treats, the column said, were less appreciated than the gift of a large container of lard, butter or margarine, followed in order of preference by canned meat, rice and other staples. The writer's poignant conclusion: ''All this may sound a bit cold and calculating, like weighing the warmth of a Christmas card. But it's only because we like food parcels so much that we criticize them a little.''

For a country that a decade earlier had boasted the world's mightiest navy and merchant fleet, that still ruled vast overseas territories and hundreds of millions of people, Britain had indeed taken a fall. The British had fought longer than any other people, and paying for their herculean effort had destroyed the nation's strong prewar position in the international market, forcing the sell-off of overseas assets and leaving Britain deeply in debt—primarily to the United States. German U-boats had sent much of the country's merchant shipping to the bottom, and the Royal Navy was worn out and stretched thin. Britain was still a world power,

with responsibilities to match, and it was a major influence in shaping the postwar world. Yet its government and people urgently needed to reconcile the contradiction between what Britain wanted and what it could afford.

At War's end the British had expected life to become immeasurably better than it had been during the years of danger and sacrifice. And the British working class, like its counterparts on the Continent, was militantly unwilling to go back to the harsh, grinding poverty of life before the War. In July of 1945 Britain voted in a Labor Party government and unseated Winston Churchill as Prime Minister just two months after the culmination of his triumph as war leader.

The new government quickly made sweeping changes that would profoundly and permanently alter the country's social structure. It nationalized the mines, railroads, the Bank of England, gas and electric industries and telecommunications. It created the National Health Service and other programs that together gave British citizens ''cradle-to-grave'' security. And it instituted new and higher taxes to pay for the social expenditures.

With its parliamentary majority based on the support of the trade unions, the new Labor government was not inclined to exhort the British to work harder and more productively than they wished. The working population was exhausted; for years, many had put in countless hours of overtime in mines, factories and fields supporting the war effort. Now, they felt little incentive to increase productivity or continue working the extra hours that Britain's aging, inefficient industries needed to produce goods for export. The economy was caught in a vicious circle: The workers wanted a better standard of living before they would be willing to work harder and increase their output; the country needed more productivity so it could afford to import the goods needed to raise the workers' standard of living.

Particularly galling to most Britons was the absence of decent housing. More then half a million British homes had been destroyed or damaged by German bombs and rockets. The government threw up some temporary shelters and new prefabricated houses, but millions of Britons still lacked proper housing during the bitterly cold winter of 1947.

The motivation of British workers was further depressed by the grim fact that even when their wages increased they could not buy much with the money. Many products of Brit-

A UNITED FRONT AGAINST FUTURE CONFLICTS

In a great London hall on January 10, 1946, Acting President Zuleta Angel, a Colombian, solemnly convened the first general session of the United Nations by quoting from its Charter: "Determined to save succeeding generations from the scourge of war," he said simply, "we have come."

The U.N., like its failed predecessor, the League of Nations, had been conceived in the heat of war as a mechanism for avoiding future wars. President Roosevelt was one of its earliest advocates; Prime Minister Churchill had passionately declared that "Twice in a single generation the catastrophe of world war has fallen upon us. Do we not owe it to ourselves, to our children, to mankind tormented, to make sure that these catastrophes shall not engulf us for the third time?"

Early in 1945, envoys of the Allied governments met in San Francisco and wrote a charter for a United Nations Organization that was subsequently signed by 51 nations. The Charter not only established principles of peaceful coexistence among nations but also promised individuals the right to basic human freedoms.

The U.N. organized itself into six units: the Economic and Social Council to improve world living standards; the Trusteeship Council to protect the interests of those living in trust territories; the International Court of Justice; an administrative Secretariat; and, most visibly, two deliberative bodies, the General Assembly and the Security Council.

The General Assembly gave every nation the chance to be heard on the world stage. The smaller Security Council was empowered to make decisions on matters of international peace and security. It originally had five permanent seats, held by the major wartime Allies (China, France, the U.S.S.R., the United Kingdom and the United States), and six rotating seats filled by nations elected for two-year terms.

However ideally conceived, no world body can be more potent than its sovereign parts allow, and the U.N. proved no exception. Seven votes were needed to pass a resolution in the Security Council, but a single "no" from a permanent member could defeat it. In February 1946, the Soviet Union became the first to use the veto: Because it considered the language weak, it killed a resolution urging the withdrawal of French and British troops from newly independent Syria and Lebanon.

Eventually the diverging interests of the Communist and non-Communist worlds, as well as such volatile issues as independence for Indonesia and the partition of Palestine, ended the U.N.'s honeymoon phase. The Soviets used the veto with demoralizing frequency, and eventually the Western powers adopted it as well.

Nevertheless, the United Nations survived, finding a permanent home in New York City in 1951, and there were those who continued to share President Harry Truman's spirited mandate to the 1945 San Francisco planning conference: "You are to be the architects of a better world. In your hands rests our future."

American delegates (from left to right) Edward Stettinius, James Byrnes, Tom Connally and Eleanor Roosevelt prepare for the opening session of the U.N.

Beneath a newly designed emblem of a world framed by olive branches, the General Assembly of the United Nations convenes in London in 1946.

ish industry—automobiles, for example—were reserved almost entirely for export in an all-out effort to increase foreign currency holdings. The most desirable items simply could not be obtained by Britishers. When in 1948 the new Jaguar XK 120 sports car was unveiled to rave notices at auto shows, frustrated Britons knew they could look but not touch—the vast majority of Jaguar's output for the next several years was destined to be shipped abroad.

Yet despite nonstop grumbling and a rash of costly strikes, the British endured their grim peace with the same spirit of fairness and cooperation they had demonstrated during the War. People who became disenchanted with the Labor government's inability to ease shortages took the good-natured viewpoint of a sign posted in many pubs: "No beer, no ale, no stout. You got 'em in, now you get 'em out."

The black market, which became for a time the main arena of economic activity on the Continent, was much less prevalent in Britain. And the British considered it bad form to use rank or privilege to get around food rationing, which showed no sign of ending. Even Prime Minister Clement Attlee and his wife, attending the 1948 Labor Party Conference in Scarborough, brought along their own little jar of sugar when they came down to the dining room for tea. They had to—whether Prime Minister or dustman, the guest would have no sugar in his tea unless he supplied his own.

In France, as in most countries, the joys of liberation and peace and even the grim elation of vengeance upon col-

laborators could not long sustain the people's mood in the face of the overwhelming problems the country faced. Shortages existed in everything, and the black market was as rife as anywhere in continental Europe.

A rare break in the shortage situation came in December of 1945, when Frenchwomen received their first ration of cigarettes since Marshal Pétain's Vichy regime had made the decision that only men should smoke. Because many Frenchwomen had no interest in smoking under whatever government, they quickly accumulated enough of the popular French brands to cut into the exclusive black market in American cigarettes run by GIs fortunate enough to be stationed in France.

Such delicacies as grapefruit appeared in French shop windows for the first time since 1939—but they cost the equivalent of four days' pay for a blue-collar worker. Fuel shortages and the shutdown of civilian automobile production during the War years meant that taxis were as hard to find as filet mignon. Until mid-1946, to get a taxi ride a Parisian had to be either a woman about to give birth, a seriously ill person or a high government official on top-priority business. Even then, application for the ride had to be made at the local police station.

The average worker's wage was six times as high as before the War, but prices in general were 14 times as high. Only farmers, able to sell their produce on the black market, were better off than before. But Premier Robert Schuman, in

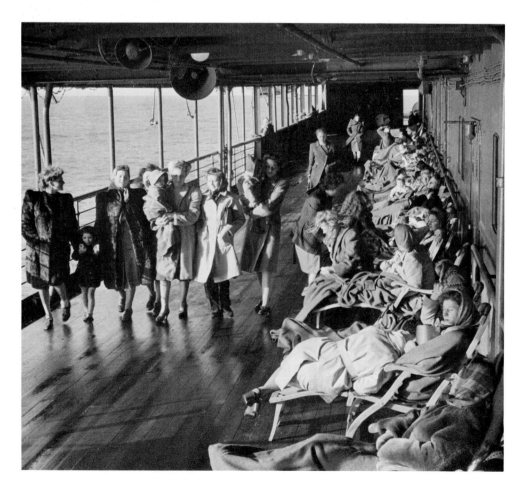

En route to New York in 1946, British war brides and their babies fill the promenade deck of the U.S.S. Argentina. Women who married American servicemen became eligible for citizenship after two years, while their children were declared U.S. citizens at birth.

an effort to undermine both the black market and the fierce inflation in legal food prices, began sending convoys of Army trucks out into the country to buy food directly from farmers, producing a rare occurrence in postwar Europe—an actual, if temporary, drop in food prices.

Perhaps the most telling indicator of France's hardships was a survey taken shortly after the War by the French Institute of Public Opinion. It revealed that a startling 21 per cent of Frenchmen would emigrate if given the chance. This radical change from generations of French insularity and self-satisfaction was borne out by the long lines that formed daily in front of the American, Brazilian, Canadian and Argentine Embassies' visa offices in Paris. For the immediate period after V-E Day, at least, many Frenchmen despaired of ever again having a good life in their own country.

An exception to Europe's privation was Belgium. Blessed by unique circumstances, Belgium enjoyed a faster and greater economic recovery than any other European country involved in the War. Unlike most of the imperial powers, Belgium had been able to retain its major colony, the Congo. Throughout the War—and the government's exile in London—profits piled up in the Congo from copper, uranium and other exports. Moreover, the government had been able to spirit much of the nation's gold reserves to safe havens in the West. Belgium's liberation from the Germans was relatively rapid and painless. Despite being the site of a German counteroffensive late in 1944, and despite suffering

a barrage of rocket hits on Antwerp, Belgium came through with less physical damage and its people suffered less from hunger than most other occupied countries.

The Belgians bucked the high tide of socialism in postwar Europe and avoided setting doctrinaire restrictions on their economy. After a quick and effective financial reform to prevent runaway inflation, the government allowed free importation of consumer goods. Belgian workers, unlike many other Europeans, could buy good things with the money they earned, and they worked hard to earn more.

Shop windows in Brussels were crowded with products—shoes, men's suits, fabrics, typewriters, radios, refrigerators, cigarettes—that simply did not exist anywhere else in Europe, or could only be had for a king's ransom in the back-alley transactions of the black market. Although prices were by no means low, these items and abundant supplies of meat, poultry and other staples were within reach of the industrious Belgians. Indeed, the ready availability of legal consumer goods brought black-market prices down almost to the level of the legitimate market. Black-market operators, dealing largely in goods stolen from U.S. Army supply dumps, were for the Belgians merely a supplementary marketplace rather than the exclusive source of unobtainable items they were throughout the rest of Europe.

Some of the countries embroiled in the War were outside the mainstream of the decisive campaigns, yet suffered grievously anyway. Finland lost a proportion of its population almost as great as that lost by the Soviet Union, and at the end of the War it lost 12 per cent of its territory as well.

The Soviets annexed Karelia, which they had occupied during 1940 and 1941, as well as the Petsamo region in northern Finland. As a result, nearly every Finnish Karelian emigrated into the remaining Finnish territory, increasing its population by 10 per cent almost overnight. The Finns had to allocate housing, allowing one room for every person over 10 years of age. Worse, they had to divide their farms to provide acreage for dispossessed Karelian farmers.

Reparations demanded of the Finns by Russia were the highest, per capita, of any defeated European country. In 1946 alone the Finns sent one fourth of their industrial output—one eighth of their entire national income—to the Soviet Union without recompense. A popular joke in the

Under protest, the mayor of the French town of Brunoy performs the wedding of a French soldier and a pregnant German woman. Beneath his official sash, the mayor wears the concentration-camp uniform he wore during the War as an inmate at Buchenwald.

postwar years concerned the large, lavender-colored Finnish 1,000-mark bank note. Pictured on it was a group of adults and children in varying stages of nakedness facing out to the sea and holding a heavy mooring rope. The scene was based on an altar fresco in a cathedral; Finns wryly said that it represented the future—their people in 1952 gazing at the last shipload of reparations heading for Russia.

Yet for all of their suffering during the War and its aftermath, the Finns enjoyed a unique distinction: Among the defeated nations, theirs was the only one not occupied. Although living under the shadow of Soviet power, and forced by that power to steer a course in foreign policy that was at least friendly to Russia, the Finns retained their independence and their democratic way of life. Communism was but a small and dwindling force in Finland after the War.

The countries of Eastern Europe and the Balkans emerged from the War with a dual burden. Not only did they have to dig themselves out from under the worst of the Continent's devastation and slaughter, they had to do so under the heavy-handed domination of the Red Army and Moscow.

In the immediate postwar period this was as true for Yugoslavia—which would later break free of the Soviet orbit—as for any other Eastern European country. Indeed, one of the most amusing, and revealing, examples of Russia's domination of its neighbors concerned Yugoslavia's Communist Deputy Foreign Minister, Aleš Bebler. At a particularly boring session of the Paris Peace Conference of 1946, Bebler dozed off during the debate on an obscure clause of the Rumanian Peace Treaty that was now being brought to a vote. He awoke to the sound of the chairman's voice calling for him to cast Yugoslavia's vote. "No," he blurted out, and then saw to his dismay that Soviet Foreign Minister Vyacheslav M. Molotov, seated across the table, was frowning severely at him. "I mean yes!" he shouted. To his horror, Molotov looked angrier than ever. "I mean I abstain," he cried, whereupon he was finally rewarded with a chilly smile from his ideological master.

Yugoslavia at this point was as devastated as any country in Europe. Like other Slavic nations, it had suffered the punishing kind of occupation the Nazis dealt out to those they considered subhuman. It had also been ravaged by a vicious, many-sided civil war among Tito's Communist Parti-

sans (the eventual victors), royalist Chetnik guerrillas, a murderous band of Croatian separatist collaborators called Ustashi, and other ethnic separatist groups.

But compared to the rest of Europe, the Yugoslavs had one great advantage—high morale. After three years of increasingly effective guerrilla warfare they had, with the help of the Red Army, won back their own country from the Germans. They had also won Stalin's agreement to withdraw most Russian military units after the liberation. Now, despite the Tito government's currently worshipful attitude toward the Soviet "Fatherland of Socialism," they enjoyed the bracing sense of being in command of their own destiny.

Within a highly regimented Communist social structure, the Yugoslavs began to rebuild with vigor and willingness. Citizens "volunteered" several hours of physical labor a week in addition to their regular work—often without being coerced. One of the projects undertaken was the construction of a road between the capital, Belgrade, and the major Croatian city of Zagreb. The 250-mile-long road had to be built entirely by hand, as there were no machines available.

Once finished, the road would mainly carry vehicles that contributed directly to reconstruction—trucks, tractors and horse-drawn wagons. Private automobiles, rare enough before the War, now were virtually nonexistent. Visitors to Yugoslavia's cities, in fact, were struck by the surrealistic sight of sidewalks teeming with people—and clean streets empty of traffic as far as the eye could see.

Nor were consumer goods in real supply. Shop windows, reflecting the Yugoslavs' zeal to rebuild, showed sparse displays of utilitarian items—plumbing fixtures, electrical equipment, technical books, tools. Such relative luxuries as bed linens and cooking pots would have to wait for better times. Even the popular drink slivovitz was scarce.

Yet the Yugoslavian government was determined to make a good impression on foreigners. While most citizens were barely able to subsist on the official daily food ration, lavish meals were available in the few hotels that were designated for foreign guests. Perceptive foreigners noticed that scraps left over from food eaten in their rooms quickly disappeared. Such pickings were a highly valued fringe benefit for the housekeeping staff.

Poland, of all the countries of Eastern Europe, probably experienced the most painful aftermath to World War II.

Fought over by their two worst enemies, the stubborn, deeply patriotic Poles were predestined to lose the War and to keep on losing after the War, no matter who won.

Liberated from the hated Germans by the hated Russians, Poland had imposed on it a Communist government that was totally at Moscow's disposal. Even before that step was consummated, the Soviets set out to make the country safe for Communism—by hunting down and shooting or deporting to Russian prisons as many officers and men of the non-Communist Polish underground, the Armia Krajowa (Home Army), as they could locate in the chaotic months after the liberation. About one sixth of the 300,000-man Armia Krajowa fell into the hands of the Russians. Many others who would have been liquidated on sight by the Soviet secret police carefully stayed out of the public eye until control of the government was handed over to Polish Communists, at whose hands they were likely to get off with a few years in a Polish prison.

Yet despite the political terror, the numbing scope of the physical devastation, the privation and hunger, the Poles were determined to dig themselves out of the rubble and rebuild. A top priority was to decide on the future, if any, of Warsaw, the nation's capital and its cultural and historic

heart. Adolf Hitler in 1939 had ordered the deliberate destruction of Warsaw; what was not bombed or destroyed by cannon fire was to be dynamited. Over the next five years the Germans, working with meticulous care, destroyed almost 90 per cent of the city's buildings before evacuating before the advancing Red Army. By 1945, more than half of Warsaw's prewar population of 1,300,000 had been killed.

The new government quickly decided that the capital would rise again. A more difficult question was, In what form? Warsaw had boasted a jewel-like medieval "Old City" of gothic palaces, churches and fortifications, as well as a "New City" dating from the 15th Century and replete with neoclassic, baroque and rococo buildings.

Both the Old City and the New City districts had, of course, been leveled by the Germans. The city fathers, though modern-day Communists to a man, made the very Polish decision to forswear the building of an ultramodern neighborhood where the Old City and New City had stood. Instead, they decided to reconstruct these quarters exactly as they had been before the War.

The Poles needed more than personal recollections on which to base the restoration. For this, fortunately, they were able to rely on the works of an 18th Century Italian painter who was born Bernardo Bellotto but was almost universally known by the name of his uncle and mentor, Canaletto. Serving as court artist to King Stanislas II Augustus of Poland, the younger Canaletto had painted architecturally precise views of much of historic Warsaw. These had been spirited away in September 1939 and safely hidden. Now they became a blueprint for a vast restoration project—one that energized the spirit of Warsaw's weary survivors. In the years immediately after the War much of Poland's depleted treasury and virtually all of its craftsmanship were invested in the rebirth of two aged sectors of the beloved capital city.

While reusable stones and bricks were pulled from the dust-choked rubble of the historic districts with loving care,

A trainload of electric cable (left) is prepared for shipment from Finland to the Soviet Union in 1948 as part of the $300 million in reparations the Finns had agreed to pay. The payments stripped Finland, and the Finns joked sourly that the nude figures reproduced on their 1,000-mark note (top) were Finnish citizens watching the last shipment of reparations disappear toward the U.S.S.R.

the rebuilding of the rest of Warsaw proceeded in a manner dictated by practicality. In the Old and New Cities, the task was to make painstakingly perfect replicas of lost buildings. In the rest of the city, it was to throw together walls and a roof wherever and however possible, just as long as the job was done quickly. As soon as any shelter took shape, people moved in.

Spectacular though the Old and New Cities' reconstruction was, it was only part of Warsaw's cultural recovery. Every conceivable landmark of Polish history and culture had been pulverized by the German dynamiters, and Communist or not, the Polish nation gave high priority to restoring two unlikely symbols of the past—its royal palaces and its churches. Unlike the Soviet Union, Poland had not had to oust its monarch in order to install Communism—the last Polish king was toppled in 1795. Thus royal palaces could be and were considered part of Communist Poland's glorious history. And the people's ingrained Catholicism had to be given its due, no matter what orthodox Polish Marxists thought of it. Thus Warsaw and the rest of Poland began the agonizing work of rebuilding, in a style as unregenerately Polish as before the Nazi and Soviet onslaughts.

No country could match the Soviet Union in lives and property lost. With western Russia a vast expanse of wreckage, with almost every family touched by violence and death, and with the standard of living in some places reduced below subsistence, the survivors of Russia's "great patriotic war" had little to look forward to.

The daily life of the average Soviet citizen, harsh and poor as it had been since before the Revolution, became much harder. Two and three years after the German surrender, many thousands of people were living in dugouts— holes scooped out of a hillside, roofed-over shell holes or ditches, cellars of bombed-out buildings.

The reactions of Russians to their ordeal differed in curious ways. Leningrad, the glittering Old World center of czarist grandeur, had set a gruesome standard for civilian suffering in wartime while undergoing a siege of bombing, shelling and blockade that lasted for 872 days. Yet the city actually experienced less physical damage than London. Its nearly one million deaths were caused primarily by starvation and cold.

Perhaps because of the slow and agonizing deterioration Leningrad's people had already experienced, life there after the War was oriented more toward the city's glorious past than toward the future. Recovery work was slow and spiritless. By contrast, Stalingrad, considered before the War a model of modern Communist urban development, suffered incredible destruction. Yet its people set out to rebuild with a cheerful energy. Stalingrad's prewar population of a half million had been reduced to no more than 22,000 when the Germans were finally driven out of the city on January 31, 1943, after five months of bitter fighting. Every industrial building had been destroyed, and 95 per cent of the housing had been wiped out.

By 1947 the population of Stalingrad had climbed to 300,000. Yet for all the cheerfulness of the people, life in the city remained harsh in the extreme. Soviet leaders had decreed a far higher priority for rebuilding industry than for sheltering the people, so although Stalingrad's industrial output had returned to 70 per cent of its prewar level, only

one fifth of the city's residences had been rebuilt. Most of the reconstructed "houses" were dugouts and tiny log huts, and the average person was allotted a living space of three by seven feet, just slightly bigger than a grave. At that, Stalingrad, as a designated "hero city," received a higher priority for new housing than most Soviet cities. And the city fathers had managed some prodigies of recovery—all of Stalingrad was back on electric service, producing the strange sight of spindly wires running into holes and piles of rubble, and little spots of light rising up at night from beneath a wasteland of destruction.

The Russian peasant suffered even more adversity than his comrades in the cities except that he ate slightly better. More than a decade after the collectivization of Soviet agriculture, the peasants still yearned for land of their own, and during the chaos of the War, 2,250,000 of them had quietly appropriated nearly 12 million acres of collective farm land for private cultivation. The Kremlin started taking it back in 1946. And although the peasants were allowed to own tiny pieces of land for their own use and profit, those who managed to accumulate any savings from their enterprise in the face of obstructive regulations lost nine tenths of it in a devaluation of the ruble at the end of 1947.

In 1920 a rural representative to a Communist Party congress had described the lot of the Russian peasant in words that still rang true in the postwar years: "The land belongs to us, the bread to you; the water to us, the fish to you; the forest to us, the timber to you." The government bought the products of the collective farms at a price it set—in 1947, it took potatoes at $5.83 a ton and sold them for as much as $1,430 on the open, or nonrationed, market. Through such economic controls, the Kremlin kept its rural peoples in a state of near-privation.

Economic conditions aside, life on collective farms that had lain helpless in the path of the German and Red Armies was bitterly hard after the War. Some farms had been totally wiped out—every building destroyed. As in the cities, first priority went to rebuilding productive facilities. Barns and silos rose from the ashes while the people were left to their improvised log huts and their holes in the ground. Unlike the cities, many of the collective farms had no electricity.

Farms in the battle zone lost virtually all of their orchards and livestock and now had to rebuild them from scratch.

The stock of chickens or pigs on a farm of several hundred people might be counted on the fingers of one hand. As soon as the numbers crept even a little above these minimums, agricultural officials would impose on the farm a production quota of eggs, hams or other foodstuffs. Sympathy for the sufferings of the people was reserved for public statements and for memorial ceremonies.

Of course the most precious commodity lost by Russia's farms was people—individuals who were deported or shot by the Germans, killed during the fighting, or called to serve in the Red Army. Few of the farms had ample machinery, and most work had to be done manually, yet many desperately needed farmhands were kept in uniform long after the fighting was over.

For in spite of its massive losses of manpower and its overwhelming need to rebuild, the Soviet Union had not disbanded its vast wartime Army. Unlike the American and British Armies, whose soldiers were demanding a speedy return to civilian life, the Red Army had not completed its mission. It occupied vast areas of land containing millions of people who, in the view of Josef Stalin, could not be trusted to be proper neighbors of the Soviet Union if left to their own devices. A joke that went around Moscow after the War defined a fascist as anyone who put the interests of his own country above those of the Soviet Union. But to Stalin that was no joke.

Just as Winston Churchill had to warm up to the Bolsheviks, Stalin had been forced during the War to be uncharacteristically civil and cooperative to the British and the Americans—hated, if respected, opponents who were temporarily his allies. With the need for such behavior now behind him, the Soviet dictator reverted to the suspicion and hostility that marked his prewar attitude toward the West.

Expecting a deterioration in relations with his former allies, and doing much to bring it about, Stalin understood better than they that although war had ended, peace had not come. Instead, a new kind of relationship between the Great Powers was emerging—an adversary relationship perhaps requiring the continued existence of large armies even if there was no fighting.

It had no name yet, this new relationship; it was still formless and beyond precise description. But it could be located. The center of the conflict was Germany.

Demonstrating American GIs march down the Champs Élysées in Paris waving sparklers and chanting "We want to go home" in January of 1946. At that time the United States still had 1.5 million men under arms, while the Soviet Union had five million.

2

Imposing a Carthaginian peace
A pervasive odor of death
A nation surviving on mess-kit scrapings
Morgenthau's punishing plan for Germany
Gathering souvenirs from Hitler's Chancellory
Conflict and compromise at Potsdam
Putting war itself on trial at Nuremberg
The titanic task of rooting out Nazism
An escape route called the Roman Way
Warning to GIs: "Soldiers wise don't fraternize"
The black-market game everyone played
Riding the Nicotine Line and the Calorie Express
A million-dollar appetite for Mickey Mouse
A pledge to return Germany to the Germans

On Tuesday, June 5, 1945, a scant year after Allied armies had launched their climactic assault on Hitler's Fortress Europe, the foremost of the Allied commanders gathered in the devastated capital of Berlin to impose their collective will on the German people. Whisked by Red Army motorcades from Tempelhof airfield to the headquarters compound of Marshal Georgy K. Zhukov in the eastern part of the city came General Dwight D. Eisenhower, Field Marshal Sir Bernard Law Montgomery and General Jean de Lattre de Tassigny, along with the deputies they had designated to be the day-to-day administrators of a Carthaginian peace.

That afternoon they would sign the Declaration on the Assumption of Supreme Authority in Germany by the Allies, a document that spelled out the intentions of the conquerors and the obligations of the conquered. Under its terms, the German people were charged with the unconditional execution of Allied Occupation directives, whose overall purposes would be to eradicate Nazism and punish its perpetrators, to exact reparations for the destruction wrought in Europe, and to ensure that Germany would be left incapable of again disturbing the peace of the world.

Two related proclamations divided Germany into four military occupation zones, one for each of the Allies, in which the individual commanders would wield supreme authority. Berlin, deep within the Soviet zone, would also be divided into four individually garrisoned sectors. There the commanders or their resident deputies would sit as the Allied Control Council for Germany, to prescribe laws and dispose of matters affecting the country as a whole until such time as the four occupying nations decided how and when German self-government should be restored.

For Lieut. General Lucius D. Clay, deputy U.S. military governor under Eisenhower, the drive from Tempelhof was a grim introduction to the city that for the next four years would be his home and his burden. He surveyed the scene with the eyes of an experienced military engineer and government expediter. Clay was no ordinary soldier. Great-grandnephew of the statesman Henry Clay, and the son of a U.S. Senator, as well as an engineering graduate of West Point, Clay was born and bred to public service. Before the War he had been General Douglas MacArthur's chief engineer in the Philippines and had also directed the massive Army and civilian construction project that tamed the Red

GERMANY'S BITTER HARVEST

River in Texas. Then he was posted to Washington, where he coordinated the Allies' vast wartime matériel procurement program, dealing adroitly with industrialists, politicians, diplomats and the military brass. His most recent field assignment had been a hurry-up job clearing the devastated French port of Cherbourg, but not even that had prepared him for the spectacle of Berlin in defeat.

"Wherever we looked we saw desolation," Clay later wrote. "The streets were piled high with debris which left in many places only a narrow one-way passage between high mounds of rubble, and frequent detours had to be made where bridges and viaducts had been destroyed. The Germans seemed weak, cowed and furtive and not yet recovered from the shock of the battle of Berlin. It was like a city of the dead."

What most bothered Ambassador Robert D. Murphy, the Department of State's European troubleshooter and Clay's political adviser, was the smell. "The canals were choked with bodies and refuse," he recorded. "The odor of death was everywhere."

Four weeks had passed since Adolf Hitler's heirs had surrendered unconditionally to the Allied armies converging from east and west, leaving Germany headless and dismembered. Communications among the four Allied commanders had become fractious after the German surrender; only now were they ready to constitute themselves as a central government of occupation.

General Eisenhower, appalled by the political and economic chaos that followed Germany's defeat, was impatient to get the Control Council organized and functioning. Clay and Murphy had come prepared to expedite the process by setting up staff offices in the sector designated for the Americans. The Soviets, however, were not to be rushed, and when the proclamations had been duly signed, Andrei Vyshinsky, Zhukov's political commissar, quickly quashed the Americans' expectations. He reminded the assembled generals that the troops of the Western Allies had penetrated hundreds of miles into previously agreed-upon Soviet areas of occupation while the Red Army was reducing the last-ditch defenses of Berlin, Prague and Vienna. Until all Western troops had withdrawn into their own assigned zones, Vyshinsky decreed that no four-power business could be conducted and no Allied soldiers would be permitted to enter Berlin except as one-day guests—and that included Eisenhower and Clay.

Zhukov was embarrassed by this Moscow-directed political stricture. He had prepared a lavish banquet for his Western guests, but Eisenhower, disappointed and disgusted by the delay, cut his visit short. He gathered his aides and flew back to his permanent headquarters in Frankfurt am Main. There he turned over to General Clay complete responsibility for negotiating Allied entry into Berlin and the procedures for setting up the Control Council. Clay had to make two additional flights to Berlin to haggle with Zhukov over Soviet-U.S. rights and requirements. Early in July, when he was finally able to move his own and Murphy's offices into Berlin, Clay again took stock of his surroundings.

"The city was paralyzed," he reported. "Shortage of fuel had stopped the wheels of industry. Suffering and shock were visible in every face. Police and fire protection had broken down. Almost 3,000 breaks in the water mains were still to be repaired. Motor ambulances were not available and transport of the sick and dead was by handstretcher or by cart. Dead bodies still remained in canals and lakes and were being dug out from under bomb debris."

Gone from Berlin was the hum of a great metropolis; there was only the noise of the grinding gears of an occasional Army truck negotiating the rubble or the growl of a military police jeep patrolling for possible diehard snipers. At night, only the rats inhabited the streets. Berlin was a microcosm of vanquished Germany, a nation in purgatory.

During the next few years, thousands of Germans would starve to death; many would survive only on the scrapings from GI mess kits; others would count themselves lucky to get one hot meal a day in return for working for the Occupation administration at penal wages. Only a few hundred Nazi leaders and war criminals would be tried, and executed or imprisoned. But hundreds of thousands of lesser Nazis would be denied a livelihood and would contribute to Germany's further moral debasement by their dealings at the criminal fringe of the Occupation economy.

Scores of war criminals would disappear abroad or buy themselves new identities at home, while ordinary civil servants, teachers, technicians and businessmen—at least in the American zone—were condemned to expiate their membership in the Nazi Party through exhausting labor on rubble-clearing crews. Not until time had moderated the hatreds of war, and administrators like Clay and Murphy had demonstrated that a pillaged and prostrate Germany was more of a burden than a benefit to war-ravaged Europe, would the economic, social and political restrictions imposed on the Germans in the Western zones be modified.

Clay at first had neither the authority nor the time to do anything positive about the Germans. With the other deputy governors and their staffs, Clay spent his first month in Berlin shaking down the mechanism of the quadripartite Allied Control Council. The Control Council's parts had to be more or less identical, because the commanders had agreed that each nation would take one-month turns chairing sessions scheduled for the 10th, 20th and 30th days of each month. And each procedural step had to be painstakingly worked out until all the delegations were in agreement, as required by what Eisenhower grumpily referred to as "the traditional but obsolete concept that international purposes could be decided only by unanimous action in committee."

As they worked, the planners anxiously awaited the outcome of the summit-level Allied conference on Germany, which was to begin on July 17 in Potsdam, a relatively undamaged town 17 miles southwest of Berlin. The leaders of Britain, the Soviet Union and the United States, it was hoped, would come to an agreement on the broad principles and specific details of four-power rule in Germany.

The Allied Big Three had given only scant attention to the administrative problems their commanders would face in Germany, and differences of national character and perspective already had led to diverse policies in the field. President Roosevelt's approach had been punitive, and most Americans seemed to agree with him. "It is of the utmost importance," wrote F.D.R. in August 1944, "that every person should realize that this time Germany is a defeated nation. The German people as a whole must have it

driven home to them that the whole nation has been engaged in a lawless conspiracy against the decencies of modern civilization." It was this policy that General Eisenhower had tried to follow as Supreme Commander of the Allied Forces in Europe when American, British and French troops under his command overran western Germany.

Prime Minister Churchill had concurred in Roosevelt's view. When the Big Three met at Yalta in February 1945, he declaimed: "Nazi tyranny and Prussian militarism must be absolutely rooted out if Europe and the world are to be spared a third and still more frightful conflict." But the British tended to take a less extreme course than the Americans in the orders they passed to their field commanders. They believed that, once the Nazi leaders had been seized and punished, "good" Germans should be allowed as soon as possible to run their country. British officials saw no reason to punish the nation for Hitler's crimes and they feared that any attempt to do so might recoil on the rest of Europe.

The French, who had not been represented at Yalta, demanded and got—through Churchill—their own zone of occupation in the Saar valley and the Rhineland. They intended to keep the Saar indefinitely and extract from it coal, labor and industrial machinery, which they loosely called reparations. And they demanded half a million German POWs as unpaid laborers to work French fields and mines in restitution for four years of German exploitation.

The Russians felt even more vindictive than the French. They had two abiding obsessions—reparations and security. At Yalta, Stalin had demanded $10 billion in reparations from Germany to pay for the ravages that the German Army had wreaked in Russia—not in cash but in industrial plants and products. His next demand was that German territory east of the Oder and western Neisse Rivers should be ceded to Poland. This would compensate the Poles for the eastern part of their country that had been taken over by the Soviet Union, and it also would have the effect of pushing Germany 200 miles farther away from the original Soviet border it had violated in 1941.

Roosevelt had only vaguely accepted Stalin's first demand "as a basis for discussion," and Churchill had vigorously debated the second. Nevertheless, Stalin proceeded as if both had been granted. As the Red Army rolled through East Prussia and Silesia, it drove the German inhabitants before it and left some of the Reich's richest agriculture and mining lands in the hands of Polish Communist administrators. Brigades of commissars and technicians followed in the Army's wake to dismantle entire German factories and ship them eastward. Their intent was to use the heavy equipment to rebuild shattered industrial cities such as Kiev and Stalingrad, but in practice much of it was left to rust on the trains on which it was moved.

None of this had been agreed to at Yalta, and Churchill bombarded Washington with cables pleading for a joint Anglo-American confrontation with Stalin. But Roosevelt died in April and his successor, Harry Truman, was not ready to confront the Russians over their Occupation policies. He was too busy trying to determine what his own administration's policy should be—and fighting an unfinished war with Japan.

A potential American policy toward postwar Germany had been formulated in a draconian plan, advanced in 1944 by Roosevelt's influential Secretary of the Treasury, Henry Morgenthau Jr. Morgenthau argued that the only way to prevent Germany from going to war yet another time was to level its factories, destroy its mines and make the country forever a pastoral state. The German leaders must be tried and hanged as soon as they were captured and the people reduced to a race of peasants and swineherds living no more than a basic existence off the land.

Truman knew that Roosevelt had at first endorsed the proposal and then quietly pigeonholed it after other members of his Cabinet rejected the policy as too harsh. What Truman did not know was that some of Morgenthau's ideas had been incorporated in a top-secret directive drafted in September 1944 by officials of the Treasury, State and War Departments and sent to General Eisenhower as Joint Chiefs of Staff Order No. 1067.

JCS 1067 specified that Germany was "not to be occupied for the purposes of liberation but as a defeated enemy nation." The country was to be disarmed, decentralized and de-Nazified. Occupation administrators would be "just, but firm and aloof" and fraternization between occupiers and occupied would be "strongly discouraged." Those who had held membership in any of 33 specified Nazi organizations were to be denied employment except as common laborers.

A Dresden couple in their seventies labor patiently in the rubble of their fire-bombed city sorting out reusable bricks and stone. Organized into groups, thousands of Germans devoted their Sundays and whatever free time they had to the massive job of salvaging the cities.

Assistance to German political institutions would be limited to that necessary to prevent civil unrest and disease and to lay the foundation for eventual democratic rule. Administrators would do nothing to revive German economic or financial institutions. Key industries were to be strictly controlled or eliminated. German living standards would not be permitted to rise above those of neighboring nations.

Secretary of War Henry Stimson had argued against the Morgenthau Plan, and now he cautioned Truman against JCS 1067. In a memorandum dated May 16 he wrote:

Early proposals for the treatment of Germany provided for keeping Germany near the margin of hunger as a means of punishment for past misdeeds. I have felt that this was a grave mistake. Punish her war criminals in full measure. Deprive her permanently of her weapons, her General Staff, and perhaps her entire Army. Guard her governmental action until the Nazi-educated generation has passed from the stage—admittedly a long job—but do not deprive her of the means of building up ultimately a contented Germany interested in following nonmilitaristic methods of civilization.

This must necessarily involve some industrialization, for Germany today has approximately 30 million excess population beyond what can be supported by agriculture alone. A solution must be found for their future peaceful existence and it is to the interest of the whole world that they should not be driven by stress of hardship into a nondemocratic and necessarily predatory habit of life.

All of this is a tough problem requiring coordination between the Anglo-American Allies and Russia. Russia will occupy most of the good food lands of Europe while we have the industrial portions. We must find some way of persuading Russia to play ball.

To Truman, this sounded like good advice, and when at last he made up his mind to meet with the Russians and the British, he approved Secretary Stimson's request to come along. When Secretary Morgenthau also insisted on joining the delegation, and threatened to resign if he could not, Truman dismissed him from his Cabinet.

Almost at the last minute, Truman named James F. Byrnes to be his Secretary of State and the principal American negotiator at Potsdam. A colleague of Truman's when both had been in the Senate, Byrnes had later served as a Justice of the Supreme Court and as Roosevelt's Director of War Mobilization. He was a master negotiator, able to formulate compromises out of seemingly irreconcilable conflicts. He had been in effect an assistant President to Roosevelt and had accompanied him to Yalta.

Truman traveled to Europe on the cruiser U.S.S. *Augusta*, and flew to Berlin on Sunday, July 15. The next day, since he was not yet due to greet Stalin and Churchill, the President set out by car for a drive through the city. The stench of burned-out buildings, bombed-out sewers and unburied bodies still prevailed. Even more depressing, Truman wrote home that night, was "the long, never-ending procession of old men, women and children wandering aimlessly, carrying, pushing or pulling what was left of their belongings." In the long run, American treatment of the Germans would be determined by Truman's instinctive sympathy for suffering people, whatever their past crimes, and the like-minded sentiments of men like Byrnes, Clay and Murphy.

Also touring Berlin that day was Prime Minister Churchill. To the people in the street, Churchill's was the better-known face; his cigar was unmistakable. At the Reichstag, where a crowd of Germans and Russian soldiers were bartering on the black market, Churchill got out of his car and climbed slowly up the steps through the crowd, a cigar firmly clenched in his teeth. It was an extraordinary moment. Many of the Germans looked away. Others stared at him with blank faces. At Hitler's Chancellery, the number of people following Churchill's progress grew. "It was frightfully hot, milling about in such a crowd," one of Churchill's companions noted in his diary, "stumbling over the dusty debris with which all the rooms and passages are littered." The Reich Chancellery's interior had been smashed in the last hours of fighting. The floor was strewn with broken glass and chandeliers, a litter of papers, ribbons and Iron Crosses. Hitler's map of the world he had hoped to conquer hung in tatters. His desk had been turned upside down and its marble top broken into hundreds of pieces. (Churchill's party quickly pocketed some of the marble, a few Iron Crosses and a piece of the map as souvenirs.)

A guide led Churchill across the Chancellery garden to the bunker where his mortal enemy had killed himself. They clambered down the concrete stairs by flashlight, breathing the dank, sour air. Three flights down, the water was rising in the lowest rooms. In Eva Braun's room they noticed a vase containing some twigs—a few months before they had been spring blossoms. Churchill could not bear to go farther. Back at the top the guide pointed out the spot where the bodies of Hitler and Eva had been seen burning. Churchill looked for a moment, then turned away in revulsion and walked back to his car without speaking. He was to write later that with the end of the War all hatred of his former enemies had drained from him.

The conference got under way July 17 at the Cecilienhof, a palace in Potsdam. There was no fixed agenda for the meeting, which was intended to take up where the Yalta Conference had left off in February and to continue in peacetime the Grand Alliance that had won the War. But all knew that one of the most important topics must be the administration of occupied Germany. Economic and political principles to guide the Allied Control Council would have to be confirmed, and the knotty question of identifying and allocating German reparations resolved. Hardly less important, in the eyes of the British and American delegations,

was a clarification of the Yalta Declaration on Liberated Europe. The Western Allies interpreted the declaration as providing for broadly based, democratically elected governments throughout the countries of the former Axis empire; in this they had to contend with the Soviets who were determined to establish a buffer of satellite states between themselves and the West. Finally, machinery for drafting and ratifying peace treaties with the former Axis countries and their allies had to be put into motion.

On all of these matters there were disagreements even within the several delegations that accompanied the Big Three to Germany, yet all had to be resolved or delegated to lower-level negotiators before the conference adjourned. Not until then could the Clays and the Murphys begin their work of rehabilitation or could the Eisenhowers and Zhukovs return home for well-deserved rest and acclaim.

In the end, Truman and Stalin dominated the proceedings, though for a time Churchill claimed center stage. Britain's redoubtable wartime Prime Minister indulged in a dogged but fruitless filibuster aimed at containing the westward spread of Soviet dominion. Then, angrily, he flew home when the conference recessed. In London, Churchill faced a far graver loss: his defeat in a general election by Labor Party leader Clement Attlee, who returned in Churchill's place to Potsdam. A reticent, pipe-smoking figure, Attlee let Truman take the lead in most of the discussions with

A Union Jack flies overhead, and a crowd of British soldiers and former inmates watch, as the last building of the notorious Bergen-Belsen concentration camp is burned to the ground in May 1945. The vermin-ridden buildings were razed to prevent the spread of disease—and also on general principles.

Stalin. But his Foreign Secretary, a tough-minded onetime truck driver named Ernest Bevin, proved a stalwart debating opponent for Foreign Minister Vyacheslav Molotov during meetings of the Allied Foreign Ministers. At Potsdam, Molotov lived up to his name—derived from the Russian word for hammer—by battering the Western delegations with Soviet demands for a free hand in Eastern Europe, a rapacious policy toward Germany, and the exclusion of Italy from the United Nations.

The conference bogged down over these three demands, and would have broken up in disorder had it not been for Secretary of State Byrnes and the American and British diplomats who labored on the subcommittees charged with working out the Big Three's disagreements. Churchill, had he remained, might willingly have debated the fate of Europe with Stalin for the rest of the summer, but both Truman and Attlee were impatient to conclude the proceedings and return home to deal with pressing domestic concerns. It was Byrnes who worked out a last-minute package in which the Western powers conceded the Soviet definition of Poland's frontiers while the Soviets accepted a compromise on German reparations in which they promised to ship food, timber and other scarce commodities to the Western zones. They also agreed to Italy's entry into the U.N. The Big Three, by deferring many unresolved problems for solution by their Foreign Ministers at later meetings, were able to end their conference with a show of harmony.

Robert Murphy had served on the subcommittee that attempted to determine the amount of German reparations, the level of its industrial production, and what the Yalta agreements had referred to as the minimum needs of the German people. He had found Potsdam to be "an arduous, tedious business." The Russians, he observed, "scored more points than we did because they were never in a hurry"; they were the only delegates "who showed no particular haste or desire for compromise." As a result, Murphy ruefully concluded, "Stalin and his group either obtained the settlements they sought or swept the ticklish questions under the rug."

Secretary Byrnes was more sanguine. When the last official photographs had been taken and the Truman party had returned to the U.S.S. *Augusta* for the voyage home, Byrnes expressed his firm belief that "the agreements reached would provide a basis for the early restoration of stability to Europe." Harry Truman was not so sure. Recalling Stalin's implacable demand for Soviet supremacy in Eastern Europe, and his own stubborn resistance, he confided to a sailor aboard the ship his opinion of the Soviet dictator: "I think he's a son of a bitch." Then Truman added: "I guess he thinks I'm one, too." The two men would never meet again.

A newly constituted Big Three, Clement Attlee, Harry S. Truman and Josef Stalin, present an affable front during the Potsdam Conference in July of 1945. The death of Franklin D. Roosevelt and the electoral defeat of Winston Churchill's Conservative Party left Stalin the only survivor of the original triumvirate.

Vanquished Germany in 1945 was divided into four occupation zones and was administered by a Central Control Commission consisting of the American, British, Soviet and French military commanders. The commission was headquartered in Berlin, which was also divided into four sectors (inset). The United States controlled the fertile south of Germany; France held the coal-rich Saar and the Rhineland; Britain governed the industrial Ruhr and most of the North Sea coast; and the Soviet Union occupied East Prussia, Silesia and Pomerania, which Poland was allowed to administer, plus a sizable portion of eastern Germany between the Elbe and Oder Rivers.

Back in Berlin, General Clay was thankful that the conference had at least produced a set of guidelines for the Allied Control Council to follow. He was grateful for the principle that Germany would be administered as a single economic unit. He was particularly pleased that Byrnes had been able to mitigate demands for reparations. The Potsdam directives also relaxed the JCS 1067 strictures against reviving German industry and had, in Clay's words, specifically charged the council "with the development of a balanced economy which would place Germany on a self-sustaining basis." Clay's interpretation of the Potsdam directives, in which his British colleagues concurred, was that "agricultural production and the peaceful domestic industries were to be maximized" and their output shared by the four zones.

It did not work out that way. True, the council meetings produced an impressive array of laws for the destruction and suppression of war potential, the punishment of war criminals and the exclusion of former Nazis from public life.

But when Clay reviewed matters in January of 1946, it would be clear to him that "almost no progress was made toward democratic political reconstruction or the development of economic self-sufficiency with a reasonable standard of living for the German people."

Both the French and the Russians contributed to this impasse. Excluded from the Potsdam Conference, French leader Charles de Gaulle simply ignored its conclusions. His representative on the Allied Control Council imposed a veto on every move to share the resources of the French zone or to establish central German political and administrative agencies. In similar vein, the Soviet Deputy Governor, General Vasily Sokolovsky, forbade Germans to cross zonal boundaries and impeded Allied access to the Soviet zone.

The Russians ignored the compromises on German reparations that seemed to have saved the Potsdam Conference. They continued to uproot utilities and factories for wholesale shipment east, while demanding food, fuel and capital

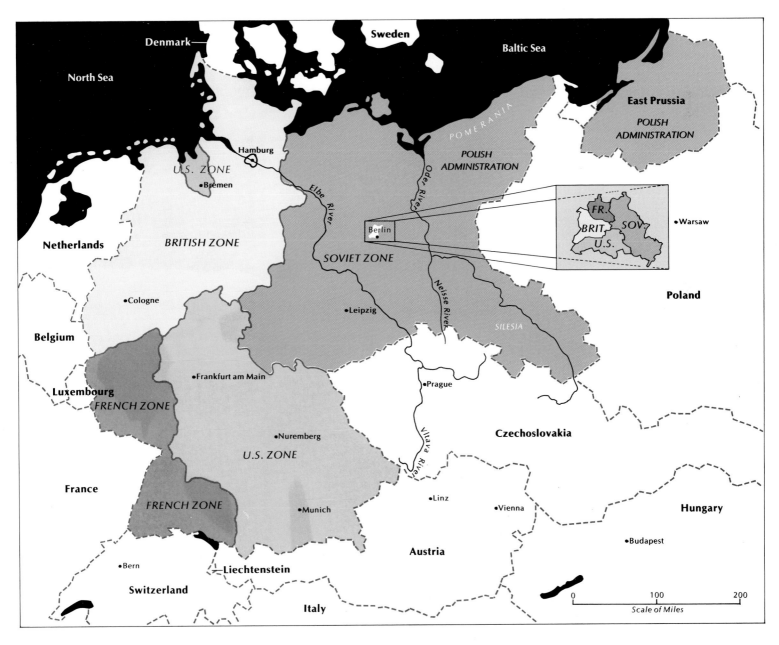

equipment from the Western zones. These Soviet attempts to extract crushing reparations from all of Germany while raising ever-higher barriers between their zone and the others would, in only two years, lead to the complete breakdown of four-power government and to the permanent division of Germany.

In every area—from ideological to purely personal—the Soviet members of the Control Council became exceedingly difficult to deal with. Calculated or not, their life style was highly annoying to the Allied officers; the Russians got up much later in the morning, ate large breakfasts and found it difficult to get to the conference table before 11 a.m. Since the Russians did not normally eat lunch until four in the afternoon, they usually insisted on working right through the Western meal hour, using the hunger pangs experienced by the other representatives as a tactical weapon in debate—or so the Westerners complained. The Soviets also endlessly exploited the requirement for double translations of all remarks by giving vent to long, polemical speeches, which then had to be repeated in both French and English; naturally, council proceedings came to a standstill.

These problems had already surfaced in November of 1945, when the Allies launched one of their last cooperative ventures: the summoning to judgment of Germany's surviving wartime leaders.

The trial of the major Nazis at Nuremberg, in the American zone, opened on November 20, 1945, before an International Military Tribunal *(pages 64-79)*. It was seen by the Allies not only as a symbolic act of cooperation but as the promulgation of a new code of law for the society of nations.

The indictments against the Nazi leaders fell into two categories. One charged the defendants with having committed mass atrocities and war crimes so monstrous that the guilt of those responsible would be self-evident. These ''crimes against humanity,'' it was argued, had to be catalogued and condemned and their perpetrators punished so that the conscience of the human race could be cleansed. The second part of the indictment charged the defendants with something quite different and less well defined—waging or conspiring to wage aggressive war.

The American prosecutor, Robert H. Jackson, described this aspect of the trial as ''mankind's desperate effort to apply the discipline of the law to statesmen who have used their powers to attack the world's peace.'' The British prosecutor, Sir Hartley Shawcross, put forward a similar view: ''It is a fundamental part of these proceedings,'' he said, ''to establish for all time that international law has the power to declare that a war is criminal.''

Four judges represented the four victorious Allied powers in Europe; their president was Lord Justice Geoffrey Lawrence, one of Britain's leading jurists. They made it clear from the outset that it was not the German people who were on trial, but their leaders, and the diplomats, proconsuls and industrialists who had abetted and profited from Nazi aggression. The defendants were to be tried not only as individuals but as symbols. Hans Fritzsche, for instance, was the relatively inoffensive head of the German Broadcasting Service, but he appeared in court in place of the dead Propaganda Minister, Joseph Goebbels.

The trial was a ghastly revelation, even to the Germans, of unspeakable crimes perpetrated in their name. Day by day for month after month, a doleful stream of witnesses, documents, photographs and newsreels revealed the nightmare of the Holocaust, and of the terror war launched by Adolf Hitler and the men now sitting in the dock at Nuremberg.

A senior Russian officer greets Lieut. General Lucius D. Clay (right) on the American commander's arrival in Soviet-occupied Berlin in 1945. At this stage, relations among the Allied armed forces in Berlin were amicable. Movement between zones was relatively unrestricted and individual officers exchanged such gifts as medals, jeeps and horses.

The events recounted in testimony included the extermination of Jews, gypsies, Slavs, prisoners of war and other captives in vile circumstances and in nauseating quantities; the terror and widespread use of torture and murder by the Gestapo, the SS and other party agencies to enforce tyranny and confirm conquest; mass deportations and mass forced labor; sadistic medical experiments and euthanasia programs; the looting of the national treasures of conquered countries and the private property of imprisoned individuals. It was an almost limitless inventory of infamy.

Considering the circumstances, the 216-day trial was conducted with reasonable, though not meticulous, fairness. The Allies were determined to have Nazi blood and they got it. The Americans and Russians in particular were outraged that even three of the defendants were acquitted. After the tribunal's 11 death sentences had been carried out, the bodies were cremated. Thus the major Nazi criminals were gone, without trace or memorial.

Other trials before and after involved Germans who belonged to indictable occupational categories—men from big business, the security service, the diplomatic corps, the officer corps and so on. Every trial produced new evidence that led to additional arrests and new trials. Men—and women—who after Germany's collapse had taken up inconspicuous lives as businessmen, lawyers, doctors, clerks and laborers, were revealed as culpable guards, prosecutors, judges, generals or scientific researchers from the Nazi period. In the American courts in Nuremberg alone, 199 such persons would be tried between July 1945 and July 1949; thirty-six of them were condemned to death, and 18 actually executed; 23 were sentenced to life imprisonment, 102 to shorter terms and 38 were acquitted. In American courts at Dachau, meanwhile, 420 Germans were sentenced to death. Similar trials were conducted in the other three Occupation zones and in other countries throughout Europe. Over the next 20 years some 20,000 Nazis would be convicted by Allied and, later, by German courts.

Meanwhile, hundreds of thousands of Germans were summoned before special "de-Nazification" courts in the British, American and French zones. Their object was the eradication of every trace of Nazism from postwar Germany. Those who were not cleared received a fine or a prison sentence; others were penalized with temporary or permanent exclusion from public employment.

The task of totally de-Nazifying Germany was overwhelming, far beyond the ability of even the large bureaucracies of the Occupation forces to cope with. The Americans were the most enthusiastic de-Nazifiers. They issued 12 million *Fragebogen*—forms containing 131 questions about the subject's past life and associations—one to every German over 18 years of age in the American zone. As a result of this campaign of self-incrimination, 169,282 persons were tried for their past Nazi and military associations.

De-Nazification had many critics. It was charged that only small fry were caught in the net—the bigger fish usually had the wits, the money and the influence to avoid it. A number of the most-wanted Nazi henchmen did escape justice—some by committing suicide, some by changing their names and identities. More than 20,000 Nazis escaped, most often to Egypt and Syria in the Middle East, or to South America, where Argentina and later Paraguay granted them political asylum. Many had arranged their escapes well before the German collapse, collecting large sums of money, false papers and useful addresses abroad. Then they made their way through Austria to Italy or Switzerland.

The routes out of Germany seemed to follow the same

Soviet Foreign Minister Vyacheslav M. Molotov welcomes his American counterpart, Secretary of State James F. Byrnes, to Berlin in July of 1945. Less than a year later, attitudes on both sides had chilled as the victorious powers differed sharply over Germany's future.

SIMON WIESENTHAL'S MISSION OF VENGEANCE

Twenty days after being freed from a German concentration camp in May of 1945, a half-starved Polish Jew wrote his American liberators to offer his services in the hunt for Nazi criminals. He appended a list of 91 SS killers he had met in 13 different camps. One, he said—an SS general—had shot and killed 13,000 prisoners. Another had won "numerous wagers by sending one bullet through two heads at a time." The letter was signed "Simon Wiesenthal (Camp Mauthausen, 127371)."

The letter launched Wiesenthal, a 37-year-old architect, on an all-consuming new career. For two years he worked for the U.S. Army, then set up his own Jewish Historical Documentation Center in Linz, Austria, to help ex-prisoners trace both their tormentors and their lost relatives. He collected thousands of affidavits, recording testimony while memories were still painfully fresh. He cross-indexed camps, SS men and survivors—using Allied, Israeli and even Nazi lists to identify the guilty. (He bought the secret SS membership roll for $500 from an SS officer.)

With single-minded fervor, Wiesenthal kept the work going by doing odd jobs, accepting donations and volunteer help. He and his family were threatened repeatedly. Yet in the first two decades after the War he exposed 900 Nazi criminals, including the Gestapo agent who had seized Anne Frank and her family (and who had gone on to a new life as a policeman in Vienna). He also helped the Israelis catch Adolf Eichmann, the man who was charged with the implementation of Hitler's "Final Solution." More important, in Wiesenthal's view, the resulting trials kept their crimes from being forgotten—and helped to immunize a new generation against Nazism.

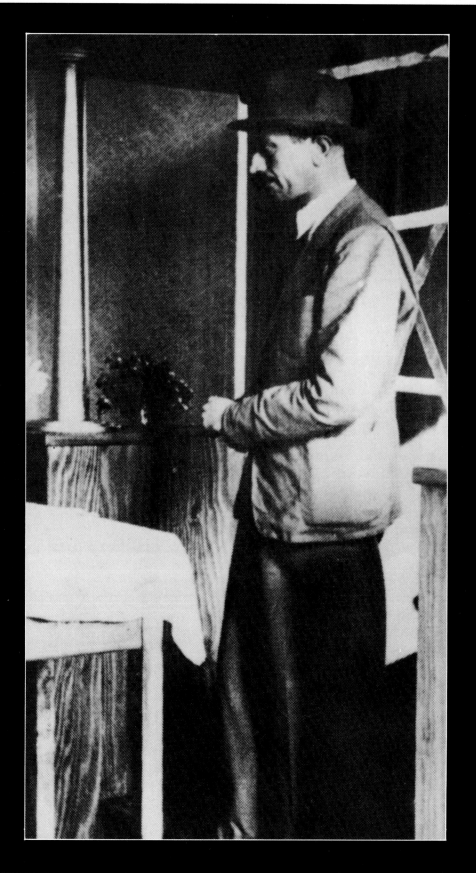

Simon Wiesenthal visits a synagogue for displaced Jews in 1946. He reported to U.S. authorities that he had actually seen many of the Nazis he was pursuing "commit murder fantastic both in number and method."

general course. They focused initially on Memmingen in the Allgäu, a secluded wooded region in southern Bavaria near the Austrian and Swiss borders. From there the route led to Lake Constance, where it divided into two, one branch leading to Switzerland, the other to Innsbruck in Austria and thence to Italy via the Brenner Pass. In Italy the goal nearly always was Rome, where a number of national committees and a papal assistance agency had been established to help refugees flee from Nazism, and later from Communism and the ruin of Central Europe. Fugitive Nazis often benefited from the same charitable mechanisms that had been set up to aid their victims. The help included warehouses full of clothes, food, toilet articles—and 2.5 million cigarettes left behind by the Brazilian Army, which had fought with the Allies in Italy. With the right connections, an escaping Nazi could procure a false International Red Cross passport, an entry visa to a foreign country, passage on a ship, and ultimately a job in a German émigré community.

Among the Germans who escaped through what they called the *Römische Weg,* or Roman Way, were two of the most wanted Nazis of all—Franz Stangl, commandant of the Sobibor and Treblinka concentration camps, and Adolf Eichmann, who had run the Jewish extermination program. Stangl, who was responsible for the murder of about one million people, was captured by the Americans shortly after the War ended and put in a camp for SS detainees at Bad Ischl, Austria. He was not brought to trial. In July 1945, Stangl was transferred to another camp at Glasenbach, then to an open prison in Linz, Austria; he escaped from the prison late in 1948 and crossed the Tyrol into Italy. Once in Rome, he secured from a German bishop a Red Cross passport, an entry visa to Syria, a boat ticket and the promise of a job in a textile mill in Damascus.

In 1949, Stangl's family joined him in Syria and in 1951 he and his family emigrated to Brazil. There, still using his real name, he again was able to get a job in textiles and later found a better job as an engineer at the Volkswagen plant in São Paulo. Stangl lived in reasonable contentment in São Paulo until he was arrested in 1967 by the Brazilian Alien Police and extradited to Germany to stand trial at last. Convicted and sentenced to life imprisonment in 1970, Stangl died in prison in Düsseldorf in 1971.

Adolf Eichmann was the head of Section B-4 of Bureau IV of the RSHA (Reich Central Security Service) and he was the person responsible for implementation of what Hitler called the Final Solution of the Jewish Problem. The end of the War found him at Altaussee in the Austrian Alps, where he and his RSHA boss, Ernst Kaltenbrunner, had taken refuge. Shortly thereafter he was captured by American troops and thrown into a prison camp for SS men. The Americans did not know who Eichmann was. Several of Eichmann's fellow inmates, however, recognized him and it was they who helped Eichmann escape early in 1946, after his name had begun to crop up with uncomfortable frequency during the trial of the major war criminals at Nuremberg.

For the next four years Eichmann lived on Lüneburger Heide, 50 miles south of Hamburg, where he worked as a lumberjack under the name Otto Heninger. Early in 1950 he, too, took the route called the Roman Way and in May passed through Austria to Italy. In Rome a sympathetic priest gave him a refugee passport in the name of Ricardo Clement and in July found him passage to Buenos Aires.

Once in Argentina, Eichmann obtained identity papers and a work permit. He worked in a laundry and on a rabbit farm and, after his wife and children joined him in 1952, he got his first steady job, as a mechanic in the Mercedes-Benz factory. He lived a dreary life in one of the poorer suburbs of Buenos Aires and took no great pains to hide his real identity. The city's Nazi colony certainly knew who he was. It was surprising, therefore, that it took justice so long to catch up with him. Not until May of 1960 was he kidnapped by Israeli agents and spirited out of the country to stand trial in Jerusalem. He died by hanging in 1962.

A few top Nazis fared better. The most notable was the Chief of the Gestapo, Heinrich Müller, who succeeded in disappearing without a trace; Allied investigators suspected that he somehow made a deal with the Soviets and lived for a while in the Soviet zone of Germany and later in Albania. The fugitive Nazi VIPs and their collaborators—fascist Croats, Italians, Belgians, Norwegians, Dutch and French—

A 1945 drawing exhibited in the French Occupation zone shows Germans scrambling to exchange their Nazi uniforms for the anonymity of civilian clothing. Many Germans, seeking to establish their own innocence, accused their neighbors of being Nazis.

eventually formed an organization called Sicherheitsdienst International (SDI) to protect themselves from agents of retribution, especially those from Israel.

Bringing every last Nazi to book proved an impossible task for the overworked Allied administrators of Germany. The Russians, French and British soon accepted this fact and let the smaller fry alone. But the Americans did their best to see that no identifiable Nazi functionary kept his job in local government, the schools, the professions, or even in the postal service and the national railways. The resulting lack of trained administrators and technicians made the difficult job of running defeated Germany even more difficult, for in theory the decisions of the Allied Control Council and the zone commanders were to be carried out by the Germans themselves. Until such time as enough non-Nazi Germans could be found or enough Nazis re-educated, the day-to-

day operation of local government fell instead to field detachments of the Allied Military Government.

When the War ended, many of the AMG units had already had several months' experience running local affairs. As the Allied columns swept across Germany, military government personnel followed on their heels. Initially the AMG's abundant tasks were purely military—to keep the lines of communication open, to prevent hordes of German civilians and foreign laborers from jamming the roads, to clear paths through the rubble of the towns, repair bridges and fill potholes, to keep law and order in the armies' rear and enforce a curfew, to find billets for headquarters' staffs, to repair the telephone system and restore electricity, gas and water, and to appoint as *Bürgermeister* some suitable non-Nazi who could pass along their orders to the German inhabitants of the captured towns.

Up until this stage any benefit the German populace

SOLVING THE MYSTERY OF "HITLER'S EVIL SPIRIT"

"The question 'Is Bormann dead?'" wrote Simon Wiesenthal, the celebrated Nazi-hunter, in 1967, "is always good for another cover story in any German mass-circulation magazine. No other prominent Nazi has been declared dead and then revived so many times."

Indeed, the abiding mystery over the fate of Hitler's secretary, Martin Bormann, made him far better known after the War than during it. On the night of May 1, 1945, as the Red Army drove deep into Berlin, Bormann and Ludwig Stumpfegger, Hitler's physician, slipped away from the *Führerbunker* in a desperate attempt to escape from the city.

Arthur Axmann, the last leader of the Hitler Youth, later claimed he saw their bodies, dead but unmarked, near a bridge not far away. But the bodies were not found, fueling the legend that Bormann, a man other Nazis called "Hitler's evil spirit," had escaped. Over the years he was variously reported as closeted in a monastery, living in Australia, Egypt, South-West Africa, Spain, Austria, the U.S.S.R.—as well as half a dozen South American republics. Unconfirmed sightings of the man numbered in the thousands.

Then in 1972, workmen digging in a Berlin freight yard near the bridge Axmann had pointed out turned up two skeletons.

After minute examination, one was identified as Stumpfegger through his dental records. Bormann's records had been destroyed but his dentist, while a prisoner of the Americans just after the War, had made a sketch of his teeth. It matched those in the other skull. Moreover, a gold bridge was identified as Bormann's by the dental technician who made it. Healed fractures in one arm and collarbone, a dent in the skull resulting from an auto accident, and diminutive thigh bones—Bormann was only five feet five inches tall—supported the identification.

Both skulls had splinters of glass between the teeth: Apparently the fugitives had bitten into glass cyanide capsules, preferring death to capture by the Soviets. Suicide fitted Axmann's description of the bodies as unmarked.

The evidence was convincing. The head of the West Berlin Institute for Forensic Medicine declared flatly: "It is Bormann. We have proved it beyond a shadow of doubt." A warrant for Bormann's arrest—he had been tried and convicted in absentia at Nuremberg—was canceled and a search of 27 years was finally concluded. Even Wiesenthal conceded that the case was closed: He pronounced himself "99 per cent" satisfied that the long-lost Bormann was indeed dead.

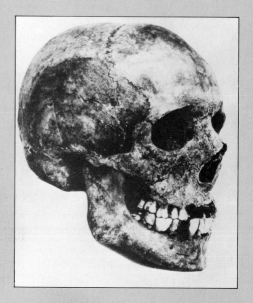

The pieced-together skull above enabled forensic scientists to identify Martin Bormann (right), whose skeletal remains were unearthed in Berlin in December 1972, only one half mile from Hitler's bunker.

received from military government was incidental. But once the front-line military government detachments moved off with the advancing armies, they were replaced by units whose task was much more concerned with civil affairs. At this point the Allied governance of Germany began.

In the American and British zones the original military government teams were usually made up of officers and men who possessed some relevant special skill but who were rated unfit for combat, most often because they were overage. The average age of officers in the early AMG teams was 45, and some of the most energetic among them were over 55. Many of them were highly qualified, successful and often wealthy men in civilian life; they included corporation lawyers, newspaper editors and university presidents. Others had qualifications as engineers, lawyers, municipal surveyors, agronomists, bankers, social workers and public-health officers. These men had volunteered in the expecta-

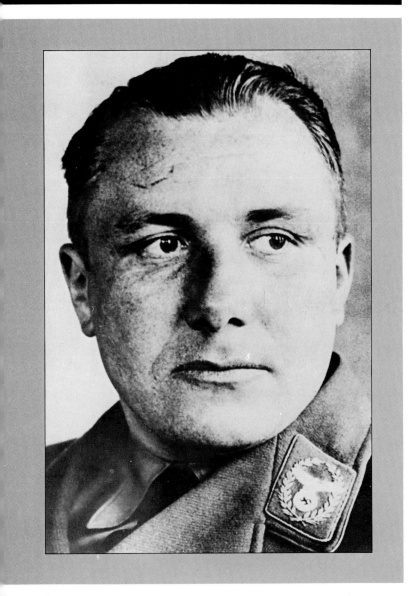

tion that they could contribute to the task of reconstructing postwar Europe, and they approached their difficult assignments with an almost missionary fervor.

Others, however, were Regular Army officers detailed from combat units because they suffered from wounds or battle fatigue or were surplus to their units' requirements—or because they had ''fouled up.'' A few who ended up in military government were rascals and crooks; these men took advantage of their privilege and power to engage in outrageous rackets and outright robberies. It was a rare AMG officer who spoke German, and although all officers had undergone a brief training course, few understood the people and the institutions they were assigned to run.

Administration within the several zones of occupied Germany varied widely. The British looked on the Germans in their zone as new subjects of their far-flung empire and treated them, albeit politely and fairly, as second-class citizens from whom they stayed aloof. The French, after defeat and four years of subjugation, were nakedly vengeful—and yet practical, in many instances hiring Germans for responsible jobs regardless of whether they had been Nazis.

The Americans ruled in accordance with the cold canons of JCS 1067 and officially were more severe than the British in their dealings with the Germans. Individually, however, they were more accessible, more lax and more generous—and they tended to appoint themselves salesmen for the democratic way of life. The Russians, by contrast, saw Germany as the hordes of Genghis Khan must have seen Samarkand; after a period of undisciplined pillage they turned to wholesale official plunder in the name of the party and the state. Their administration evolved into a ruthlessly calculated and coldly executed design for molding what remained of their zone into a future Marxist satellite.

The German reaction to their conquerors mirrored these different attitudes. ''The British like us but don't always notice that we are there,'' one German commented. ''The Americans like us but treat us like badly behaved children. The French hate us on equal terms.'' It was for the Russians that the Germans reserved their utmost fear and loathing, reinforced by the age-old Teutonic hatred for the Slav. ''One was freest in the British zone,'' recalled a German writer, Hans Werner Richter, ''best off in the American zone, and most at risk in the Russian zone.''

After Potsdam, military government grew in both size and efficiency, but in the American zone it always suffered from understaffing and even at its peak had only 12,000 officers and men working for it. By contrast the British zone had nearly 26,000 and the French were so numerous in their zone that in Baden-Baden, their headquarters town, the 7,600 French outnumbered the Germans who lived there. The Russians ran their zone largely through hundreds of German Communists who had spent the War years underground or in exile. They also welcomed into the party Nazi administrators who were willing to change their loyalty.

But nowhere were there enough administrators to implement the Potsdam protocols or even to deal adequately with immediate problems. The most pressing of these included bringing in the harvest, clearing rubble from the streets, restoring public services, organizing a new police force, repairing bridges, roads and railways, clearing the rivers for navigation, selecting new teachers and reopening the schools, rounding up and confining Nazi officials, destroying German military matériel (U-boats, ammunition dumps, weapons), and dismantling war plants and heavy industry. The list ran on and on.

An estimated 400 million cubic meters of rubble covered the devastated areas of Germany. Though much of the countryside was spared, not one of its great cities had escaped destruction by bombing and the ground fighting that

followed. In Cologne, 66 per cent of the residential structures had been destroyed. In Düsseldorf, 93 per cent of them were uninhabitable. In Nuremberg, only one house in 10 was undamaged. In Frankfurt, only 44,000 of the city's 177,000 houses were still standing. In Berlin, 95 per cent of the city center had been destroyed; in the rest of the city, only one house in four was habitable.

Not just houses, but all manner of structures had been obliterated. Gone were offices, churches, shops, theaters, schools, universities and much of the industrial infrastructure—power plants, transport and communications, including most docks, railway bridges, canals, telephone switchboards, even the post offices. The nearly total disruption of wheeled transportation and electrical communication brought civilized life to a virtual halt.

As Clay and Truman had observed, countless thousands of dead still lay under the rubble; in the first summer after the War the sweet stench of decay hung above the ruins like a pall. The living, crowded together in improvised quarters in the basements and bunkers beneath the rubble, accommodated themselves as best they could; many fashioned precarious caves in the debris, where they lived an almost Stone Age existence amid the tangled remains of what had once been Europe's most advanced industrial state; some had no shelter at all.

Fifteen million urban Germans had fled from the cities to escape the bombings. Of those who remained, five million had been made homeless, and their number was more than doubled by the millions of refugees who had fled from the Red Army in the East or were still being expelled from western Poland, Czechoslovakia and other parts of Eastern Europe. All of these people competed for what little shelter remained. The best of the undamaged houses were requisitioned by the Occupation armies as billets, messes and offices, and their German inhabitants were turned out into the street. The majority of Germans in the smaller towns also were living in squalor and penury, often in condemned quarters, and usually in a state of severe overcrowding. In Germany as a whole, 10 people were now living where six had lived before, and some places were worse than others—in Düsseldorf the average living space was reduced to four square yards per person.

A Jewish visitor to the British zone, English publisher Victor Gollancz, was appalled by the way Germans were forced to live. He wrote home to his wife:

"On your way from Düsseldorf to Aachen you come upon what is perhaps the most ruined town in Germany. Julich is 93 per cent destroyed.

"We began to walk among the rubble. A minute later we came upon a sort of stovepipe sticking out of the ground. It took us a little time to find the entrance to what was clearly some kind of underground dwelling, a narrow incline tunnelled in the earth. The cellar consisted of two tiny rooms housing seven people. Six of them were in what I suppose must be called the sitting room, which was about the height of a man; they could just cram into it—the parents, two adult sons, and two younger children. (The seventh was out.) In the adjoining hole you could just make out a dim hell of wooden beds and dirty bedclothes. They had neither water nor lavatory; for excreting they used either a pail or, more commonly, the rubble outside. The clothes they stood up in seemed their only possessions."

In the first summer after the War, even the solution of Germany's dreadful housing shortage seemed a less pressing priority than the provision of food, coal, communications and essential services. And as winter drew closer, the Allied Military Government realized that a widespread disaster was looming.

General Eisenhower had sounded the warning when he told the Germans in August: "The coming months are going to be a hard test for you. You will just have to be tough—there is no alternative. Every sign indicates a severe shortage of food, fuel, housing and transport. It is therefore up to you to alleviate your hardship by working very strenuously and helping one another. So to bring in all the harvest it will be necessary for the townspeople to go out into the country and give a hand there. There will be no coal available for heating homes this winter. To meet your basic requirements in the next few months you will have to go into the woods and cut your own firewood. A third priority is the provision of living accommodations. As far as the weather allows, damaged property must be repaired to offer as much protection from the winter as possible. To this end you will have to collect scrap material over the widest possible area and gather dead wood in the forests. These are your problems.

Returning Hermann Göring's private hoard of stolen art, American soldiers in June of 1945 lift a painting of Venus and Adonis onto a waiting truck; still to be loaded are a white stone Madonna and a statue of Saint George and the Dragon. While searching caves in southern Germany for stolen gold, the Americans had uncovered $200 million worth of fine art that Göring had appropriated from collections throughout Europe.

Their solution depends entirely on your own endeavors."

The cold and damp of life in squalid, unheated ruins might have been more bearable if the inhabitants' food ration had been sufficient to sustain life, but it was not. In July, before the harvest, the ration scale in the Western zones dropped to 950 calories per day—less than half the calories considered necessary to sustain a person through an average working day, and one third of the average calorie level in the United States. In Berlin the official food ration was 1,240 calories a day, but in reality people received only two thirds of this, a starvation diet of barely 850 calories. As a result, 4,000 of them died each day in August, and fully half the babies born that month failed to survive.

The first postwar German grain harvest fell 15 per cent below estimates, and it became clear that famine would engulf the nation if there were not massive imports of food. General Clay summarized the situation: "We had to have food. West Germany had never been self-supporting. Even Germany as a whole could not raise enough to sustain its people. Now their principal producing farmlands located in north-central and eastern Germany were much smaller because of the severed Eastern Territory. Moreover, their produce was not available to the Western zones. Yet the population of these zones had increased by about four million and was to increase still more."

Nor was it easy to find food abroad. The shortage was worldwide, and several of the Occupation powers found it hard to feed their own people, let alone their former enemies: Parts of the Soviet Union were on the verge of famine and in Britain the food situation was worse than at any time during the War—so bad, in fact, that bread had to be rationed for the first time in history. The French, whose soldiery in Germany lived off the land, were consumers of German calories rather than providers. Between the summer of 1945 and the spring of 1946 one million tons of food was imported into the British zone and half a million tons into the American zone. With difficulty, the average German ration in the two zones was maintained at 1,500 calories per day during the first postwar winter, still well below the minimum necessary for adequate subsistence. By comparison, German farmers, who could eat their own produce, got 3,000 calories per day and soldiers of the U.S. Army 4,200 calories per day.

The subsequent months were worse. In March 1946 a critical shortage of grain at home forced the United States to stop all shipments to Germany. As a result, the ration in the Western zones fell even lower. More and more Germans learned to live on a single daily meal of watery soup with— if they were lucky—one marble-sized meatball. In the French zone the public-health situation was described as "frightful." In the British zone the ration dropped in some instances to a mere 400 calories per day—one half the figure for inmates of the Bergen-Belsen concentration camp under the Nazis.

For those Germans who were obliged to live on such perilously scant and monotonous fare, life became a losing struggle. People no longer had the strength to work for more than a few hours a day and they collapsed at their jobs. Typhus, spread by lice, began to appear among those who were too listless and demoralized to keep themselves clean.

"We could not hope to develop democracy on a starvation diet," General Clay wrote later. "We could not even prevent sickness and discontent." Undernourished bodies, living in cold, damp, unsanitary conditions, could offer little resistance to disease. The incidence of tuberculosis, typhoid, dysentery and skin diseases, fostered by malnutrition and overcrowding, rose sharply; in Hamburg in October of 1946 there were nearly 17,000 diagnosed cases of TB, five times the prewar level.

Victor Gollancz, the English Jew who had taken up the cause of the defeated Germans in the British press, was particularly touched by the fate of Hamburg's children. "I have just returned from visiting a bunker—a huge air-raid shelter, without daylight or air, where 800 children get their schooling," he reported. "In one class of 41 children, 23 had had no breakfast, and nothing whatsoever until half past two; then they had the school meal of half a liter of soup, without bread. Seven of these children had the ugly skin blemishes that are mixed up in some way with malnutrition; all were white and pasty. Their gaping 'shoes' mean the end of what little health they have when the wet weather comes." Many children had no shoes at all and went barefoot—three quarters of a million in Schleswig-Holstein were in this state. Few had winter coats of any kind.

By contrast to the Germans, the men of the occupying ar-

A REBORN ARTIST'S TOUR OF THE LANDSCAPE

In 1933, the Nazis declared the respected German painter Otto Dix "degenerate": His fiercely critical view of mankind's folly—above all the folly of war—offended the Nazi dream of militancy. Dix was forbidden to teach or exhibit and was "exiled into landscapes," as he put it. More than 260 of his earlier works were burned.

In 1945, discovering a use for Dix after all, the Nazis drafted him into the *Volkssturm,* the home-defense militia. Within a month he was captured, and in a French POW camp he painted his first free work in 12 years—a triptych for the prison's chapel called "Madonna behind Barbed Wire." The paintings shown here and on the following pages reflect Dix's work in the immediate postwar years: a grim yet nascently hopeful view of the smashed human landscape of Europe.

A grizzled Otto Dix (left) glowers in his "Self-Portrait as a Prisoner of War." Dix was a prisoner until February 1946.

In Otto Dix's 1949 painting entitled "Cripple in the Ruins,"
a German beggar whose legs have been amputated sits upon a fallen
column, his hat resting in his lap, seeking alms.

Masked and menacing figures revel in a "Carnival in the Ruins" —a
1946 work reflecting Dix's ambivalent attitude toward the struggle
to establish a life of pleasure amidst the rubble of vanquished Germany.

Showing off their legs —and hard-to-get silk stockings —a pair of flashy women smile from a 1946 canvas called ''And New Life Blooms upon the Ruins,'' disregarding the wreckage of war around them.

His body covered with sores and his clothing in rags, a man looks heavenward in hope of succor. Dix entitled this painting ''Job,'' after the Biblical tale of affliction, tested faith and eventual redemption.

mies were living well. They had the best food and drink left in Europe, and even junior officers were billeted in requisitioned houses with as many as four German servants. Yet their lives were not exactly joyous. The gray, shattered towns of Germany were depressing places to be stationed and there was little to do in the beginning but drink. The Occupation soldiers were haunted by a sense of impermanence and isolation. Few of them spoke German and fewer still were ready to like Germans. Their clubs and messes were off limits to Germans and German bars were off limits to them. For Americans, Germany in 1945 was not like France or Italy, and certainly not like England, where no GI ever had to be lonely or without feminine companionship. Fraternizing with a German woman was *verboten* by order of the Joint Chiefs of Staff.

When the first American soldiers crossed the Rhine, they carried in their helmet liners a pamphlet derived from JCS 1067 that strictly forbade contact with any German man, woman or child outside the narrow requirements of duty. There would be no shaking hands, no idle talk, no visiting German homes or playing with German children. And, it was stressed, no going out with German girls. The punishment for that offense was a $65 fine—a month's pay for a private—and striking up a conversation with a *Fräulein* came to be known as the "$65 Question."

"Don't get chummy with Jerry," the Army newspaper *Stars and Stripes* exhorted its GI readers. "In heart, body and spirit every German is Hitler," the troops were warned. "Don't make friends with Hitler. Don't fraternize. If in a German town you bow to a pretty girl or pet a blonde child you bow to Hitler and his reign of blood."

For a time the savagery of the German Army's resistance and the universal horror aroused by the discovery of concentration camps like Belsen and Buchenwald turned many soldiers against all the German people. But nonfraternization was against ordinary human nature and could not last. Once the War was over the rule was widely disobeyed. Under a Burma Shave-like sign on the autobahn proclaiming "Soldiers wise don't fraternize" a GI soon scribbled: "This don't mean me, buddy."

"No one could help it," explained one soldier. "The girls were pretty and they didn't wear much, and we'd been through hell, living hard, in the open." Said another: "When we came up against our first 19-year-old Rhineland blonde with blue eyes, pink cheeks, plaits, and very desirable, we were just clean bowled over."

These were disciplined combat veterans, and they did their best to obey the nonfraternization order—at least in public. But by the time they started going home—as they soon did by the millions—nonfraternization had become a dead letter, through common consent and the good sense of General Eisenhower. First the Supreme Allied Commander conceded that it was permissible to talk to German children. In July of 1945 he extended the rule to German

Obeying orders, GIs pass without speaking to a young German woman sun-bathing in a park. Fraternizing in the first months of the Occupation brought fines for enlisted men; for officers it was a court-martial offense.

adults—you could stand with them, walk with them, even talk with them, but you could not sit with them on a park bench or hold their hands. Then in August, Eisenhower declared: "Members of my command are now permitted normal human contacts." It was the best Eisenhower could do about an impossible situation. But it would be more than a year before American soldiers—unlike the British, who had never accepted this aspect of JCS 1067—would be allowed into German movie houses or Germans into American theaters and snack bars.

In the meantime, the young men drafted to replace the homeward-bound veterans were arriving in Germany by the thousands with nothing in their helmet liners but an easily turned head and a Hershey bar. It did not take them long to meet young women who were as well brought up as the ones back home, but for whom a small square of chocolate was the equivalent of a meal, and a can of Spam a family banquet. *Schockolade* and *Zigaretten* needed no translation; for one Saturday-night date with an American or British soldier, a woman could cadge at least a pack of cigarettes, and a pack of cigarettes sold on the black market would keep her for a week.

Author Wilfred Byford-Jones's poignant account of a British private's relationship with an 18-year-old Berliner in the autumn of 1945 was typical of the experiences of thousands of Allied soldiers and their German women:

"She looked every bit like an English girl of twenty-two or three," the soldier recalled, "and was fair, with blue eyes, but was pale. I'd seen her several times in the same café drinking colored water, and she'd always been alone. She couldn't speak a word of English and I couldn't speak any German. I met her several times and we always did the same thing, went to a cinema and had a drink or danced. All the time I could see she was hungry. Somehow I began to feel sorry for her; then I felt responsible for her.

"It was forbidden to go into German houses," the British soldier continued, "but one night, because it was raining, she took my arm and led me to the block of flats where she lived. The block had been hit by artillery, the two top rows were burnt out. She lived on the third floor. There were two rooms and a small kitchen. There were no panes in the windows. One room was a bedroom, but there were no beds, only two settees, which she pushed together. She had lived

with her mother, whose photograph was there. Her mother had poisoned herself on April 25, when the Russians were attacking Berlin. There was a photograph of her father. He had been killed. The Russians had taken much of the furniture for their barracks. The place was cold—no wood or coal. I made a sign to ask if there was any food in the house, and she thought I wanted to eat. She went to a cupboard. In the cupboard were a few potatoes, a cupful of flour and some salt. Half a loaf of bread was wrapped in newspaper. I felt a bit sick at times about the power I had over that girl. If I gave her a three-penny bar of chocolate she nearly went crazy. She was just like my slave."

At about this same time, a German police official was lamenting to his superiors:

"It is impossible to distinguish between good girls and bad girls in Germany. Even nice girls of good families, good education and fine background have discovered their bodies afford the only real living. Moral standards have crashed to a new low level. At the present rate, in two months I wonder if there will be a decent moral woman left."

What kept most urban Germans alive—and enriched many an Allied soldier—was the black market. In time this illegal activity evolved into a highly organized underground economy, a triangle of market forces in which the immutable law of supply and demand was worked out between three main groups—the people of the towns and cities, the people of the countryside, and the soldiers of the Occupation armies. The half-starved townspeople traded away their valuables —jewelry, watches, furs, Leica cameras, Zeiss binoculars, *objets d'art.* In return they received the soldiers' post-exchange commodities—coffee, sugar, chocolate, white bread, nylon stockings, C rations, cigarettes—or stolen military stores such as gasoline, coal and Spam. The country people traded their potatoes, bacon, poultry, fruit, flour and eggs for the townspeople's valuables or the cigarettes and other scarce goods they had obtained from the soldiers. For this process of barter the Germans coined a new word, *kompensieren,* from the English "to compensate." A columnist for the Berlin newspaper *Der Telegraf* reported a typical black-market chain of compensations:

"A hungry friend of mine was offered a pound of butter for 320 reichsmarks. As he did not have enough money on him he bought it on credit; he would pay the next day. Half the pound went to his wife. With the remaining half we went out to 'compensate.' At a tobacco shop we got 50 cigarettes for the half pound. Ten cigarettes we kept for ourselves. With the remainder we went into a bar. For the 40 cigarettes we received a bottle of wine and a bottle of schnapps. We took the wine back to the house, but the schnapps we took out into the country. Before long we found a farmer who would exchange the schnapps for us for two pounds of butter. Next morning my friend took the pound of butter he had been offered originally and returned it on the grounds that it was too expensive. Our 'compensating' had brought us in 1½ lbs. of butter, a bottle of wine, 10 cigarettes and the pleasure of a tax-free bit of business.''

Though black-marketeering was officially banned and often severely punished, everyone engaged in it—poor and well-to-do Germans alike, private soldiers and high-ranking Allied officers. For the soldiers, who had easy access to PX goods and unused quartermaster supplies, the black market brought huge windfalls. For most Germans, who lacked the barest necessities of life, it was the only source of luxuries, clothing and medicine—and the constant trading for ad-

vantage made an intolerable existence tolerable. In the beginning, ironically, it was the ex-Nazis who were most active in the trade. Denied employment until overworked de-Nazification courts could clear or convict them, they could spend their days scavenging for salvage, trekking back and forth between town and country, and haggling tirelessly between buyer and seller. When Germany's trains began to run again, it seemed that the entire nation had joined the black market. A visitor from Switzerland reported:

''Day after day, night after night, the people crowd onto the railway platform by the hundreds, many with small children, all with suitcases or rucksacks on their backs. They have heard that somewhere—perhaps 100, perhaps 300 kilometers away—there is a village where potatoes or flour or a bit of pork fat can be got on the black market. So there they are going. If the trains run at all they run two to 10 hours late. They are unlit and, because of the coal shortage, unheated. The people are squashed into the carriages like sardines into a tin. Such is life in Germany today. The German goes hungry. He freezes. He sees his children die. He has become like a helpless, hunted animal.''

All the trains had nicknames. The one from agricultural

Lower Saxony to the industrial Ruhr was known as the Potato Train. The fast train from the hungry cities of Cologne and Hamburg to the bountiful area around Munich was the Calorie Express. The Vitamin Train ran from Dortmund to Freiburg, where the cherry harvest was the main attraction. The Nicotine Line took its passengers to the tobacco fields around Pfalz. The interzonal train from Osnabrück, near the North Sea, to Berlin was known as the Fish Express; on its return it was known as the Silk Stocking Express. During the potato harvest, it was estimated that 80 per cent of train travelers were "calorie seekers" and that by making repeated trips the average traveler managed to carry home 600 pounds of potatoes. When there was no room inside the train, the passengers stood on the running boards and clung precariously to the sides of the cars or huddled on the roof. It was not surprising that Germans had little time for work while their days were taken up with scouring the countryside in their search for food.

Food and other basic essentials were what most Germans sought from the black market. But there were some who looked for more, and there was virtually nothing that could not be obtained, from women's hose and fresh trout to priceless drugs like insulin and penicillin, houses, travel permits and title deeds to bombed-out dwellings. For some of the millions of Germans displaced by the War, the black market even offered a unique opportunity to assume a new identity with new qualifications, and to make a new start in life higher up the ladder with the help of bartered documents. An enterprising medical corpsman who had learned to set bones and stitch up wounds in a German Army field hospital bought himself a set of papers of such surpassing authenticity that he was selected over 50 other candidates for the post of chief surgeon of the Baden-Baden city hospital. Local investigators eventually unmasked him—along with 392 false doctors of philosophy, two unconsecrated priests and 300 commoners with fake titles of nobility.

More prized than a new identity was a whitewash of the old one. The so-called Persil Certificate—named after a commercial laundry soap—was a document issued by the Allies that officially cleared the bearer of any complicity in Nazism during the Hitler era, and was eagerly sought after on the black market by ex-Nazis on the run.

The black-market economy was personally and socially demoralizing and economically destructive. No modern industrial society could possibly run for long on a barter system, but it remained necessary as long as the official economy was based on bureaucratic order rather than financial incentive. It derived largely from the Allies' rigid monetary controls designed to prevent a repetition of the inflation that had ravaged Germany after World War I and fostered the conditions that brought Hitler to power. But the Allies' extreme monetarist policy backfired badly. A United Nations economic survey summarized what happened:

"The practice of 'suppressing' inflation was carried *ad absurdum,* to the point of strangling economic activity. The military administrations brought with them the respectable dogma that price inflation is wicked and antisocial under all conditions. However, under conditions of starvation, and in the absence of well-established government machinery, the attempt to run the economies of the different Occupation zones by detailed military orders only perpetuated the paralysis of the economy." The results, the report concluded, were probably far worse than any that normal inflation might have caused.

After the War the average monthly income in Germany remained at its wartime level of about 200 reichsmarks—just about enough to acquire a pound of butter or a bottle of wine—or a single American paper dollar. Officially the reichsmark had kept its nominal wartime value, but in practice it was virtually worthless because no one trusted it and no one wanted it. Money, one of Western civilization's main foundations, had ceased to serve its usual purpose. In their day-to-day transactions, the Germans were no longer paying cash in the official economy but were bartering on the black market: A Persian rug could be bought for 100 pounds of potatoes, a bicycle for a piano, and virtually anything, from diamonds to sex, could be had for American and English cigarettes.

Of all trade goods it was the cigarette that was the most highly prized unit of exchange and came nearest to supplanting the mark as a universally recognized currency. Like currency, the cigarette had the advantages of constant demand, controlled supply, convenient size and relative durability. And it had one more quality—in the last resort it could be lighted and smoked to allay the pangs of hunger.

A thriving black market attracts German civilians and soldiers of the Occupation forces to the Tiergarten, Berlin's famous park, in the summer of 1945. The Germans typically traded their remaining cameras, household goods and heirlooms for Allied cash, or for cigarettes that they then exchanged in the countryside for desperately needed foodstuffs.

Very few cigarettes, however, were smoked by the person who first bought them. More often they were passed from person to person at a profit or for barter and changed hands a dozen times before coming to rest. Germany became virtually a cigarette civilization, and there were times when it seemed the fate of the nation was bound up with such names as Lucky Strike, Camel, Chesterfield and Pall Mall. Tobacco plants bloomed in Rhineland vineyards, in suburban gardens and in city window boxes. Two new folk figures emerged—the tobacco baron at one end of the scale and at the other the *Kippensammler,* the collector of discarded *Kippen,* or cigarette butts. The tobacco from seven butts plucked from the sidewalk could be turned into one cigarette, and with one cigarette anyone could be an entrepreneur. Germany had become a nation of bowed heads.

For an Allied soldier with an entrepreneurial bent, cigarettes could be the coinage of great wealth. In Berlin during the summer of 1945 an American or English cigarette sold for two reichsmarks, and in 1946 this price tripled and quadrupled. In a city where even necessities had to be trucked in from the American zone, a cigarette became worth more than double the pay for a hard day's work clearing rubble, which was the only job available to most city dwellers. For 25 cartons of cigarettes costing $20 in the PX, a GI truck driver could buy a Leica camera in Berlin and mail it home to his wife or a friend, who could sell it in the States for $600. For $600 the same GI could buy 750 cartons and trade them for 30 Leicas worth $18,000. With that he was well on his way to swinging a truly big deal in antiques, fine art, Meissen porcelain, or whatever. Even a high-quality diamond could be bought for no more than two kilos of coffee and 50 cigarettes.

It was no wonder that many ordinary soldiers, as well as officers of all ranks, took this almost effortless chance to set themselves up for life. In Berlin alone, some six million cigarettes each week flowed out of the PX and its British equivalent and circulated at an estimated value of 40 to 60 million reichsmarks. The French and the Russians made out less well, because the Germans preferred the milder British and American brands—a pack of 25 Russian cigarettes,

made of the best Bulgarian tobacco, rarely traded for more than 40 reichsmarks.

But the Russians profited in other ways, thanks to a bit of unintended largesse from the same Henry Morgenthau who wanted to turn Germany into a nation of shepherds. The Allies had planned to replace Nazi bank notes with a common Occupation currency. Printed in the United States, the currency would be issued to the occupying armies at an exchange rate of four marks to the dollar. The Russians balked at this arrangement until, early in 1945, Secretary Morgenthau presented the Soviet government with a set of the engraving plates used to print the new money. The Soviets were supposed to keep track of the value of the bank notes they printed and issued to their troops and reimburse the U.S. Treasury accordingly, but they never rendered an accounting. Instead, the Russians ran off an endless stream of marks and used them to pay off their troops.

The Russian soldiers' level of pay was not very high. But they had been unpaid for so long—a year, even three or four years in some instances—that when payday finally came their knapsacks were stuffed to overflowing with Occupation marks. The money had to be spent in Germany, for the Soviet government had decreed that it could not be exchanged in Russia. But the GIs were under no such restriction. The result was an explosion of private dealing in goods and marks between Russian and American soldiers, especially in Berlin where contact was closest. The Russians would pay the equivalent of $300 to $400 in Occupation marks for an American fountain pen. They would pay as much as $1,000 for a cheap Mickey Mouse watch from the PX and much more for a quality timepiece with ruby bearings set in its wheels and balances. (When the GIs discovered this, they took to stippling the movements of ordinary watches with red fingernail polish.)

The Soviet appetite for watches was inexhaustible and the American soldiers made fortunes out of it. In July alone the GIs were paid nearly one million dollars in Allied Occupation marks, but they sent back to the States almost three times that much, converted into hard-currency U.S. dollars in the Army Post Offices. The two-million-dollar balance represented Russian-printed Occupation marks acquired from the German black market or directly from members of the Red Army. During the first four months of the Occupa-

tion, American military personnel sent home $11,078,925 more than they were paid. When a maximum of $100 was put on individual money orders, some men showed up at the post office with 500 orders at a time. Eventually, the U.S. Army had to reimburse the U.S. Treasury a staggering $250 million for Allied Occupation marks, while the Soviet government paid nothing.

In the opinion of General Clay and his superiors in Washington, the Soviets had deliberately embarked on a campaign to exploit the good will of their allies and prolong the sufferings of Europe in order to assure themselves of a dominant position in the postwar world. Before the War, German industry had supplied the European economy with coal, steel, chemicals and such high-technology products as the intricate flood-control machinery that kept the Netherlands from disappearing beneath the North Sea. In return, Europe had stocked Germany with its agricultural output and raw materials. Now this interlocking trade on which the life and health of Europe depended had ceased. Under Moscow's interpretation of the Potsdam agreements, which its representatives argued ceaselessly in the Allied Control Council and at meetings of the Allied Foreign Ministers, it seemed unlikely that Europe's economy would ever revive.

In the spring of 1946, General Clay had discussed the problems of Germany with Secretary Byrnes; he followed up the discussion with a long memorandum to the Department of State urging a merger of the four zones and an easing of the Allies' repressive treatment of the Germans. If the Soviet Union and France would not agree, he argued, the United States and Britain must form their own cooperative zone without delaying further. "We face a deteriorating German economy," Clay wrote, "which will create a political unrest favorable to the development of Communism in Germany and a deterrent to its democratization. Failure to obtain economic unity before the next winter sets in will make it almost unbearable. The sufferings of the German people will be a serious charge against democracy and will develop a sympathy which may well defeat our other objectives in Germany."

In July, Byrnes got direct confirmation of Clay's fears as he listened to a speech by Vyacheslav Molotov at a meeting of the Council of Foreign Ministers in Paris. The Ministers

With a frontier guard in hot pursuit, a young German makes a run for it after dropping the sack of coffee he was trying to smuggle in from Belgium in 1947. Starving German parents, and black marketeers, commonly employed children under the age of 14 as couriers because, if they were caught, they were less likely to be prosecuted by the Allied authorities.

had gathered for the second in a series of attempts to agree on preliminary terms for a peace treaty with Germany, and now Molotov was revising in public the positions his government had taken in private. Significantly, a translation of the speech had already been released to the foreign press—"an act as unusual for Soviet diplomats as it was routine for us," Byrnes reflected.

Molotov's surprising theme, which he reiterated in many variations, was that the Soviet Union opposed any policy that would make Germany an agrarian state, annihilate its factories or inhibit its industrial production. These were obvious references to the much-discussed, though now rejected, Morgenthau Plan. But Molotov's remarks also described what would certainly be the effect of current French and Soviet actions in the Allied Control Council. "We should not," Molotov insisted, "put obstacles in the way of the increase in the output of steel, coal and manufactured products of a peaceful nature in Germany," and he charged that the Allied Control Council had done just this.

Byrnes knew that it was the Soviet representatives in Berlin who had tried to set a ruinously low ceiling on German industrial production and that it was General Clay who had finally, over Soviet protests, ordered a halt to further dismantling of factories in the Western zones. With rising indignation, Byrnes recognized what Molotov's speech was intended to do—blame the Western Allies for Germany's enforced stagnation, while delaying indefinitely the peace treaty the Foreign Ministers were supposed to be expediting.

Before the Soviet Union would talk about a peace treaty with Germany, Molotov concluded, many years would have to pass during which Germany would have to demonstrate its ability to govern itself and fulfill its obligations to the Allies. "Above all," he declared, "it will be bound to carry out reparations deliveries."

As Byrnes later recorded, it was clear at this moment that the Soviets "would utilize their veto power in the Allied Control Council and in the Council of Foreign Ministers to secure adoption of their conception of a 'democratic' gov-

Hungry, cold and impoverished, urban Germans scrabbled to survive. At top, a German carefully scrapes up sugar spilled into the gutter from a passing truck. The man at center stoops to retrieve a cigarette butt that he can exchange for food. At bottom, an old woman chips small pieces of wood from a tree stump in Berlin's Tiergarten to heat her home.

ernment; to secure a part in the control of German industry, and to enforce the payment of $10 billion in reparations.''

It was equally clear that Molotov was raising the ghost of the vindictive Morgenthau Plan to frighten the German people into supporting Communist candidates for the local elections that at last had been scheduled to establish representative government in Berlin and the Western zones. It was time for the United States to reverse course.

Two months later, after another meeting of the Foreign Ministers at which Molotov again refused to discuss Anglo-American proposals for a peace treaty, Byrnes delivered his country's response in the heart of the U.S. zone, at Stuttgart, where Clay had gathered American Military Government administrators and U.S.-appointed senior German officials.

To focus attention on his visit, the Secretary of State arrived in Stuttgart via Berlin, where, along with U.S. Senators Tom Connally and Arthur Vandenberg of the Senate Foreign Relations Committee, he boarded Adolf Hitler's special armor-plated train. The train's luxurious fittings included lavendar-tiled bathrooms and black-marble bathtubs. The setting for the speech at Stuttgart also was dramatic. Clay recalled that ''the streets leading to the Opera House where it was delivered were lined with immaculate troops from the U.S. Constabulary, and with armored cars at the intersections. Behind these aligned troops were thousands of Germans. The auditorium was filled with officers, soldiers and civilian officials of the military government, and with invited German officials who were seated in a reserved section in the front orchestra rows.''

Byrnes's speech was a historic turning point. In essence he held out the hope of a revived, free and independent Germany run by Germans. Americans had learned, he began, that they lived in one world in which peace and prosperity were indivisible; ''our peace and well-being cannot be purchased at the price of the peace and well-being of any other country.'' He promised that Americans would ''continue our interest in the affairs of Europe'' and would maintain troops on German soil for many years to come in order to ensure the hard-won peace. He pledged that the present suffering of the German people, largely a consequence of the failure of the Allied Control Council to agree, would not be allowed to continue. ''Germany is a part of Europe,'' he declaimed, ''and recovery in Europe will be slow indeed if Germany with her resources of iron and coal is turned into a poorhouse.'' If Germany could not be made an economic whole, America would do all it could to unite as much of it as possible. The United States was willing to unify its zone with any or all of the other zones, Byrnes said, and the British had already accepted the offer.

Byrnes concluded: ''The American people want to return the government of Germany to the German people. The American people want to help the German people to win their way back to an honorable place among the free and peace-loving nations of the world.''

The speech was a triumph—''the major development of the Occupation so far,'' according to Clay. It was heard not only by the audience of 1,500 in the Opera House but by millions of Germans listening to a simultaneous translation on the radio. Most were deeply moved, for here at last was the outstretched hand they had been waiting for.

At the end of Byrnes's speech a band struck up ''The Star-Spangled Banner,'' and everybody, including the 150 Germans in the audience, stood. As Byrnes left the podium many of the Germans were openly weeping—and even Clay's eyes were moist. ''I walked backstage,'' the American general later wrote, ''to congratulate him on a speech that I believed would live through the years.''

The speech marked the end of the negative phase of the Occupation and the beginning of a more positive one. Far ahead lay the reconstruction of Germany with American aid, German self-government, and a self-generated economic miracle. But it would be two more years before the essential ingredients of change—still-larger imports of food and raw materials, and currency reform—would have their impact. Till then there could be only hope.

JUSTICE AT NUREMBERG

In the courtroom at Nuremberg, U.S. prosecutor Robert H. Jackson, standing at center, examines a witness (top) during the trial of 21 ranking Nazis (left).

NAZISM ON TRIAL BEFORE THE WORLD

The presiding judge, Britain's Lord Justice Geoffrey Lawrence, spoke slowly and calmly: "This trial is unique in the history of jurisprudence," he said, "and of supreme importance to millions of people all over the globe." Thus, on November 20, 1945, in battered Nuremberg, commenced a trial in which not one nation but rather civilization itself, as the American prosecutor, Robert H. Jackson, said, was "the real complaining party." For the next 10 months, the city in which the Nazi Party had held its annual rallies saw leading Nazis tried for their crimes against world peace, against the rules of warfare, and against the 11 million Jews, Slavs and other "undesirables" they had murdered.

Not all the top leaders could be tried, of course. Hitler, Himmler and Goebbels had already become their own executioners. But 21 others—among them Reich Marshal Hermann Göring, Foreign Minister Joachim von Ribbentrop and Germany's ranking admirals and generals—survived to be judged by the International Military Tribunal, composed of four distinguished jurists from the United States, Great Britain, the Soviet Union and France.

Each of the four powers had its own staff—the American contingent, the largest by far, numbered more than 600 lawyers, investigators and aides. American military police guarded the immense courtroom, which held 600 people, and escorted the prisoners to and from the adjoining prison. Translators rendered the gruesome evidence intelligible in four languages simultaneously.

The task of collecting, sifting and assimilating the evidence had been colossal. Documents on the SS, the Nazis' elite security force, filled six freight cars. Nearly 300,000 affidavits were introduced as evidence and the final transcript ran to 10 million words. But the verdicts were easily tabulated. Three defendants were acquitted and seven others sent to prison. Eleven were sentenced to death. Only one of them, in his last words to the court, acknowledged the justice of his punishment. "A thousand years will pass," said Hans Frank, the notorious Governor-General of Poland, "and still this guilt of Germany will not have been erased."

In a surrealistic painting, the grim evidence of wartime devastation intrudes upon the prisoners arrayed in the courtroom at Nuremberg.

Standing around a bonfire on execution eve, children from the city of Nuremberg silently hang an effigy of Hermann Göring, the second-ranking Nazi

A DISPARATE BAND OF DEFENDANTS

The men tried at Nuremberg had little in common. They ranged from relatively innocuous careerists like the diplomat Constantin von Neurath, to Himmler's assistant, Ernst Kaltenbrunner, the brutal chief of the Central Security Service.

The defendants varied greatly in age, temperament and appearance—often in ways that seemed to fit their crimes. Jew-baiter Julius Streicher (a man who was obsessed with the sexual aspects of racial purity) looked to British writer Rebecca West like "the sort of old man who gives trouble in parks." Youthful and servile Baldur von Schirach, onetime leader of the Hitler Youth, had a face and figure that to one observer "suggested a surfeit of cream buns." At first, drug addict and gourmand Hermann Göring looked "exquisitely corrupt and soft amid the austerities of Nuremberg." But thanks to a prison diet—and no morphine—he lost 120 pounds.

The prisoners did not get along well together. The military men maintained an icy isolation; the others—trusting and liking no one—resorted to backbiting or fantasy. Ribbentrop complained about being tried with Göring; banker Hjalmar Schacht called Göring an ignoramus in economics and told the prison psychiatrist that the snobbish Ribbentrop "should be hanged for his stupidity." Rudolf Hess, who had flown to Britain in 1941 believing that he could talk the British out of the War, continued to have problems with reality. He spent much of the trial feigning amnesia.

Some of the defendants had attempted suicide when first captured. Hans Frank, the "Butcher of Poland," slit his throat and wrists—but was clumsy about it. He survived. Labor leader Robert Ley was more successful and escaped trial: He stuffed his underwear in his mouth and hanged himself with a towel in his Nuremberg cell.

The whereabouts of a 22nd defendant were still a mystery. Hitler's secretary Martin Bormann, who vanished as the Reich collapsed (page 48), was tried, convicted and sentenced to death in absentia.

In a uniform stripped of all but buttons, Hermann Göring arrives in court on November 26, 1945. The slimmed-down Göring, who struck American writer John Dos Passos as "a leaky balloon of a fat man," still had to turn sideways to fit through the narrow elevator doors.

Grand Admiral Karl Dönitz, U-boat fleet commander, later Navy chief

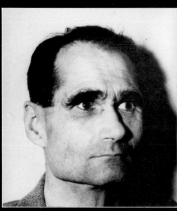

Rudolf Hess, Deputy Führer until his flight to England in 1941

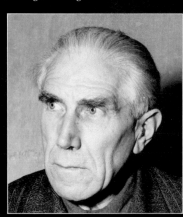

Franz von Papen, former Chancellor and Ambassador to Turkey

Hjalmar Schacht, Reichsbank President and Economics Minister

Hans Frank, Minister of Justice and Governor-General of Poland

Wilhelm Frick, Interior Minister and Protector of Bohemia and Moravia

Hans Fritzsche, radio propagandist and deputy to Joseph Goebbels

Walter Funk, successor to Schach as Reichsbank President

General Alfred Jodl, chief of operations for the High Command

Ernst Kaltenbrunner, leader of the Reich's Central Security Service

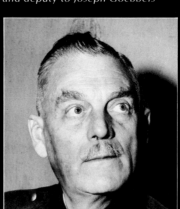
Field Marshal Wilhelm Keitel, chief of staff of the High Command

Constantin von Neurath, diploma and Protector of Czechoslovakia

Grand Admiral Erich Raeder, head of the German Navy until 1943

Joachim von Ribbentrop, wartime Foreign Minister

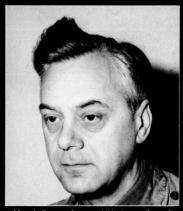
Alfred Rosenberg, Minister for the Occupied Eastern Territories

Fritz Sauckel, manpower organize and procurer of slave labor

Arthur Seyss-Inquart, German Commissioner for the Netherlands

Baldur von Schirach, Hitler Youth leader and Gauleiter of Vienna

Albert Speer, chief Nazi architect and Production Minister

Julius Streicher, anti-Semitic editor and Gauleiter of Franconia

After the suicide of Robert Ley, the already strict security at Nuremberg prison became even more rigorous. Shifts of alert MPs stood guard day and night outside each cell, keeping constant watch on the prisoners, who were ordered to keep faces and hands visible even while they slept. Such potentially harmful items as pencils, eyeglasses and suspenders were removed each night, and meals in GI mess kits came with spoons only, lest someone try to kill himself with a knife or fork.

The accused men occupied part of a wing that previously had held political enemies of the Reich. The building also housed lesser prisoners, including a group of female concentration-camp guards and some witnesses whose incriminating testimony during the trial had led to their own arrest. The structure itself was guarded as carefully as the prisoners, lest any diehard Nazis try to free the accused or disrupt the trial. Five American tanks protected the prison and the adjoining Palace of Justice, whose hallways were guarded by sandbagged machine-gun emplacements.

The prisoners had to sweep their cells daily and wear black-dyed GI fatigues except during court sessions, when they appeared in their customary civilian clothes or military uniforms. They could talk with one another in court, at meals and in the exercise yard—as long as they behaved themselves to their guards' satisfaction.

The Nazis adapted in different ways to the regimen. Ribbentrop became slovenly, while General Alfred Jodl maintained his cell, uniform and person in perpetual inspection order. Rudolf Hess goose-stepped around the exercise yard and complained that the same Americans who were anxious to prevent his suicide were secretly adding poison to his food. Julius Streicher, editor of the strident *Der Stürmer,* was reduced to faking nightmares and awakening everyone with his screams to get attention. Hjalmar Schacht complained petulantly that his sleep was disturbed by the guards, who, he said, chewed their gum and played their radios too loudly.

It was a dim and shrunken existence for men used to extreme power. Almost all the accused attended Sunday church services, if only to escape their cells. Some, like Göring and Albert Speer, took to pacing their 9-by-13-foot quarters—"at first back and forth," Speer wrote, "and then, the better to utilize the space, around and around."

Inside the prison at Nuremberg, American MPs on no-cell-block watch during their three-hour

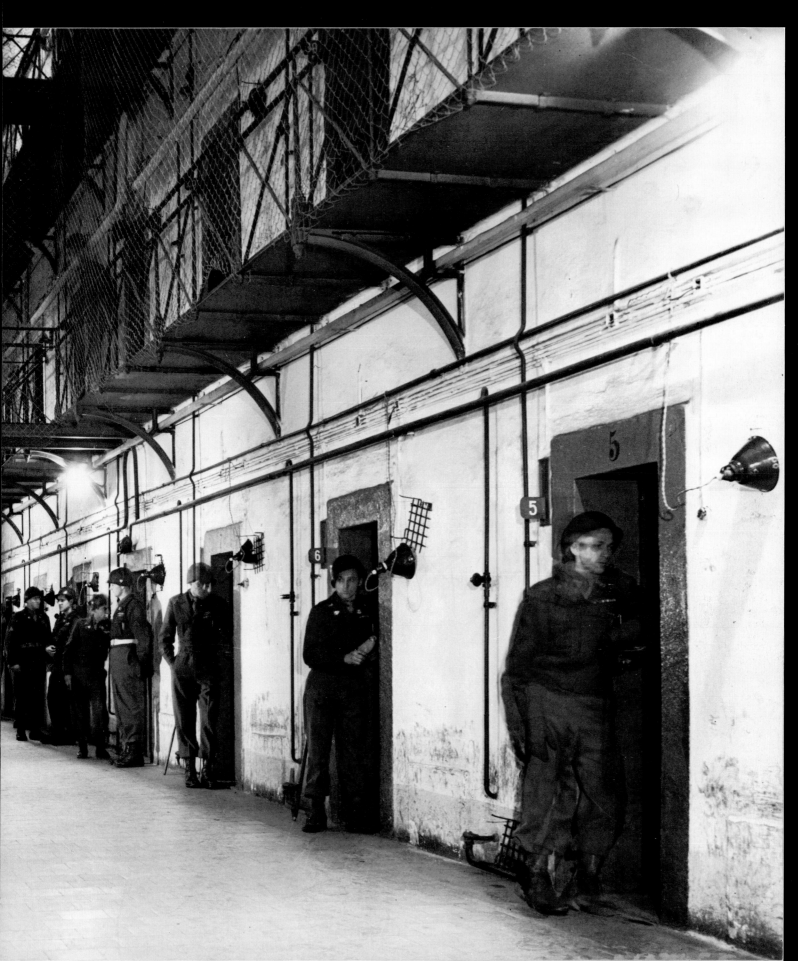

shift. The guards used the hand lamps by the cell doors to check the prisoners at night. Wire mesh was hung on the walkways above to prevent suicide attempts.

Chuckling at a translation error, Göring (left), Hess, Ribbentrop and Keitel sit in the dock's first row, Dönitz, Raeder, Schirach and Sauckel behind them.

NERVOUS LAUGHTER AS THE EVIDENCE BUILDS

'I could feel the presence of dead millions,'' recalled a British attorney. ''They were there throughout the trial, sad phantoms from the gas chambers come as witnesses to Nuremberg.'' The evidence, often grisly, piled up day after day. And still the unbalanced Hess read novels or slept. Göring hissed ''S____'' at a wit-

ness he disliked, and all laughed at the occasionally botched translation *(above)*. Although blind to his own crimes, Ribbentrop pettily dismissed his attorney when the man neglected to wish him a Happy New Year for 1946.

One by one, the defendants were examined. Göring, who went first, dueled stubbornly with the prosecutors but refused to shift blame to the absent Hitler. Few others were so highly principled. Their denials of responsibility provoked Speer to de-

nounce his fellow prisoners sardonically as ''letter carriers on high salaries.'' Ernst Kaltenbrunner disowned his signed name so many times that even the defense attorneys began referring to him as ''the man without a signature.''

To dodge was useless. The defense of acting on ''higher orders'' had been expressly forbidden by the four-power agreement that established the tribunal—which left most of the Nuremberg prisoners with no defense at all.

The chief American prosecutor, Robert Jackson (left), and the Soviet deputy chief, Colonel Y. V. Pokrovsky, listen intently in court. Jackson was on leave from his duties as a justice of the U.S. Supreme Court.

Seated on the witness stand, Wilhelm Keitel, formerly chief of the High Command, confers with his German attorney during a recess. The defendants chose their own lawyers from a roster approved by the Allies.

DEATH BY THE ROPE

The judgments at Nuremberg ranged a full gamut. Hess, Funk and Raeder were sentenced to life in prison, Speer and Schirach to 20 years each, Neurath to 15, Dönitz to 10. Papen, Schacht and Fritzsche—acquitted of major crimes—were later tried and given short sentences by German denazification courts. The rest were condemned to "death by the rope."

In the early hours of October 16, 1946, the doomed men crossed the yard to the dingy prison gymnasium, where eight correspondents, 10 official witnesses—two of them German—and three new gallows awaited them. Guards and chaplains escorted them up the 13 steps to a platform. Hangman John Woods adjusted the noose, bound each man's feet with a web belt, and placed a black hood over his head. A U.S. officer made a cutting motion, and an assistant executioner sprung the lever. The drop opened and the condemned fell.

No man showed cowardice. Ribbentrop—the first executed—wished "peace to the world" as he left it at 1:14 a.m. Streicher screamed "Heil Hitler!" Jodl—who had agreed with his wife to regard the tolling of the cathedral bell at midnight as their last communication—whispered "I greet you, my Germany."

One Soviet and one American physician stood by to pronounce death. Theirs was sometimes a long wait. The hastily built gallows evidently allowed for an insufficient drop, and several of the condemned men died of slow strangulation rather than broken necks. Ribbentrop swung for 19 minutes, Keitel for 24. Streicher groaned audibly through his hood. But by 3 a.m. the last of them were dead. They were laid atop plain wooden coffins at the far end of the gymnasium, where a U.S. Army photographer snapped their death portraits as proof that the sentences had been fulfilled.

Master Sergeant John C. Woods of San Antonio, Texas, readies his noose. Woods, official executioner for the U.S. Army, commented later: "I hanged those 10 Nazis and I am proud of it!"

WILHELM FRICK

HANS FRANK

ALFRED JODL

ARTHUR SEYSS-INQUART

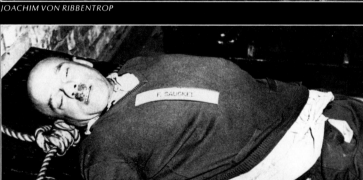

JOACHIM VON RIBBENTROP

ERNST KALTENBRUNNER

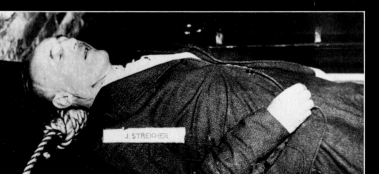

FRITZ SAUCKEL

WILHELM KEITEL

JULIUS STREICHER

ALFRED ROSENBERG

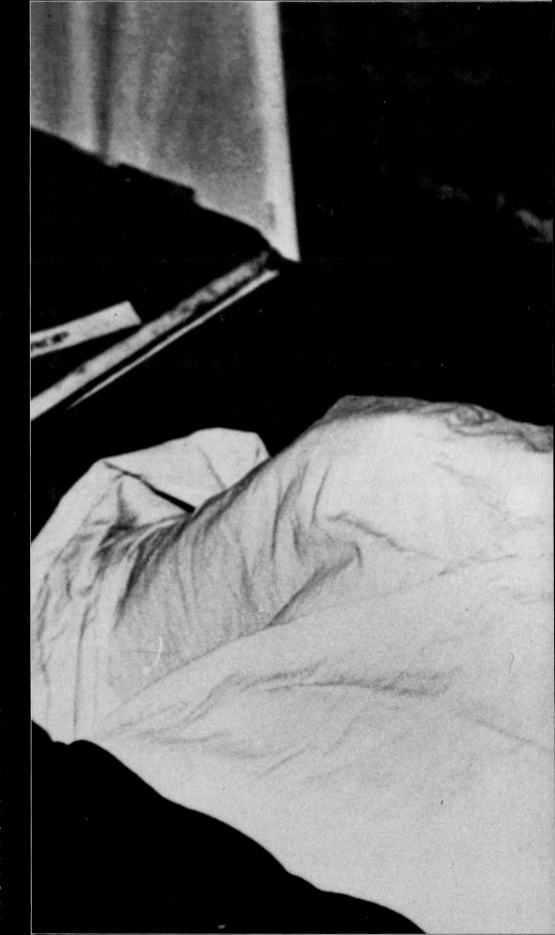

HOW GÖRING EVADED THE HANGMAN

One of the condemned men had cheated the hangman. Hermann Göring had bitten into a cyanide capsule two and a half hours before he was to be executed.

No one knows how Göring got the poison. One vial had been found taped to his navel when he was captured. There was some speculation that a visitor might have smuggled him the second dose, but Allied investigators concluded that he had probably had the two-inch glass capsule all the time, hiding it variously in his alimentary tract and beneath his toilet.

Göring had boasted to Albert Speer that his remains would be honored as a national treasure. Instead, his stiffening body, turned pale green from the poison, was carried over to the gymnasium to be photographed with the others. Then all the bodies were loaded aboard two guarded trucks and carted to the former concentration camp at Dachau, where the death ovens had been relighted especially to cremate them. The ashes were scattered in the Isar River, leaving no relics, no graves, to inspire any future Nazis.

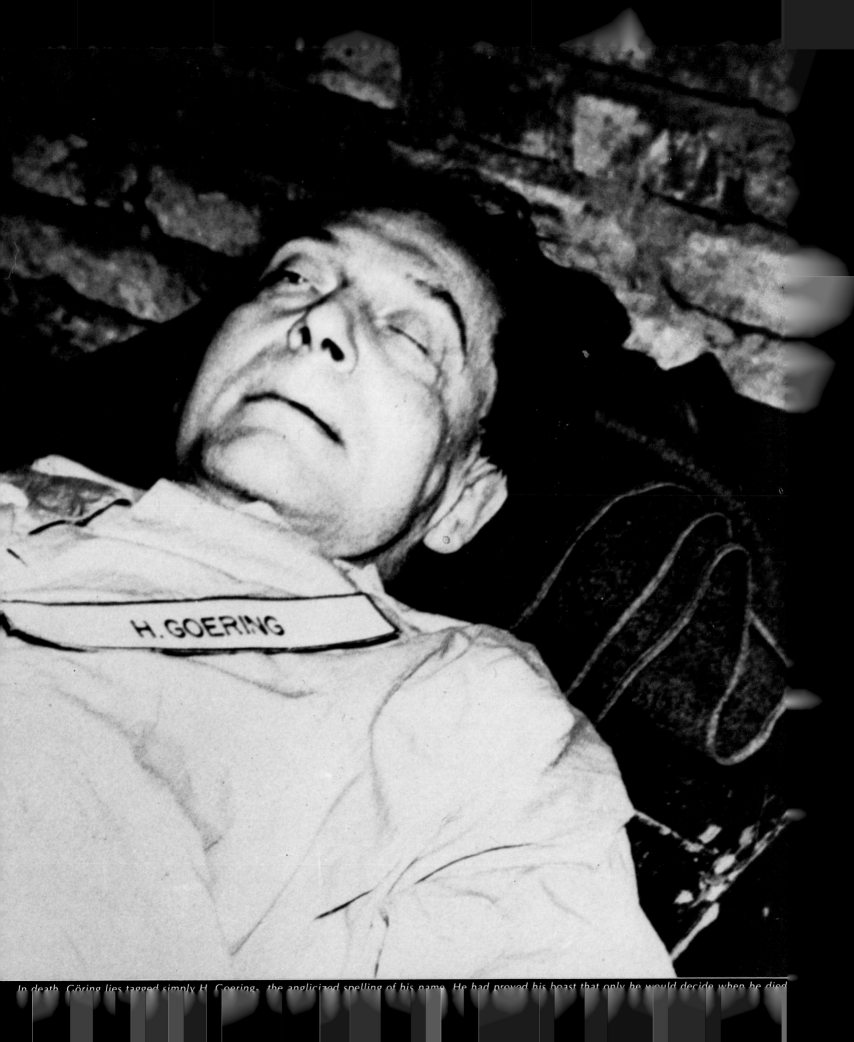

In death, Göring lies tagged simply H. Goering, the anglicized spelling of his name. He had proved his boast that only he would decide when he died.

3

Ordeal of the "compass-point" citizens
Shipping the hated Germans home
Brass bands and firing squads in Murmansk
The British decision that doomed thousands of Cossacks
UNRRA's massive effort to house the homeless
Years of waiting and hoping in DP camps
Where is the city of Texas?
Braving the underground route to Palestine
"You can shoot us, but we're not going back"
Joyful landfall in the Promised Land

The coming of peace to Europe brought the greatest and most agonizing cross-migration in human history. The survivors among the more than 50 million people who had been uprooted during six years of war all seemed to be on the move at once. People of every European nationality were struggling to return home or reach some other haven. Among them were civilians who had fled bombardment, slave laborers, concentration-camp inmates, prisoners of war, German-speaking émigrés forced out of Eastern Europe, and countless others who had been caught up in the maelstrom of battle. The roads of Europe were jammed with columns of people trudging on foot, on bicycles, in horse-drawn wagons and in automobiles that in many cases had been stolen. At the same time, freight cars that once had carried troops to war and Jews to slaughter now hauled an army of what one American observer called "compass-point citizens" north, south, east and west across the ravaged face of Europe.

Thirty-five million of these displaced persons, or DPs as they were called, had fled to another part of their own countries during the War. For them, the road home was relatively easy, and they soon settled down much as dust settles after a windstorm. The remaining 15 million found themselves in alien lands, a great many in Germany, the hated nation that had devastated their lives. Among them were Jews who had survived the Holocaust and were waiting to emigrate to Palestine, Eastern Europeans who were reluctant to go home to life under a Communist government, and those who simply had nowhere to go in the aftermath of the War. These unfortunates were destined to live in "temporary" camps for months or even years.

Alongside the victims of the Third Reich surging across the countryside were millions of displaced Germans. These hapless souls included *Lebensraum,* or "living space," Germans whom Hitler had sent to colonize conquered land in the East; *Reichsdeutsche,* Germans from the portions of Germany proper now under the heavy boot of the Red Army; and *Volksdeutsche,* ethnic Germans whose ancestors had settled in Poland, Hungary and Czechoslovakia. Their migration had started in the autumn of 1944 when Soviet forces had first stormed into Eastern Europe. Millions of these Germans fled rather than face vengeful Russian soldiers, who had been given a free hand to kill and to plunder.

ARMIES OF WANDERERS

At the same time, Allied leaders—commencing to redraw the map of postwar Europe—were discussing the forced resettlement of the ethnic Germans who had remained in the East. In December 1944, Winston Churchill called for a "clean sweep" of ethnic Germans from Eastern Europe. Eduard Beneš, who was leader of Czechoslovakia's government-in-exile, had been even more blunt. Beneš detested the Sudeten Germans who—like many ethnic Germans in Eastern Europe—had embraced Nazism, and had then lorded it over their oppressed countrymen. Said Beneš, in an angry radio speech: "We must get rid of all those Germans who plunged a dagger into the back of the Czechoslovak state in 1938."

In February 1945, Roosevelt, Churchill and Stalin met at the Soviet Black Sea resort of Yalta to plan the final campaign against Germany and to chart the course of postwar Europe. At the meeting's conclusion, the three leaders agreed that "Poland must receive substantial accessions of land in the north and west" to make up for land lost to Russia in the east, and to punish a defeated Reich. The Poles themselves were not consulted about the arbitrary exchange, and when their government-in-exile protested the permanent loss of the eastern territories, Churchill replied that Poland had no say in the matter. "Unless you accept," he warned, "the Russians will sweep through your country and your people will be liquidated."

Five months after the Yalta Conference, at Potsdam, Churchill, Stalin and Roosevelt's successor, Harry S. Truman, spelled out the details of ceding German land to Poland and Russia and sending Eastern European Germans to a truncated Germany. Territory the Poles were to control included the Baltic port of Danzig, the industrial province of Upper Silesia and the coastal province of Pomerania. Poland was ceded most of East Prussia, the Soviets the rest. At one point in their discussions, Truman asked how many Germans were left in the region between the Oder and Neisse Rivers, which also was to be ceded to Poland. Stalin replied that no Germans were left in the area; those who had not been killed had fled. In fact, there were nearly five million Germans remaining in that one region and anywhere from one to three million elsewhere in the East. All of them were destined to be transported forcibly to the West.

Churchill, in spite of his earlier call for a clean sweep in the East, confessed at Potsdam that he had "grave moral scruples about vast movements of population." "The uprooting of millions," he said, "was too many and would be morally wrong." Despite Churchill's misgivings, the Allies eventually agreed, in Article XII of the Potsdam Protocol, that "the transfer to Germany of German populations, and of elements thereof, remaining in Poland, Czechoslovakia and Hungary will have to be undertaken. The transfers should be effected in an orderly and humane manner."

But the transfers—which the jubilant and vengeful Poles, Czechs and Hungarians had begun to press even before the conference at Potsdam—would prove neither orderly nor humane. Eventually nearly two million people would perish in that deadly hegira.

In many cases the ethnic Germans were expelled almost without warning, forced to depart with little more than the clothes on their backs. In Brno, Czechoslovakia, for instance, members of the newly formed National Guard—inspired by hatred for the Germans—decided one night to "purify" the town. "Shortly before 9 p.m.," recalled one witness, "they marched through the streets calling on all German citizens to be standing outside their front doors at 9 o'clock with one piece of hand luggage each, ready to leave the town forever. Women had 10 minutes to wake and dress their children, bundle together a few possessions and come out onto the pavement.

"Here, they were ordered to hand over all their jewelry, watches, fur and money to the guards, retaining only their wedding rings." Then the Germans were marched at gunpoint out of town toward the border.

Similar scenes were repeated throughout Eastern Europe. "These uprooted masses wandered along the main roads, famished, sick and weary, often covered with vermin, seeking some country in which to settle," reported a delegate of the International Committee of the Red Cross. "Wherever they appeared, they were passed on, now in this direction, now in that. A man and a woman expelled from Silesia got as far as Mecklenburg, where they received orders to return to Silesia. The man returned to his cart and placed his wife in it since she could no longer walk. Then they returned to Silesia. No sooner had they arrived than they were once more rejected."

German refugees herded onto trains fared no better than their compatriots on foot. In Breslau, Poland, militiamen rounded up 130 Germans, took most of their valuables and packed them into cattle cars for the trip west. The journey lasted 11 days, remembered one refugee, during which he and his fellows were robbed of what little remained to them. The plundering of such trains was commonplace. On one journey, reported a refugee, "hundreds of bandits—many of them 12 to 16 years old—sprang like cats onto the train and took away absolutely everything from the voyagers, un-

dressing them to shirt and underwear. Terrible cries of distress were raised as the Poles trampled upon children and old people in their lust to loot."

At night the freight cars usually were shunted off to a siding to make way for other trains. The passengers slept where they were. On one occasion they spent the night in the ice-cold waiting room of a station where, one of them graphically recalled, "the loud groans of the half-clothed people slowly congealed into occasional whimpers. Throughout the night, Polish bandits and soldiers conducted searches to see whether any useful objects had been overlooked or to fetch women into the next room to be violated."

The trains brought thousands of German émigrés into Berlin every day. "The journey takes several days, during which no food is provided," wrote British philosopher Bertrand Russell after visiting Berlin in 1945. "Many are dead when they reach Berlin; children who die along the way are thrown out the window. A member of the Friends Ambulance Unit describes the Berlin station at which these trains arrive as 'Belsen over again.' "

Even after reaching Berlin, many of the displaced Germans did not live for long. Under the bomb-wrecked roof of the Stettin Station, British reporter Norman Clark saw scores of people, "all ravenous and starving," for whom "nothing could be done—until death." These people, he wrote, were but a fraction of "the dead and dying and starving flotsam left by the tide of human misery that daily reached Berlin." Throughout the summer of 1945, that tide deposited nearly 20,000 German émigrés per day inside Germany's four zones of occupation. In the Soviet sector, the authorities provided subsistence rations for the émigrés and quickly put them to work. They viewed the newcomers not as a burden but as a commodity—additional labor for the Communist state they were creating. "No distinctions were drawn between them and ordinary German citizens," noted historian Malcolm Proudfoot. "Lack of land and property meant little, since both belonged to the state and were being redistributed. The German refugee problem was thus, in a very real sense, peculiar to Western Germany."

There, in the American, British and French sectors, local authorities found themselves on the horns of a dilemma. On the one hand, here were desperately needy people; on the

In this poignant sequence of photographs taken in late October of 1945 a cluster of German mothers and children (top) arrive in a railroad yard in the British sector of Berlin—the only survivors from a group of 150 who had been evicted from Lodz, Poland, 270 miles away. One more perished even as these pictures were taken: A young mother striding ahead of her companions to seek help for her three year old clasps him tighter for warmth (center). Then, realizing he has died, she pillows his head on a rail (bottom) as another mother and child join her in grief.

other hand, the Allies were determined not to be overly generous to their erstwhile enemies. "Until the misfortunes of those whom Germany oppressed and tortured are obliviated, it does not seem right to divert our efforts to Germany itself," President Truman told a U.S. Senator who wanted to initiate private relief efforts for Germany in the harsh winter of 1945-1946. Thus, American military authorities in Berlin halted International Red Cross relief shipments earmarked for Germany and ordered them sent to other needy areas of Europe.

Not until thousands had perished from disease and starvation did the Allies relent. They then allowed groups such as CARE, the International Red Cross, the Swedish Red Cross, the American and British Friends Service Committees and several other private aid organizations to distribute food and clothing to the émigrés and to other needy Germans. The shipments of food lifted the specter of mass starvation that had been hanging over western Germany and allowed German authorities to turn to a long-range problem: how to absorb the millions of newcomers, whom many western Germans viewed as a threat to their survival.

It was immediately evident that the cities could not hold the refugees. In most cities at least half the dwellings were in ruins; commerce and municipal services were virtually nonexistent. Thus, German authorities decided to divert as many émigrés as possible to small towns and villages that had not been so badly damaged by the War. Every town was given a quota of people to feed and shelter—and, presumably, to absorb.

The displaced Germans, however, fared little better in the countryside than in the cities. Most towns were already desperately overburdened with refugees who had evacuated the cities during the War. In one tiny Schleswig-Holstein village, the two waves of refugees swelled the population from 890 to more than 3,000. To shelter them, every structure in the village was put to use—including stables and pig sties. A visitor to the village in 1946 noted grimly that "there is not a barrack, not a public hall nor an air-raid shelter, not a factory room or shop that has not been used as an emergency accommodation." In their makeshift homes, the refugees crowded together with little semblance of normal life. "There is no privacy, no possibility of retreat," said one. "No one can be alone, even for a few minutes."

Jobs in the crowded countryside were as scarce as decent housing. German farmers—like farmers all over postwar Europe—were handicapped by a lack of fertilizer and equipment, which meant that they had lower crop yields and fewer jobs to offer. There were few jobs in the cities, either. Under the terms of the Potsdam Agreement, 15 per cent of the factories still standing in the western zones were dismantled and shipped to the Soviet Union as war reparations; another 8 per cent were sent to countries that had been occupied by Hitler's armies.

Many of the émigrés thus were doomed to live in poverty for years—existing on CARE packages and, eventually, on relief payments from a nascent German government that could ill afford them.

As Germans migrated westward, an equally arduous population shift was under way eastward. Five million Russians—slave laborers, prisoners of war, refugees and many thousands of disaffected men who had fought in the German Army—had been outside the Soviet Union when the War ended. More than two million of them were in territory under British, French and American control. The Soviets quickly shipped the 2.9 million displaced Soviet citizens in territory they controlled back to the U.S.S.R. The disposition

Still in shock, a teen-age German girl is helped away from a railroad station in Berlin; she had been raped by a gang of Polish youths on the train that brought her out of Poland. Such gangs, made up mostly of youngsters orphaned by the War, regularly boarded westbound trains to rob and molest dispossessed Germans all the way to Berlin.

of those in Western-occupied areas, however, became a matter of long and acrimonious debate. Moscow demanded that all its citizens be repatriated—even those who did not wish to return home. Eventually the Western Allies agreed. They fully expected Stalin to mete out swift and deadly justice to any Russian captured in a Wehrmacht uniform. But they either did not realize or chose to ignore the fact that Stalin was planning to treat virtually all of his returning countrymen—not just those who had taken up arms against him—as traitors deserving of a traitor's fate.

The story of these displaced Russian citizens is one of the grimmest of the postwar years. Advancing through France in 1944, the Allies had captured thousands of Russians serving in the German Army and sent them to prisoner-of-war camps in Britain and the United States. As their numbers grew, the British government became concerned over what to do with those prisoners being held in England. At a Cabinet meeting on July 17, Foreign Secretary Anthony Eden proposed deferring the entire matter until the War ended,

while Churchill suggested simply notifying Moscow that Russian prisoners were in British hands—in effect leaving the next move up to the Soviets. Churchill's view prevailed, and three days later the British informed the Soviets of the prisoners' existence. Moscow replied that all of the prisoners should be repatriated "at the earliest opportunity."

In the meantime, Lord Selborne, the Minister for Economic Warfare, stepped forward to champion the Russian prisoners. In a letter to Eden, Selborne argued that repatriation should be on a voluntary basis only. Most of the Russians, he contended, had enlisted in the Wehrmacht at gunpoint, and only after weeks and months of savage treatment. One of his aides had interviewed several of the prisoners, Selborne said, and almost to a man they did not want to go home for fear they would be executed or condemned to slave labor in Siberia.

Eden disagreed. "A large proportion of the prisoners are willing and even anxious to return to Russia," he blandly told Selborne. In any case, Eden continued, "They were

captured while serving in the German military or in para-military formations. We cannot afford to be sentimental about this." Eden pointed out that thousands of British and American soldiers were being held prisoner in eastern Germany and Poland—areas the Red Army was likely soon to liberate. If Britain delayed in releasing the Russian prisoners, he said, the Soviets might well respond in kind.

On September 4, Eden argued his case before the full Cabinet. The Foreign Secretary conceded that many of the Russian prisoners had been subjected to brutal treatment at the hands of the Germans and were likely to be ill treated further if they went home. Nevertheless, he recommended that "the Cabinet should accede to the Soviet request to repatriate their prisoners irrespective of whether these men wish to return."

The Cabinet approved Eden's recommendation but took no action to implement it. A month later, Churchill and Eden flew to Moscow to meet Stalin and Soviet Foreign Minister Molotov. Among other issues, they were to discuss the return of Soviet POWs and of British prisoners in German camps about to be liberated by the Red Army. Stalin had little trouble persuading the British leaders to repatriate all Soviets they had captured wearing German uniforms. Four months later, at Yalta—after they had already sent back a group of prisoners—the British tried to persuade the Americans to make a similar concession.

Roosevelt and the American delegation had a much different attitude toward repatriation. They wanted to send back only those men who really wanted to return home. They contended that under the Geneva Convention, Russians captured in German uniforms could claim German citizen-ship and be treated as such. Moreover, they feared that forcible repatriation of any man in a German uniform might bring reprisals against American POWs still in German hands. The British failed to bring the Americans around to their position, and at the end of the conference the two Western powers signed separate agreements with the Russians covering only the mechanics of liberating prisoners of war. Both agreements stated that Soviet representatives would be admitted immediately to camps where Soviet citizens were concentrated.

By April, however, with the end of the European war only days away, the American position had shifted. A paper prepared by Supreme Headquarters, Allied Expeditionary Force, detailed U.S. policy toward refugees and displaced persons. It addressed the issue of Russian nationals unequivocally: "After identification by Soviet representatives, Soviet displaced persons will be repatriated regardless of their individual wishes." In mid-May, an agreement incorporating this policy was signed by Soviet and American representatives at Halle, Germany.

Acting U.S. Secretary of State Joseph C. Grew explained the American about-face in a letter to Secretary of the Navy James V. Forrestal. "Now that all American prisoners of war held by German armed forces have been liberated," Grew wrote, "there no longer exists any danger that German authorities will take reprisals against them." At the Potsdam conference in July, the Americans joined the British in endorsing forced repatriation while limiting its application to "Soviet citizens originating within the 1939 boundaries of the Soviet Union."

Thus both Britain and the United States acquiesced at least indirectly in the eventual imprisonment or execution

German farmers and miners gather with their families and cartloads of belongings at Bamberg, a rail junction in the overcrowded U.S. zone. As essential workers, they were given permission to migrate to the French zone, where skilled labor was in short supply.

Searching for loved ones, German DPs scan a public bulletin board where members of separated families have posted notices in hopes of tracing wives, husbands and children.

of millions of Soviet subjects then in territory under their control. To Stalin, it mattered little that many Soviet citizens had remained loyal to the U.S.S.R. despite the appalling brutality they endured in German captivity. In his twisted view any Soviet citizen—soldier or civilian—who had caught even a glimpse of life outside Russia without the guidance of political commissars was no longer trustworthy.

Red Army soldiers captured in battle, even while unconscious or severely wounded, were especially despised. In Stalin's eyes they had surrendered when they should have died fighting, and he had no use for them. On several occasions, the Red Air Force had strafed Soviet POW camps in German territory. And when Stalin's son Yakov was captured, the dictator chose to let him die a prisoner rather than exchange him for Hitler's nephew, then in Russian hands.

Many Soviet prisoners of war, obligingly sent back by the British soon after Churchill and Eden's visit to Moscow in October of 1944, had already met a traitor's fate. On Octo-

ber 31, nearly 10,000 Russian prisoners sailed from British ports to Murmansk. Witnesses noted that virtually all of them went willingly; only a dozen had to be put on board by force. Most apparently were unaware—or at least unsure—of what awaited them.

They were not long in finding out. The first shipload of prisoners came ashore in Murmansk on November 7. There, noted an American diplomat, they were welcomed "with a brass band and then marched off under heavy guard to an unknown destination." For some of the prisoners that destination was the front line: They were rerecruited for the final drive on Berlin. (Those who survived the fighting were subsequently sentenced to 25 years' forced labor for treason.) Many others were immediately stripped of the heavy winter clothing the British had given them, were issued the rags that served as Russian prison garb and put on trains for the labor camps of Siberia. In some cases, the Soviets simply slaughtered the returnees as soon as they had debarked.

By the end of 1945, the British had repatriated 32,000 Russian soldiers from camps in England, while the Americans returned 4,454 from camps in the United States. The British also sent back 50,000 Cossacks who had been in Austria when the War ended and who had placed themselves under British protection. Unlike the Russian POWs, the Cossacks fought bitterly to stay in the West. A fierce warrior people who had once held sway in southern and southwest Russia along the Don and Dnieper Rivers, the Cossacks had chafed under Moscow's rule for nearly 400 years. When Hitler invaded the Soviet Union in 1941, the Cossacks had greeted the Germans as liberators and they were now well aware that they faced death or imprisonment if they were returned to the Soviet Union.

The two large groups of Cossacks who found themselves in southern Austria when hostilities ended were the 15th Cossack Cavalry Corps, commanded by General Hellmuth von Pannwitz, a German, and the Cossack Division, led by White Russian officers who flocked to the Nazi banner in hope of fighting the Communists as they had done during the Bolshevik Revolution. The Cossack Cavalry Corps had fought in Yugoslavia against Marshal Tito's partisans; the Cossack Division, though part of the German Army during the siege of Stalingrad, never saw combat.

After the collapse of the Stalingrad campaign in 1943, the Cossack Division had retreated westward, traveling slowly with its women and children in great caravans of wagons, horses, cattle and even camels. In May of 1945 the division surrendered to the British at Lienz, Austria—15 miles from the Italian border. After the trials of their lengthy retreat, life in Austria was idyllic for the Cossacks: There was lush pasturage for their animals, ample Red Cross supplies and neither guards nor barbed wire. Few even entertained the notion of escape, for it seemed unnecessary. They hoped fervently that the British would offer them asylum or invite them to join in a new war against the Soviet Union. All agreed that they would never return home.

On May 27, the Cossacks' hopes were cruelly shattered. The British ordered the division to hand over its weapons and told the officers to report for a parade before Field Marshal Sir Harold Alexander, a man they admired because he had fought on the czarist side during the Russian Civil War. The next day the British transported 1,600 of the division's officers to the town of Oberdrauburg. Waiting to greet them was not Alexander but Brigadier Geoffrey Musson, commander of the British 36th Infantry Brigade.

Musson's announcement was devastating in its brevity: "I have received strict orders to hand over the whole of the Cossack Division to the Soviet authorities. The order is categorical. Good day."

On the 29th of May, the British trucked the Cossack officers across a bridge and delivered them to the Soviets at the town of Judenburg. The British soldiers could not see what happened to the Cossacks once they were in Soviet hands—but they could hear. That night and throughout the following day the sound of small-arms fire came from across the river, accompanied by a lusty male choir. After each burst of gunfire there would come a huge cheer from those who had not yet been killed. Clearly, the Cossack officers knew how to die bravely.

Forewarned, the remaining Cossacks decided to resist. On June 1, they gathered in the town square in Lienz to pray, the men forming a barrier around the women and children. The British were forced to pry the men loose with rifle butts and clubs to load them on waiting trucks. Many of the Cossacks chose quick death to a delayed one. A man shot his family one by one, then killed himself; several women cut their infants' throats, then took their own lives in the same way. Over the next two weeks, the British delivered more than 20,000 Cossacks into Russian hands, although several thousand managed to escape into the surrounding forests and mountains.

In similar fashion, the British handed over 17,000 men of the Cossack Cavalry Corps, whom General von Pannwitz had led into Austria as the War ended. On May 25, the British—having told the Cossacks they were being sent to Italy and thence to Canada—marched them instead to Soviet captivity at Judenburg. The 3rd Battalion of the Welsh Guards, meanwhile, forced another 10,000 men of the Cossack Cavalry Corps into trucks at gunpoint for delivery to the Russians—a job their commander called "the most ignoble task I could ever give them."

Like their brethren in the Cossack Division, many of Pannwitz' Cossacks were immediately executed. The remainder were shipped to slave-labor camps in Siberia and Arctic

A Russian private stands guard in late May of 1945 as displaced civilians and demobilized German soldiers trudge homeward across the bridge over the Mulde River separating the recently established Soviet and U.S. Occupation zones. The Russian-language banner reads: "Welcome brothers and sisters freed from German fascism by the Red Army."

Russia. Years later, one officer who survived recalled the taunts of his captors as he was sent off to the Gulag: "A spell of timber-felling, a spell in a mineshaft with water up to your belt. You will feel your legs turn to macaroni, but you'll work. Hunger will make you."

Through no fault of their own, most of the two million Russian civilians whom the Germans had shipped to the Reich as forced labor shared a fate similar to the Cossacks'. The Soviets were eager to put them to work rebuilding their own country and they stridently demanded that those in the Allied sectors be returned immediately.

Once liberated, all Soviet civilians who had labored in the Third Reich underwent similar processing. They were funneled into giant collection centers in Germany and Austria; the center at Wiener Neustadt in the Soviet zone of Austria alone held 60,000 people. There, all so-called undesirables were executed. The rest underwent stiff interrogation. Virtually without exception, all of them—even the survivors of concentration camps—were deemed enemies of the state and loaded onto prison trains for the trip back to the Soviet Union. Well into the winter months, wired and barred cattle trains—guarded by machine gunners—could be seen chugging through the southern Polish countryside carrying prisoners on the first leg of a journey that ended in labor camps in Siberia or in war-devastated areas elsewhere in the U.S.S.R. A Soviet intelligence officer who later defected offered a breakdown of what happened to these people. Of the 5.5 million Soviet citizens who were repatriated, he said, 20 per cent were sentenced to death or to 25 years at hard labor—which amounted to slow death; 15 to 20 per cent were given shorter terms of forced labor, from which it might be possible to emerge alive; 10 per cent were exiled to Siberia; 15 per cent were sent to help rebuild war-torn towns and cities; and 15 to 20 per cent were allowed to return home. The remaining 15 to 25 per cent either escaped or died in transit.

In the confusion surrounding such a massive transfer of people, many non-Soviet refugees were swept along to meet the same fate as Russian citizens. Among them were thousands of citizens of the Baltic countries of Latvia, Lithuania and Estonia, which the Soviet Union had annexed in 1940. Hitler later evacuated 133,000 ethnic Germans from the Baltic States and resettled them in territories newly annexed by Germany. In 1944, threatened by the prospect of Soviet occupation of their countries, an additional 36,000 Baltic civilians fled to Sweden via Finland and the Baltic Sea. When the War ended, most of them vigorously resisted being sent back to their homelands. Soviet officials fought equally hard to scoop up these Baltic refugees in the dragnet of repatriation.

In Sweden, the fate of 167 survivors of the 15th Latvian Division of the Wehrmacht became a cause célèbre. The division took refuge in Sweden in May of 1945. The soldiers claimed they were not subject to repatriation to the Soviet Union because the Baltic States had not been part of the U.S.S.R. in 1939—the cutoff date set by the Allies at Potsdam. For months, the Swedish public debated their case while the Soviets demanded their return. The soldiers went on a hunger strike and one tried to kill himself by driving a sharpened pencil through his right eye. Miraculously, he survived and later escaped to England along with several comrades in a tiny fishing boat.

The remainder of the division was not so fortunate. In January 1946, the Swedes finally bowed to Soviet pressure and shipped the hapless soldiers to Russia. Most of the Baltic civilians, however, were allowed to remain in Sweden and eventually became citizens.

A young woman named Asja, from the Latvian city of Riga, was typical of the Baltic people who resisted repatriation to the expanded Soviet Union. The Germans had drafted her into the Wehrmacht as a nurse, and when the War ended she found herself in Pilsen, Czechoslovakia, where she was taken into custody by an American unit. Asja's initial euphoria at avoiding the Russians faded when an American officer informed her that a panel of three Allied officers—one British, one American and one Russian—would determine her fate. "My heart was filled with despair," she recalled. "I was haunted by the thought that the Russians would snatch me away." Asja decided she would pose as a German. She thought the ruse might work because she spoke fluent German.

A week after she was captured, Asja was called to appear before the panel. The American officer began the interview with three simple questions: Name? Occupation? Length of service?

"I am a nursing sister of the Wehrmacht," she stammered. "She's no German," the Russian interrupted. "She's a Balt in disguise. She comes from one of the Baltic States. And I will be responsible for sending her back there."

The room fell silent. The American's boyish face seemed to age years in a second, Asja recalled, as he realized that he might be determining whether she would live or die.

"Well," countered the American, "the girl's evidence is that she is a German and in the absence of any other evidence I am prepared to believe her. My vote is that she is a German national."

"And my vote is for her repatriation to the Baltic States, where she belongs," the Russian shouted.

The two officers glared at each other for what seemed to Asja to be hours. Then the silence was broken by a precise British voice:

"I say she is German. That makes two votes to one."

"I heard the scratching of pens on paper before anybody spoke again," Asja later wrote. "Then the Englishman, without a change in the tone of his voice, addressed me. *Fräulein*, we have decided that you will go to Hanover as soon as transport is available."

Swedish policemen escort protesting former members of the Wehrmacht's 15th Latvian Division from an internment camp at Rinneslatt to a Russian ship. The police had to intervene swiftly to prevent wholesale suicide when the soldiers learned they were to be repatriated.

In British-occupied Hanover, Asja was enrolled in a relocation camp, just one of a million displaced persons who languished in similar camps throughout Germany and Austria waiting for what they referred to as their "second liberation"—the first had been from the Nazis, the second would be from the camps themselves.

"Smoke was still curling from the blasted ruins of Germany when the first teams began probing the desolation in search of this new kind of debris of modern war, the displaced ones," recalled Kathryn Hulme, an American who was sent to Europe in June of 1945 to work for the United Nations Relief and Rehabilitation Administration (UNRRA). Hulme would live with the DPs for nearly five years as an administrator and friend, sharing their moments of tragedy and of eventual triumph.

The Allies had established UNRRA in November 1943 as a gigantic welfare agency for displaced citizens of the nations then fighting the Axis. Money to run it came from the governments of 44 nations and from private welfare organizations. By the summer of 1944, UNRRA had begun small-scale relief operations in Italy, but its biggest task came the following year when it sent scores of "spearhead" teams into Germany to run DP camps in abandoned German Army barracks, factories and even concentration camps, in cooperation with the Allied Military Government.

In these bleak surroundings, UNRRA workers fed and sheltered the nearly two million people who either balked at returning home or had nowhere else to go. These people—the so-called hard-core DPs—entered the camps by the trainload immediately after the War and waited there to be resettled. For the most part, the DPs were assigned to camps by nationality, but they had a goal in common, expressed best by a Latvian refugee who lamented to an UNRRA worker: "If I could only go some place where I could be a person and not a DP."

Kathryn Hulme had been at Wildflecken—a typical DP camp established in a converted Wehrmacht barracks in northern Bavaria—for less than 10 days when the first big influx of Polish DPs was announced. The hapless Poles, many of them forced laborers, had been stranded in the Czech city of Pilsen when hostilities ceased. "Four thousand, maybe more," a Military Government official informed the camp with a terse telephone call. "In batches of five hundred. By rail."

The next day at dawn, Hulme and a caravan of trucks drove 35 miles to the nearest intact railhead to await the trainload of DPs. A short time later, an old steam locomotive appeared, pulling several cattle cars. When the train stopped, a horde of gaunt, ragged people poured out of the cars—"men, women, children and gigantic bundles," Hulme recalled, "issuing continuously as in old comedies of movie slapstick, but with a peristaltic rhythm as bodies and baggage momentarily cleared the car door and made room for more to surge forward from the rear corners."

When all of the refugees had detrained, the UNRRA workers found themselves with not 500 new charges but at least 1,000. One woman had given birth during the journey and several more women had gone into labor and were about to deliver, according to the American officer who had shepherded the train from Pilsen, Czechoslovakia.

Throughout the day and far into the night, convoys of trucks delivered the Poles to Wildflecken. These first arrivals, Hulme wrote, were only the prelude to "prolonged and frantic activity." The UNRRA team was expected not only to settle thousands of DPs at Wildflecken but to persuade 1,500 of them to repatriate voluntarily each week until the weather closed the camp in for the winter. Surprisingly, Hulme recalled, the first batch took little persuading, "even when the stay-behinds goaded them about Russians waiting to receive them into boxcars labeled for Siberia. For better or worse, their peaceful faces said, we are going home where we belong."

Over the next few months, more than 10,000 Polish DPs passed through Wildflecken. Then, as winter approached, the number of those willing to return home slowed to a trickle. Hulme was puzzled until one refugee explained by pointing at a map of Poland's new boundaries, which had been posted to encourage repatriation.

The man ran his fingers down Poland's new eastern frontier, which followed the Bug River. Then he pointed to a village a few miles away on the Russian side of the river. The village, he claimed, was no longer in Poland, but in Russia. And if he set foot anywhere in Poland, he would be sent there to live as a Soviet citizen. For this reason, many Polish DPs not only refused repatriation, but forged identity papers and birth certificates lest UNRRA try to send them to what was now the Soviet Union.

As repatriation halted, Wildflecken's 12,000 DPs settled in for their first postwar winter. Food was in very short supply, recalled Kathryn Hulme, despite a steady flow of Red Cross food packages into the camps. The packages were welcomed, she said, "but a thousand other things were needed, and these we had to hunt for ourselves from Germans living nearby." The DPs tried to barter cigarettes and chocolate from their Red Cross packages for fresh meat and milk, which were especially scarce. If the Germans refused to trade, the DPs stole what they needed. UNRRA officials soon found themselves fielding complaints from local farmers over the disappearance of their precious hogs and cattle. Once, Hulme recalled with amusement, U.S. Army MPs came barreling into the camp in search of two pigs taken from a nearby farm. They searched from top to bottom the barracks where the pigs reportedly had been hidden, "poking into every room, every wardrobe, every crate and sack." A zealous MP captain even searched the men's and women's latrines—but to no avail. Later, Hulme learned, "the two old ladies we had intruded upon in the women's toilets, crouched over the seats with shawled heads, were the pig carcasses we sought, dressed and posed with such realism that even our captain had leaped back in embarrassment when I pulled open the doors."

Wildflecken survived another unexpected intrusion that winter. At Christmastime a large detachment of U.S. troops marched into camp to conduct a surprise inspection of the DPs' possessions in hopes of uncovering goods filched from neighboring German villages and from a nearby Red Cross warehouse. The Army investigators located a huge cache of food and clothing, but were embarrassed to discover that they were part of a special holiday shipment of Red Cross parcels. In all, the Army's raid netted one stolen horse, three goats and numerous bottles of bootleg schnapps.

When spring arrived, the repatriations began anew—but at a glacial pace: Only 220 Poles volunteered to leave Wildflecken on the first train of 1946. To speed the process, the Military Government tried shuffling the DPs from camp to camp, wrote Hulme, "uprooting them as soon as they had tacked up a private-room partition or strung a light bulb, giving them no chance to create a temporary home, in the hope that they might begin thinking of their real homes in Poland and go there, if for no other reason than for the peace of staying put."

When that strategy failed to produce the necessary numbers, the Military Government offered a 60-day ration of food to any DP who returned home before the end of 1946. The bribe had the desired effect: By October, the homebound movement was again in full swing, as Polish DPs voluntarily left camps all over Germany and Austria at the rate of 800 a day.

As the repatriates traveled toward Poland, they crossed paths with numerous other Poles, as well as Czechs and Yugoslavs, who had decided to flee westward as it became evident that their countries soon would have Communist governments. Many of these people had been DPs only a few months earlier; now they were being displaced again—this time by ideology. "It was like seeing ghosts," wrote Kathryn Hulme. "The returnees stayed only long enough to whisper their warning to trusted friends, and then disappeared." In early 1947, UNRRA closed its camps to newcomers in an attempt to discourage this new wave of DPs. When the refugees arrived, they were turned away. They were told that they would have to survive as "free-livers" in the poverty-stricken German economy, waiting, like their countrymen inside the camps, for the offer of a job in the West and the chance to start life anew.

With millions unemployed worldwide, jobs for displaced persons were painfully scarce. In their eagerness to leave the melancholy half-life of the camps, the DPs clutched eagerly at any opportunity. Whenever overseas jobs were offered, an overabundance of applicants rushed forward; real qualifications mattered little. "When we posted the news that Canada would accept qualified tailors, everyone who had ever sewed on a pants button was a master tailor," recalled Hulme, who had been transferred to the Aschaffenburg camp near Frankfurt am Main in the spring of 1947. "Our DP nurses swore they had done a bit of tailoring before they studied nursing. Ace mechanics in our garages dropped their tools and lined up at our unemployment office to have the record on their work card changed from mechanic to tailor."

The DPs' subterfuge was for naught: The Canadians took

only six tailors from a population of 7,000 at Aschaffenburg—the majority of whom, for the moment at least, were "master tailors."

"Again and again, we picked up and dusted off the rejected ones," Hulme later wrote. "The more highly educated the DP, the more absolute was his hopelessness. One Ukrainian doctor wept like a child when he was rejected from a scheme calling for hard-rock miners for Canada."

Throughout 1947, job offers trickled in from Belgium, Canada and Australia, but a hoped-for deluge never materialized. There were still one million DPs in the camps and many of them had resigned themselves to permanent residence in their "temporary" quarters. At least, wrote Hulme, they were inside "the only places on the planet that were safely theirs until tomorrow." The long-term DPs did their best to transform the camps into real communities: Businesses such as barber and cobbler shops sprang into existence, rival camp newspapers argued bitterly over camp

elections, and lawyers were kept busy with divorce cases and litigation of every sort. The DPs even rearranged their clothing-distribution warehouses to resemble department stores, with separate counters for men, women and children, and curtained dressing rooms. "Visitors always stared with astonishment," Hulme later wrote. "They had not expected to find camp life 'so normal.'"

Hulme and the other relief workers buoyed the lagging spirits of the DPs with one strong ray of hope: An emigration bill was being debated in the United States Congress. Near the end of 1947, news had reached the camp that the bill in its final form would require every DP emigrant to have a sponsor in the United States. "We began asking our DPs whom they knew inside the U.S.A.," Hulme related. "We passed out stamps and free advice on how to broach to a fifth cousin in Iowa (possibly with a mortgage over his head and 10 dependents of his own to support) the subject of guaranteeing jobs and housing to some forgotten kinfolk."

The replies from America began arriving with the first snows of November and their recipients deluged Hulme with questions: Where is the city of Texas, the state of Minneapolis? Is the weather there like Latvia's? Are there forests like Estonia's?

The DPs treated the first letters as though they were tickets and they already had one foot on the gangplank. Finally, on June 25, 1948, their hopes were realized when Congress passed Public Law 774, the Displaced Persons Act, which provided for more than 200,000 DPs to enter the United States over the next two years. While generous, the act did not open wide the door to America for all DPs; it was strewn with clauses that eliminated many of them from consideration. Forty per cent of the visas allocated by the Act, for example, were to go to persons "whose place of origin or country of nationality has been de facto annexed by a foreign power." This meant that a large portion of the visas would go to Balts, whose countries the Soviets had annexed. Another 30 per cent were allocated, in a so-called farmer clause, to persons who had been "previously engaged in agricultural pursuits." Third on the priority list were DPs who had relatives in the United States.

Even if a DP fell into one of those priority categories, he still might be frustrated by a clause that limited immigration to people who had entered Western Europe after the 1st of September, 1939—the date of Hitler's invasion of Poland. The clause eliminated everyone who had migrated before the War began.

Once a prospective immigrant was selected, he still faced a grilling by U.S. immigration officials about his morals and political beliefs, and a rigorous examination by U.S. Public Health Service doctors. Only then was the precious visa granted. Hundreds of thousands of DPs—dismayed by the tangle of red tape involved in getting an American visa—emigrated instead to Australia, Belgium, Canada and several other countries with less stringent entry requirements.

Since early in the War, the Polish Army-in-exile had fought as elements of the British armed forces. Now the British welcomed the Polish veterans and their dependents. They came 100,000 strong, their numbers augmented by thousands of Polish refugees who had attached themselves to the Polish Army at the end of the War rather than remain in DP camps. The British, despite their own straitened circumstances, found temporary housing for the newcomers and helped them prepare for life in a strange land. Schools were established for children, taught in Polish with English as a second language. Adults were offered classes in English, in skills that could lead to jobs, and in the complexities of the British way of life. After a relatively short time, the Poles were assimilated into British society.

The passage of the Displaced Persons Act in the United States came less than two months after another event that made 1948 a watershed year for DPs: the creation of the State of Israel, a new Jewish homeland carved from British-controlled Palestine. Before Israel's birth, many Jewish refugees had waited in stateless limbo in the DP camps of Europe, their numbers continually swelled by Jews fleeing an outpouring of postwar anti-Semitism in Eastern Europe. At the same time, several thousand Jews chose not to wait. Instead, they traveled clandestinely and illegally through Europe to Palestine, even though they knew that at the end of their perilous journey, they might be turned away.

More than three million Jews somehow survived the Holocaust, and at the end of the War many of them joined the mass movement of displaced persons across Europe. In many cases they had returned full of hope to their towns and villages, only to find that their homes had been destroyed and their families were scattered or dead. In many places they also found themselves the targets of a new wave of anti-Semitism. Those two factors convinced the majority of them that there was no place for them in postwar Europe.

By the beginning of 1947, one quarter of a million Eastern European Jews had emigrated west, flooding the DP camps. Most of them, said one, were "filled with one longing—to go home." That home was now Palestine, the Biblical land of "milk and honey" that their ancestors had struggled to reach thousands of years earlier. But immigration to Palestine in the first three years after the War presented many difficulties. The British, who governed the place under a mandate from the old League of Nations, had imposed a strict quota on the number of Jewish immigrants in order to placate Palestine's Arab majority. Only 1,500 Jews per month were allowed to enter. Thus, the only recourse for most European Jews was to slip into Palestine.

As the War was ending, the Haganah—the Jewish na-

Grim-faced relatives attend the mass funeral in 1946 of Jews killed when anti-Semitic violence erupted in the Polish city of Kielce. Although the pogrom's leaders were tried and convicted, such stark examples of renewed anti-Semitism persuaded thousands of Polish Jews to emigrate.

tional defense movement in Palestine—began planning the secret routes that would transport the Jews of Eastern Europe to Palestine. The Haganah had been formed in the 1920s to protect Jewish settlements in Palestine from Arab attack. Now it had a more complicated kind of fight on its hands. Agents of the Haganah traveled through Eastern Europe—organizing groups, providing money and documents, bribing border guards, arranging train and truck transportation, and finding ships to carry their fellow Jews on the last leg of the journey to Palestine from Atlantic, Mediterranean and Black Sea ports.

Between the end of the War and the creation of Israel, more than 70,000 Jews would undertake the *aliyah*—literally, the going-up—in an attempt to reach the promised land. Their journeys usually were cloaked in secrecy, but in the spring of 1946, an American journalist named I. F. Stone persuaded the Haganah to let him travel with a group of immigrants from Europe to Palestine to chronicle one such journey. The only proviso was that names and places be disguised to prevent the British from uncovering the operation.

In May, armed with a British visa for Palestine, and an unofficial Haganah passport, Stone arrived in the American zone of Germany. He visited several Jewish DP camps—including a model kibbutz set up on a farm once owned by Julius Streicher, the magazine editor who was perhaps Nazi Germany's most notorious anti-Semite. After several weeks in Germany, Stone made his way across Czechoslovakia to a small town on the Polish border, one of the most active crossing points for the Haganah underground out of Poland.

There—in a town he called Anton—Stone introduced

American journalist I. F. Stone interviews young émigrés (above) during their harrowing journey from Central Europe to Palestine. On the crowded deck of a refugee ship in the Mediterranean, Stone (at right center, his back to the bulkhead) applies a wet compress to the head of a passenger overcome by heat.

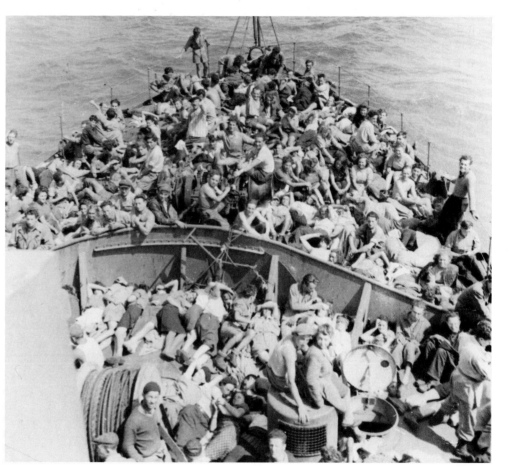

himself to "Schweik" and "Hacak," two remarkable Czech Jewish brothers, survivors of Auschwitz, who ran this stage of the route to Palestine. "First," Schweik told him, "people came through on their way back to Poland, but pretty soon a movement began in the opposite direction. Polish Jews began to return from Poland. They would tap on the windows in the middle of the night and ask for shelter. During the winter some came to us barefoot in the snow. The stories they told were much alike. They could find no trace of their families. The Polish government was not anti-Semitic, but some of the Polish people were. They preferred to return to the camps in Germany and wait for a chance to emigrate abroad to America or Palestine."

The help that the brothers gave the refugees—food, shelter, transport, border crossings, all paid for with cigarettes sent from the United States—made them legendary figures in Poland's Jewish community. In the year prior to Stone's visit they had sped 5,000 refugees down the Haganah trail. The refugees were a mixed lot. They included Polish Jews who had found life intolerable in postwar Poland, Eastern European Jews who had fled to the Soviet Union at the outbreak of war, and those who had lived in eastern Poland, which the Soviets had annexed in 1939. Somehow, Stone reported, the Jews from Russia had survived as families. "Only among these refugees did one see fathers and mothers with children." For a chance to reach Palestine, many of them had traveled fantastic distances—from Siberia, from the easternmost Soviet provinces, even from Tibet.

Bidding farewell to the brothers, Stone caught a train bound for Bratislava, the capital of Slovakia, 180 miles to the south. He was dressed in the uniform of a U.S. Army military correspondent—an unusual sight in that part of Europe. As Stone swung on board the last car of the train, a decrepit and dirty third-class car, a passenger exclaimed: "Look! The American is coming with us." Friendly hands grabbed his bags and helped him on board. In the car, Stone found 53 Polish Jews who had managed to cross the border into Czechoslovakia. The frontier, they told him, was a dangerous place for refugees. The Polish guards frequently shot the men and beat the women and children. Sometimes the Jewish refugees could bribe a guard to let them through, but at other times they had to wait in the woods for days or weeks before they had a chance to slip across the border.

The group Stone joined had twice been ordered back to Poland by the Czech police. "You can shoot us," the Jews told them defiantly, "but we're not going back." The police relented and put them on the train for Bratislava. From there they hoped to cross into the Russian zone of Austria and proceed to Vienna. From Vienna, the Haganah underground route would take them to an Italian port where they would find a ship to carry them across the Mediterranean. If their ship could slip through the British naval blockade off the Palestinian coast they would be "home."

"I was aware of the trials which lay ahead," Stone wrote. "I had heard of the dangers and delays which beset the underground route to Palestine, but there was no apprehension among my fellow voyagers. They felt themselves on their way. Behind were the green hills of the treacherous Czech border. Ahead somewhere were security, freedom and a new home."

On their short journey to Bratislava, the Jewish DPs passed thousands of other refugees. "At every station and on the sidings to which we were shunted to let more important trains pass, we saw other trains loaded with refugees," Stone wrote. "In ancient third-class carriages like ours, we saw Poles going east, and in battered freight cars, *Volksdeutsche* going west. Sometimes our trains and the trains carrying the other refugees stopped on opposite sides of the same platform, and people from both got out to stretch their legs. But there was no mixing. No one shouted across the platform from one train to the other. Their mutual misery created no common bond between peoples who regarded each other as oppressors and oppressed. The hate and fear that flowed between us was almost tangible."

There were no lights in the carriage and when night fell the refugees began to sing in the dark. "I have never heard singing that touched me so much," Stone recalled. "The songs I heard were songs that had sprung from the Nazi-created ghettos, the concentration camps, and the forest hideouts of the Jewish partisan bands. Many were spontaneous creations of anonymous longing. On their way out of Europe, the songs they sang said farewell to vanished homes and parents. Every once in a while someone would retreat into the shadows and I would see a head bend and shoulders shake. I stood watching the rails stretch out behind us in the darkness until the sky began to grow gray with the first hints of dawn.''

At 5:30 a.m. the train pulled into Bratislava. The refugees detrained and walked through the streets to rendezvous with 200 more Jews who had reached the Slovakian city by different routes. A young Haganah agent guided the refugees onto four old freight cars that had been added to the end of a train bound for Austria. After a short run the train reached the end of the line in Slovakia, and the refugees got out and proceeded on foot down a dusty country lane, a strange, shambling column trailing behind two carts piled high with their luggage and the youngest of their children. It was a particularly hot day. ''Sweat poured from us,'' wrote Stone, who by now had changed into civilian clothes. ''The gravel crunched beneath our feet. I don't think I shall ever forget that steady tramp, tramp, tramp as we marched toward the border.''

On the Czech side of the border three guards sat idly on a railing and watched them pass. On the Austrian side a long bridge led over a broad marsh. There were no guards in sight, either Austrian or Russian, at the other end of the bridge. The Haganah agent called out each refugee's name and one by one they slipped across the border into the Soviet zone of Austria. There, unhindered, they re-formed the column and marched on. It was to prove the easiest border crossing of the entire trip. At 4 p.m. that day, they reached a railway station two and a half miles inside the border. Here they unloaded the baggage from the carts and boarded the third-class carriages of a train bound for Vienna. Within a few hours the train reached a suburban station in the city's Russian zone, where the refugees piled into two trolley cars and rode unchallenged into the American zone.

Vienna had become the great crossroads of the Jewish exodus—an exodus far greater in both magnitude and misery than the ones centuries earlier from Egypt and Spain. In Vienna were to be found Jews from virtually every country in Europe. The huge Rothschild Memorial Hospital in the American zone of the occupied city was the hub of the Jewish migration. There the new arrivals received a physical examination and an UNRRA identity card. This granting of an identity card was a momentous event. ''To march across borders illegally, stateless and homeless, without documents, and then to come at last to a place were one meets a friendly reception, where one is given an identity card, is something only a refugee can fully appreciate,'' wrote Stone. ''One suddenly becomes a person, with a name, a number, and a *paper*. One now has a right to move freely in the American zone of Austria.''

Jewish refugees arriving in Austria had two alternatives. They could enter DP camps there or in Germany and en-

The spray from fire hoses mingles with black funnel smoke as a Royal Navy minesweeper swings close aboard to intercept a ship carrying Jewish refugees toward Palestine in 1947.

A British soldier at Haifa confronts angry refugees, one holding an infant suffocated by tear gas when their ship was boarded at sea.

dure the interminable wait for inclusion in the British immigrant quotas for Palestine. Or they could take a chance and continue along the underground route in the hope of entering Palestine illegally in a matter of a few weeks or months. When Stone arrived in Austria, there already were 34,000 Jews waiting in camps in the American zone alone. Some of them were living in relative comfort—in spas or in hostels like Camp New Palestine, a former residence for SS troops in Salzburg—but they were still not home, not in Palestine, and many thus chose the illegal route.

From Vienna, the next stop on the road to Palestine was Italy, generally reached by truck across the Brenner Pass. I. F. Stone, anxious to continue his underground journey with the least possible delay, parted from his companions and set off for a small port in Italy, where he was advised that an illegal refugee ship would soon embark from a town he referred to only as "X."

A few nights later, as a group of refugees was boarding the ship at a lonely cove 20 miles from "X," the usually indifferent Italian police arrived to halt the operation. Stone interceded, and while he remonstrated with the authorities,

the ship's crew cut her lines and sailed without him, but with 1,200 refugees safely on board.

Stone's contacts then informed him that another illegal ship, the *Haganah,* was on the point of sailing from a French port not far away. Stone reached the ship the next day and sailed down the coast to yet another nameless port; on board were a crew of 24, and life belts enough for an ocean liner full of passengers. The accommodations aboard the *Haganah,* a 750-ton freighter, were hardly up to a liner's standards, however. Bunks four and five deep had been rigged in every available space below and above decks. In the main storeroom was a cache of canned goods, bread and powdered eggs. In the galley were two enormous stew kettles: one for those who ate only kosher food and one for everyone else.

A few minutes past eight the following morning, one of the crewmen shouted: "Here they come!" A line of 10 trucks jammed with refugees drove up to the terminal at the tiny port. Many of the refugees had been traveling all night, standing upright in an open truck while a fierce rain beat down on them. One of the refugees' Haganah escorts

gave Stone his impression of this stage of the exodus:

"Imagine a dark night and a lonesome corner of a small town," he related. "The dirty little streets are unlighted. One sees no living soul as one drives into the town. Our three big trucks turn into a courtyard. I see a long line of people, like shadows along the wall. They stand in silence, their baggage already on their backs, their backs bowed. At a signal the people begin to climb onto the trucks one by one, like soldiers on the eve of an invasion. I stand by the trucks and watch a group of women and children climb on the trucks, children without mothers, and mothers without children. There are packs on their backs and a hot fire in their eyes. Some smile. Others cry with joy. Some hug and kiss each other and hold hands. Nobody says a word. I ask a small girl near me—it is a cold night, with rain and a chilling wind—'Are you cold?' She answers in a whisper, 'How can I be cold on a night like this?' "

On the pier of the French port, the Jewish émigrés formed ranks to board the ship. At a signal from the ship's captain, the boarding began. The first refugee to board was a young Pole named David Pickman, who had fought with the Polish partisans. Six hours later, the last passenger—a stocky Belgian named Victor Baumgard—walked up the gangplank. There were 1,015 DPs in all.

When the ship was ready to sail, the refugees were ordered below, out of sight of any coastal patrols. Then a pilot boat took the *Haganah* slowly out to sea. "A few minutes before 6 we dropped the pilot and headed south into a driving wind and rain," Stone later wrote. "Down below, the people were packed in like the cargo of an African slaver. At 6:30, when we could see nothing but the highest mountains and there were no other boats in sight, the captain blew a whistle as a signal that people could come up from below. Our passengers streamed up on deck to look with wonder on that great sea. For them it was the sea which washes the shores of Eretz"—of Biblical Israel.

During the voyage, Stone had time to survey the passengers; he found them a microcosm of those who had lived through the Holocaust. They came from 16 different countries; more than half of them were Poles, but there were many Czechs, Dutch and Germans and even a smattering of Greeks and Swiss. Sixty per cent of the DPs were men, while 80 per cent—the healthiest and strongest of both sexes—were under 30 years old. The oldest passenger, a Russian who had converted to Judaism, was 78; the youngest, a Polish girl whose parents had been gassed at Treblinka, was 10. "This child," her aunt boasted to Stone, "has crossed five borders illegally on her way to this ship." More than 300 of the refugees had fought during the War—in the Red Army, the Polish Army, the Czech Army or as partisans.

On the eighth day of their voyage, the refugees were transferred in lifeboats to a battered Turkish freighter less than half the size of the *Haganah*. For two days, the ancient ship, her engines "wheezing like an asthmatic old woman," wallowed across the eastern Mediterranean. Finally, on a brilliant July morning, the Turkish ship neared the port of Haifa. Stone vividly recalled the landfall:

"Shortly before dawn I went to sleep for a while on top of the wheelhouse. I woke to see the dim outlines of a mountain toward the southeast. As the light increased and the sun rose, a cry ran over the ship—'It's Israel.' "

The distant mountain was Mount Carmel, which dominates the Haifa skyline. A last obstacle lay ahead. As the ship entered the harbor, said Stone, it appeared that an entire British naval task force was waiting for one tiny vessel.

"The refugees cheered and began to sing *Hatikvah*, the Jewish national anthem," Stone wrote. "We pulled down the Turkish flag at our helm and raised the Mogen David and the Union Jack side by side. People jumped for joy, kissed and hugged each other on the deck. So singing, we moved into the arms of the waiting British."

Stone's shipboard companions were fortunate. After a short stay in a Haifa detention camp, they were permitted to remain in Palestine—the last illegal immigrants allowed to do so. A few weeks later, the British announced that henceforth any "illegals" caught in their naval blockade would be interned on the island of Cyprus. But the British announcement would only spur Jewish determination. Over the next two years, 56 more ships would test the British blockade as thousands of Europe's last DPs tried to reach Palestine, in hopes of beginning their lives anew.

With an emotional embrace, a husband and wife are reunited in Haifa after five years. The Polish couple had been separated by the Nazis in 1941 and each believed the other dead. The wife had made her way to Palestine and her husband found her there in May of 1946.

VOYAGE INTO ADVERSITY

Its decks overflowing with refugees, the ship Exodus 1947 arrives in Palestine after being intercepted by the British on its unauthorized voyage from France.

A REFUGEE SHIP'S TORMENTED PASSAGE

They came from Poland, Germany, Hungary—from every nation where Jews still lived with the stench of the Holocaust in their nostrils. Many were "Jews of the miracle," inmates of death camps who had somehow survived. Now, on July 18, 1947, arriving in Haifa, they sang the Zionist anthem and descended the gangway to touch the soil of Palestine. It might have been the fulfillment of a dream.

Instead it was part of a long nightmare. The 4,554 men, women and children aboard the *Exodus 1947* were illegal immigrants, part of a deluge of European Jews seeking a new life in the land of their forefathers. The British, who governed Palestine, feared a rebellion among the majority Arabs if Jewish immigration was not controlled. Thousands of "illegals" had slipped through the British blockade, and thousands more had been diverted to camps in Cyprus to await legal entry—a wait that might take years.

The harried British decided to make an example of the *Exodus,* a Chesapeake Bay excursion boat bought in the United States by agents for the Haganah—the Jewish underground army. The British had pressured the French, unsuccessfully, to impound the *Exodus* in Sète, the port where the passengers boarded, and the Royal Navy dogged the ship across the Mediterranean. Then, early on July 18, as the *Exodus* neared Palestine, two British destroyers rammed its sides and 40 Marines and sailors rushed aboard. Three hours later, after a desperate battle in which passengers pitched tins of corned beef at boarders wielding truncheons and firing tear gas, the ship surrendered. Two refugees were dead and a crewman—his skull fractured—died later.

The battered *Exodus* limped into Haifa that afternoon, looking to one observer "like a matchbox splintered by a nutcracker." The American captain and officers were arrested, and the passengers were transferred to three waiting British transports. That their stay in Palestine was so brief was the least of their sorrows. Ahead lay a voyage under guard not to Cyprus, as they thought, but back to France—and then, in a move that shocked the world, to a place the refugees thought of as "the bloody graveyard": Germany.

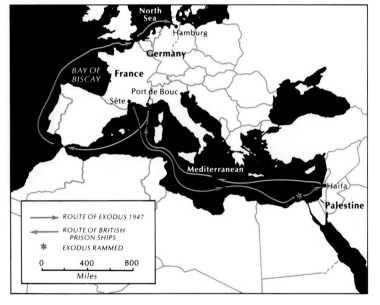

The Exodus 1947 (red route) departed for Palestine from the port of Sète in southern France. British warships that were tracking the Exodus eastward captured it in a sea battle (red asterisk) and escorted it to Haifa. The refugees were put aboard transports (blue route) and taken first to Port de Bouc in France, then north to Hamburg, Germany.

Acetylene torch in hand, a British soldier opens a jammed cargo port so that refugees in the hold of Exodus 1947 can disembark, temporarily, in Haifa.

FORCED REJECTION FROM HAIFA

In Haifa, the Jews were separated first from their baggage and then from one another—the males to be searched by the soldiers, the females by Arab women. Then all of them were deloused with DDT powder. Sharp objects, identity cards and cameras were confiscated. Water bottles belonging to the refugees were smashed on the dock; no one was to retain the means for independent movement.

Not all of the Jews left the *Exodus* or boarded the nearby prison ships without a struggle. Several had to be carried both off and on. The wounded were taken to a Haifa hospital, the dead to Martyr's Row in Haifa Cemetery, where 15,000 mourners attended their funeral.

Somehow, 41 people managed to hide until the last British search party had left the ship; then, in clothes smuggled aboard by a Jewish cleanup crew, they walked boldly ashore as part of the work detail.

A refugee's broken water bottle lies on the Haifa dock.

Using a painful arm lock, a British soldier forces a refugee across the dock at Haifa to an interrogation area. It took the British 12 hours to clear the ship.

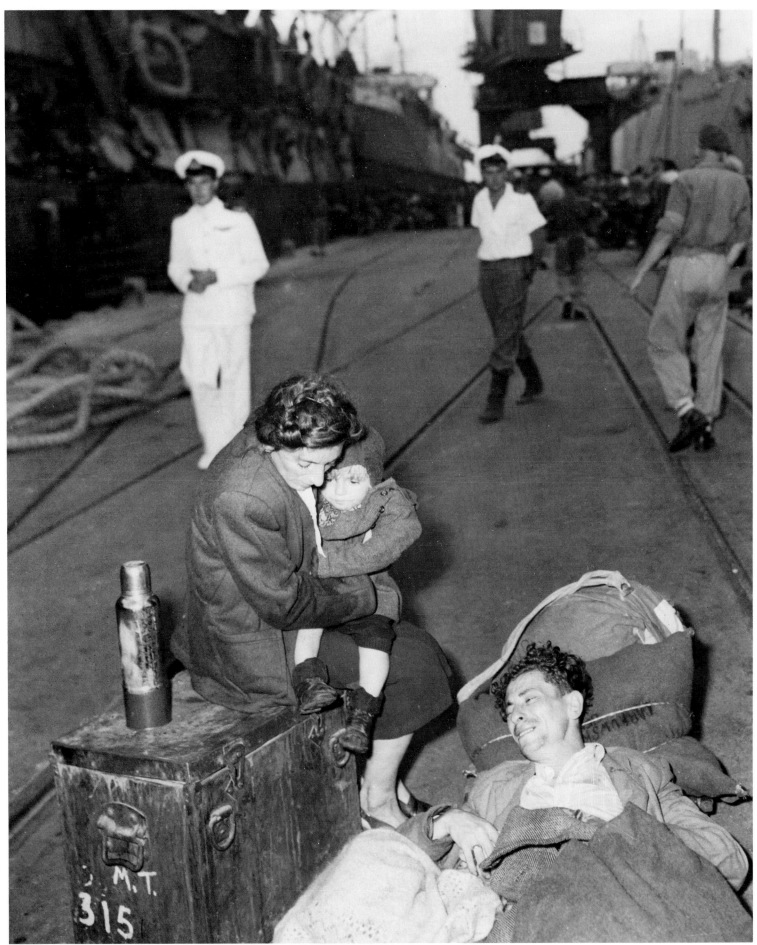

With his family and their sparse belongings, a wounded refugee waits for an ambulance. The damaged Exodus (left rear) was towed to a ships' graveyard.

Refugees on the caged foredeck of the prison ship Runnymede Park hold aloft a homemade banner that bitterly combines the British Union Jack and the Nazi

A BATTLE OF WILLS ABOARD PRISON SHIPS

The British marked the refugees' baggage "Cyprus" and told them they were being taken to the island to await entrance to Palestine. Instead the prison ships sailed to Port de Bouc, France, where the refugees were ordered to go ashore. All but 159 of them refused, swearing to set foot nowhere but in Palestine.

The British then waited for the terrible conditions on the ships to drive the Jews off. One American observer described the fetid holds and caged deck areas in this way: "Picture yourself on the New York subway. It's August, and it's rush hour. They've turned off the fans, slammed the doors, and you're left standing up against each other for five weeks." Yet most of the refugees stubbornly held out.

At last the British issued an ultimatum: Debark or be taken to Germany. Even that did not work. Only seven passengers—all of them sick—got off.

Observed from the stern of an escorting British frigate, the three prison ships steam toward Gibraltar en route to Germany. Once in the Atlantic, they hit heavy weather—adding seasickness to the refugees' miseries.

swastika. The Jews spent nearly a month anchored off the coast of France.

British soldiers move past a train filled with refugees waiting to board trucks for the last leg of their journey to a camp for displaced persons. On some of the

DETENTION IN A DESPISED LAND

At dawn on September 8, 1947—almost two months after leaving Haifa—the prison ships arrived at Hamburg in the British zone of occupied Germany. The British had sealed off the dock area and had assembled a welcoming party of 2,500 soldiers armed with truncheons and tear gas. Six medical squads stood by.

Most passengers on the *Ocean Vigour* and the *Empire Rival*—the first to dock—left peacefully. But the 1,485 refugees on the *Runnymede Park* took down the ladders to the hold and refused to budge. Eventually they were dragged off, screaming, kicking and spitting at the soldiers.

Once the refugees were on shore, they passed through cloth-covered wire corridors directly onto waiting trains that took them to camps outside Hamburg. British troops traveled in boxcars between the railway coaches, and armored cars guarded the route. All glass had been removed from the train windows, which were covered with heavy mesh screens. But the refugees remained fiercely adamant. "We have no life in Europe or Germany," said one Jew, "nowhere but Palestine."

trains angry Jews kicked at the wire window screens until they fell off.

A struggling Jewish woman is taken off the refugee train by a British MP.

Silhouetted on his elevated guard post, a British sentry armed with rifle and searchlight scans the grounds of the camp for displaced persons at Poppendorf in northern Germany.

A DEFIANT SHOUT: "PALESTINE!"

The refugees were taken to two camps, one built by the Nazis to house slave laborers, the other built by the British to shelter liberated Allied prisoners of war. Both had armed guards, searchlights and barbed wire. Inside, the refugees lived in tents or crammed 80 to a Quonset hut. Many, in tears, refused to eat their first camp meal because the food had been touched by German hands.

The British held off issuing ration cards until they had interrogated the Jews, hoping to identify the Haganah agents among them. But the refugees refused to divulge even their names, and when asked their nation, shouted "Palestine!" The British gave up and issued the cards.

The British jailers gave up in other ways too, becoming increasingly bored—and lax. The Jews began to slip away, doggedly heading once more for Palestine, and within a year all of them were gone.

A teen-age refugee defiantly shakes his fist behind the barbed wire that

holds him and his friends prisoner. The Exodus refugees joined more than 165,000 other homeless Jews still languishing in camps across Germany in 1947.

A NATION BORN IN VIOLENCE

עליה בכל הד
ובכל הג

Palestinian Jews in 1946 march beneath a banner demanding free immigration. The British at that point allowed only 1,500 Jews a month to enter Palestine.

SOLOMON'S JUDGMENT ON SOLOMON'S LAND

A Haganah soldier—tattooed at Auschwitz—does sentry duty in Jaffa. The 60,000-man Haganah became the Israeli Army after independence.

Nowhere did the passions ignited by the War flame more fiercely than in Palestine, a tiny patch of land on the eastern shore of the Mediterranean. Jewish survivors of the Holocaust were determined to enforce the long-standing claim of Jews everywhere to a homeland. But the Arab residents of Palestine, a 2-to-1 majority, bitterly resented any influx of Jews and demanded to know why they should have to pay for Hitler's crimes. In the immediate postwar years, Jews and Arabs viciously attacked each other, and both in turn vented their rage on the hapless British, who since 1923 had governed Palestine under a League of Nations mandate.

Palestine became a vexing international problem that required what one journalist called "Solomon's judgment on Solomon's land." The obvious solution was to share the land. But ethnic hatreds ran too deep, with extremists on both sides resorting to any tactic to increase their portion. And Britain, war-weary and financially bankrupt, was not up to the role of Solomon. Most of the 100,000 Britons serving in Palestine felt like the Tommy who wrote home: "Dear Mum, I am in Bethlehem where Christ was born, but I wish to Christ I was in Wigan, where I was born."

Before the War, violence had been largely an Arab tactic. But after 1945, when Britain refused to fling open the gates of Zion, the Promised Land, the Jews also turned militant. Many still hoped to shame Britain into honoring its pledge to establish "a national home for the Jewish people" by encouraging illegal immigration, which helped rally world opinion to their side. But others secretly armed and trained the Haganah, or Jewish underground army, to fight the British, and extremists organized groups known as the Irgun and the Stern Gang to drive the British from Palestine by terrorism. The Irgun—led by a refugee Polish Jew named Menachem Begin, later Prime Minister of Israel—blew up a wing of British headquarters in Jerusalem, the King David Hotel, killing 91 Britons, Arabs and Jews. The Solomon-like decision by the United Nations in 1947—to partition Palestine—led in the next year to an independent Jewish state and the evacuation of the British. But it did not bring peace.

Pedestrians in Jerusalem flee for their lives as the King David Hotel blows up on the 22nd of July, 1946. The explosion was the work of Jewish terrorists.

THE END OF AN INFORMAL ALLIANCE

Palestinian Jews had fought alongside the British in North Africa and Italy. But that alliance of convenience ended with the defeat of the common German enemy. Following the War, Jews turned their military prowess to wresting an independent homeland from the British.

The earliest raids, under the direction of the Haganah, were undertaken to help illegal immigrants reach Palestine. Haganah raiders sank patrol boats, attacked coastal radar stations and freed immigrants who were penned up for deportation.

Jewish activists soon expanded their attacks, bombing oil refineries, troop trains and RAF airfields. In well-organized raids they blew up bridges, mined roads, and cut telegraph wires and oil pipelines—proving that they could isolate both Palestine and the British within it.

A Royal Air Force truck burns on the Allenby Road in Tel Aviv after being overturned and set afire by Jewish activists. By early 1947, the Jewish underground had caused an estimated $2.4 million in damages.

A Palestinian policeman guards workmen removing the wreckage of an express train carrying British troops from Cairo to Haifa that was sabotaged by the Jewish underground in April of 1947. Five soldiers and three civilians were killed in the derailment.

AN EYE
FOR AN EYE

Not all Jewish zealots limited their attacks to government targets, or sought, as did the Haganah, to avoid causing casualties. Members of the Irgun and the Stern Gang went straight for the British jugular in both their rhetoric—labeling the British Nazis —and their tactics.

The Irgun numbered about 2,000 members, the Stern Gang about a tenth of that. But they made themselves felt. Introducing guerrilla warfare to the cities, they tossed hand grenades into police stations, planted mines inside Army posts, left bombs in train depots, tax offices and banks—often killing civilians as well as soldiers, Jews as well as Britons and Arabs. Members of the Stern Gang machine-gunned policemen from rooftops and robbed banks and armored cars to finance their campaign of urban terror.

Jewish raiders often wore British uniforms or flowing Arab robes to help them reach their targets unnoticed and to incite hatred of their enemies. One terrorist band used a kidnapped British policeman as a human shield during an attack on a police patrol. The Irgun and the Stern Gang went so far as to send letter bombs to prominent officials in Britain; none injured their targets. But other officials in Palestine were not so fortunate; by the end of 1946, Jewish assassins had claimed 373 victims.

The terrorists operated on the ancient principle of an eye for an eye. When the British condemned three convicted terrorists to death, the Irgun kidnapped two British sergeants, Clifford Martin and Mervin Paice, as they left a café in Natanya. Two days after the terrorists went to the gallows (shouting ''Avenge our blood!''), the sergeants were discovered hanging in a eucalyptus grove with Irgun execution orders pinned to their flesh. When British officers cut down the first body, it blew to bits, wounding an officer. The Irgun had mined the surrounding ground.

Heads wrapped in their own khaki shirts, British Sergeants Clifford Martin and Mervin Paice, both aged 20, dangle from trees in a thicket 18 miles north of Tel Aviv. On the day that the bodies were discovered—July 31, 1947—off-duty British troops rioted in Tel Aviv, killing five Jews and wounding 15 more.

"YOU HAVE TURNED THE COUNTRY INTO A JAIL"

The British tried hard to control the Jewish guerrillas. They established a curfew that turned nighttime Jerusalem into a ghost town, and their armored cars prowled the streets night and day. Surprise raids kept the underground unsettled. After incidents of violence, the British cordoned off neighborhoods and swept them clear. Thousands were detained and questioned.

The sweeps uncovered immense arms caches and netted dozens of terrorists who were tried under laws mandating death for carrying firearms. Still the ugly warfare went on. The frustrated British levied a so-called sabotage tax on all civilians to pay for terrorist damage. British women and children were evacuated; those left behind moved into fortified zones, called "government ghettos" by the Jews. "You have turned the country into a jail," gloated one captured terrorist, "and now have to lock yourselves up inside it."

A British soldier hands up a rifle from a secret arms storeroom—one of dozens uncovered in a raid on the Jewish cooperative farm at Yajur in 1946.

An Orthodox Jew is searched before entering a British compound for questioning after the bombing of a British officers' club by terrorists in Jerusalem. The bombing was one of 16 attacks on British targets on a single day—March 1, 1947—that killed 22 people.

Weapons drawn, British policemen prepare to enter a suspected terrorist hideout during a night raid in Jerusalem in October of 1946. An operator in a radio car (rear) stands by to call for help if necessary.

In a photograph taken during riots in Jerusalem following the U.N. decision to partition Palestine, an Arab stabs and seriously wounds a Jewish journalist.

A Jewish-owned taxi burns in front of Jerusalem's Damascus Gate, the entrance to the Arab section of the city. The vehicle was seized and set afire in retaliation for a raid in which taxiborne Jewish terrorists killed 15 people in the Arab market.

A SEASON WHEN "WISE MEN STAYED INDOORS"

"Let them celebrate today," muttered an Arab housewife watching Jews in Jerusalem cheer the United Nations vote to partition Palestine. "Soon they'll all be dead."

Her words were all too prophetic. The morning after partition was announced on November 30, 1947, seven Jews died in random killings throughout Palestine. Two days later an Arab mob rioted through Jerusalem's business district, stabbing and stoning Jews, looting and burning Jewish shops. Jews hit back, burning an Arab theater and other establishments.

In spite of the British curfew, the fighting continued to flare sporadically. In the month after partition was announced, 489 people of all faiths died in the violence. "This Christmas week in the Holy Land," wrote an American journalist, "shepherds went armed, travelers to Bethlehem were shot at, and wise men stayed indoors."

Rescue workers begin to sift the rubble of Ben Yehuda Street in Jerusalem on February 22, 1948, after Arab terrorists in British uniforms set off bombs that took 57 lives. Enraged Jews, duped by the ruse, then killed nine Britons.

OPENING STRIKES IN A HOLY WAR

As 1948 began, Palestine's civil strife accelerated into civil war. Both sides set up recruiting offices to enlist volunteers. Arab youths crossed into neighboring Syria for a month's training with the Syrian Army, while Syrian and Lebanese guerrillas entered Palestine to raid Jewish settlements. The Haganah came out into the open, both to restrain Jewish mobs and to protect Jews from Arab mobs and raiding parties.

Arab and Jew alike prepared for the British evacuation, scheduled for the spring. Haganah agents scoured Europe for arms, purchasing a huge supply from Czechoslovakia. (The Czechs also sold armaments to the Arabs, but the Jews intercepted the shipment before its arrival in Palestine.) Arabs throughout the Middle East called for *jihad*—a holy war against the Jews. But their war council betrayed a disarray that would eventually guarantee the survival of Israel: They could agree on little except the undesirability of a Jewish state. Nevertheless, Egypt, Jordan and others alerted their armies, as much to grab parts of Palestine for themselves as to stop the Jews in the name of Islam.

Moments after the bomb explosions by Arab terrorists, adults clutching children seek cover on Ben Yehuda Street in the Jewish shopping district of Jerusalem.

A British tank rumbles through battered Jerusalem on May 14, 1948, the day Britain's mandate over Palestine ended. That afternoon, Jews raised the new

Israeli flag (inset), proclaiming their first independent state in 1,878 years; on May 15, they went to war to defend Israel—successfully—against Arab invaders.

4

Truman's bold doctrine of intervention
A momentous proposal for European recovery
The rise of home-grown Communism
General de Gaulle's unswerving faith
"A state of insurrection exists in France"
Italy starts over at "year zero"
An unruly coalition of the Left
"Occupy the land of those who have too much!"
A guerrilla army's bid to seize Greece
Training and sanctuary beyond Communist borders
Merciless strikes by a phantom general
The Communists' last stand on Tsarno Ridge

The call from the British Embassy in Washington to the U.S. State Department came in just after lunch: Britain's Ambassador, Lord Inverchapel, requested an immediate appointment with Secretary of State George C. Marshall. He had two notes from his government that he wanted to present to Marshall before the day was out.

As it happened, Marshall had already left his office that Friday afternoon—the 21st of February, 1947—to go to Princeton University and receive an honorary degree. In his absence, Under Secretary of State Dean Acheson suggested that the Ambassador send a representative with copies of the notes. Late in the afternoon the First Secretary of the British Embassy arrived at the imposing structure on Pennsylvania Avenue that housed the Department of State. He was escorted to Loy Henderson, Director of the Office of Near Eastern and African Affairs.

The two notes the First Secretary handed to Henderson dealt, respectively, with Greece and Turkey. Although dryly diplomatic in language, they were momentous in impact. They announced that Britain and its shrinking empire no longer had the resources to combat Communist pressures in the eastern Mediterranean, for generations a sphere of strong British influence. On April 1—39 days hence—Britain would be compelled to end all financial and military aid to Greece and Turkey, leaving them in danger of Communist domination. The British government hoped that the United States would be willing to assume the burden of protecting them.

The State Department team that assembled over the weekend to prepare recommendations for Marshall's attention on Monday knew very well that the problem went far beyond Greece and Turkey, and Britain's inability to support them. Two years after the War it was obvious that Europe was not recovering as rapidly as Western statesmen had hoped and expected. With industrial and agricultural production still far below prewar levels, the Continent was manufacturing only half the consumer supplies it had produced in 1939. Highways and bridges were still being rebuilt, and in the devastated cities mountains of crushed masonry were still being shoveled away. Moreover, in January of 1947 the magazine *World Report* published a survey indicating that in country after country businessmen suffered from a crippling lack of confidence in the stability of

POLITICS OF CONFRONTATION

prevailing governments. "What Europe finds," *World Report* concluded, "is that disorganizations in normal life are proving much harder to overcome than the physical destruction caused by war."

The disarray of Western Europe ranged from Britain's near bankruptcy to the political chaos of France and Italy, where it seemed that at any moment Communist-dominated governments might come to power. To the east, Greece was being torn apart by civil war. And if the Communist guerrilla armies there defeated the government, Turkey would be at risk. After that, the whole of the Middle East as well as Italy and France would be in danger of falling under the hammer and sickle. Washington's view, in Acheson's words, was that "one rotten apple would infect the whole barrel."

On his return Monday, Marshall met briefly with the British Ambassador to hear his evaluation of the situation. Then, a little before noon, he went to the White House to tell President Truman what he had just learned.

The internal debate that the British notes had set in motion led in a remarkably short time to a fundamental shift in U.S. foreign policy. Appearing less than three weeks later before a special joint session of Congress, President Truman asked for $400 million in aid for Greece and Turkey. For the most part, noted one observer, "he dealt with the world crisis as if it were a question of repaving a highway in Missouri." But at one point, in the middle of his text, Truman uttered a sentence that defined what would later be known as the Truman Doctrine: "I believe that it must be the policy of the United States to support free peoples who are resisting attempted subversion by armed minorities or by outside pressures." He added that the support should come "primarily through economic and financial aid."

While Truman spoke, Marshall was in Moscow, attending a meeting of foreign ministers. There he met with Josef Stalin and came away profoundly, if unfavorably, impressed. What particularly struck him was that Stalin seemed totally indifferent to the ministers' inability to agree on issues affecting the recovery of Europe. What difference did it make that there was no agreement, Stalin asked: "We may agree the next time, or if not then, the time after that." To Marshall, it was clear that Stalin preferred to let Europe drift—presumably in expectation of a general collapse that would bring Communist governments to power. Marshall talked

about Stalin's cynical attitude all the way back to Washington, recalled Charles E. "Chip" Bohlen, who was Marshall's chief adviser on Soviet policy.

Once back at the State Department, Marshall asked his staff to draw up a plan for assistance to Europe. His trip, he reported, had convinced him that the situation was urgent: "The patient is sinking while the doctors deliberate."

What emerged from the consultations of Marshall and his staff was a speech delivered by the Secretary of State at Harvard University's commencement exercises on June 5, 1947. He mused over the text on the plane to Boston. In its final form it was short, simple and so deliberately understated that neither those who heard it at Harvard nor the journalists who commented on it next day fully understood how monumental a commitment Marshall was proposing.

He began by describing the dislocation of Europe's economy and the demoralization of its people, and he noted the adverse effects Europe's troubles had on the economy of the United States. It was logical, he said, "that the United States should do whatever it is able to do to assist in the return of normal economic health in the world, without which there can be no political stability and no assured peace."

Marshall suggested that the European nations, acting together, draft a program of recovery which the United States would then underwrite "so far as it may be practical for us to do so." He deliberately avoided naming sums—saying only that Europe "must have substantial additional help"—and he threw the program open to any nation, including the Soviet Union.

In due time, Congress approved Marshall's historic proposal. Sixteen European nations and the three Western zones of Germany applied for and received Marshall Plan aid. The Secretary and his advisers were worried at first that Russia might decide to join the Plan, which would almost surely have guaranteed its rejection by Congress. In fact, as Bohlen later conceded, the Plan was framed in such a way as to "make it quite impossible for the Soviet Union to accept." Among its stipulations was that the United States would have the right to verify the use of goods and funds—a condition that the secretive Russians would never agree to. In addition, the Soviets were not anxious to see their privileged trading area in largely rural Eastern Europe integrated into industrialized Western Europe. They rejected the Plan and forbade any of their satellites to participate.

The Marshall Plan and the Truman Doctrine that preceded it were, in Truman's words, "two halves of the same walnut." Taken together, the two policies constituted an abandonment of isolationism and the beginning of a foreign policy of involvement and intervention. Both the Truman Doctrine and the Marshall Plan conceived of the intervention in economic terms, but the Marshall Plan was far broader in its reach—and had the rehabilitation of all Western Europe as its objective.

Although the Plan was not specifically anti-Communist, as was the Truman Doctrine, neither was it the "no-strings" policy that its planners at first pretended. Its recipients understood that if their governments were to become Communist, Marshall Plan aid would immediately cease. Because the Truman Doctrine was more limited in its aims, its immediate effect was easier to measure. The Soviet Union had been waging a war of nerves against Turkey in order to obtain a Navy base on the Turkish straits and had massed troops on the Turkish frontier. The United States poured $100 million in military aid into Turkey, and within a year the Russians—faced by a vastly improved Turkish Army and Navy—dropped their campaign of intimidation. They quietly let it be known that they no longer had any claim on the Dardanelles.

As might be expected, the Truman Doctrine and Marshall Plan accelerated the division of Eastern and Western Europe into opposing camps. One of the first Soviet reactions was to establish in Belgrade the Communist Information Bureau, or Cominform, with broad authority to coordinate the activities of Communist parties in both the East and West. In the crucial year that followed, the United States was to pour $6 billion in Marshall Plan aid into Europe. Although that massive investment—augmented in subsequent years by another $7 billion—would eventually help save Europe from economic ruin and launch a vigorous revival (pages 152-163), few people in the spring of 1947 were confident enough to predict what would happen. As they looked out

at Europe's chaotic condition, neither those who offered the aid nor those who received it would have sworn that the Plan would be successful.

In the Western European countries that the Marshall Plan was trying to reach, the overriding fact of political life was a massive shift to the left. The prewar parties and politics were everywhere rejected. "During the catastrophe," wrote France's Charles de Gaulle, "a great change had occurred in men's minds. To many, the disaster of 1940 seemed the failure of the ruling class and system in every realm."

Before the War, the parties of the Left had drawn much of their support from the working classes of the cities. But the wartime resistance movements thrust together urban workers and rural peasants, intellectuals and aristocrats, the young, the middle-aged and the old. Not all who fought in the Resistance automatically voted for the Left after the War. But almost all of them shared a yearning for change.

The Communists were particularly skillful at exploiting this new mood. The Italian Communist Party prided itself on reaching beyond the cities to recruit members from the independent-minded peasantry, the *contadini*. "In population percentage," boasted Italian Communist leader Palmiro Togliatti in 1947, "our strongest local federation in Italy is in Siena—in the heart of Tuscany's vineyards and olive groves. And I'm not sure there's a single factory there."

Speaking to a journalist many years later, an Italian shepherd named Mario Cecchi recalled the heady sense of brotherhood and common purpose that drew him into the Communist Party when he came back to his town in Umbria after the Italian surrender in 1943. "The party was already organizing when I came home," he said. "We had a perspective that was better, from the War. We had a vision of a better life. The church made a Madonna and paraded her through the valley on Saturday nights, saying, 'Drive out the Communists! Vote Christian Democratic! Save your immortal souls!' But we Communists kept on. Important men told us that for the party to grow and be strong it was necessary for people like us, who were poor and uneducated, to take the advice of people who knew. There were still *padroni* who would knock on your door and if you didn't give them your wine and olive oil you were out. But the party changed that. It made us all brothers."

For many, Communism in those turbulent years had a messianic appeal that went far beyond politics. In an interview, the French singer and actor Yves Montand described the highly emotional attraction to Communism that he and many others of his generation in France felt as the War was ending. "I come from a poor family," he said, "and I grew up fighting for something to eat. At that time, it seemed very simple and clear. Marx was going to solve everything. He had replaced God. There would be happiness and food and no more prostitutes. Man would be perfect. This faith we needed to survive."

In country after country, Communist parties whose influence had been negligible before the War emerged as powerful political forces. Membership in the Italian Communist Party jumped from 10,000 in 1944 to more than one million by 1946. The Communists became the largest party in postwar France. Even in Belgium, the Netherlands and the Scandinavian countries, where Communism had always been notably weak, the Communists made important gains in postwar elections, becoming for the first time an opposition party to be reckoned with. In conservative Holland, postwar circulation of the party newspaper rose rapidly to a quarter of a million.

In all countries, the Communists benefited greatly from the important role they had played in the Resistance. But they were not the only Left-Wing group swept to prominence by what the Italians called the *vento del nord*—the wind from the Alpine north that symbolized the pressure for change. There were also the Socialists, and a broad spectrum of Catholics known in most countries as Christian Democrats. Critical of both capitalism and Marxism, the Christian Democrats attempted to steer a middle course based on many of the progressive and reformist policies demanded by the Resistance. Although the Christian Democrats' crusading Left Wing was dominant immediately after the War, the party also drew support from some Right-Wingers who had no other place to turn once their parties were banned or discredited.

Political activity in virtually all the countries of Western Europe immediately after the War consisted of a bitter struggle for power among these three groups. Against them, old-fashioned liberals and the entrenched conservatives were powerless because of their prewar failures.

Under a sign announcing the "Berlin Emergency Program, with Marshall Plan aid," German men and women shovel dirt from the foundation of a bombed-out apartment house. By May 1950, American aid had funded 300 housing projects in Berlin alone.

The three parties shared roughly three quarters of the popular vote in Europe's first postwar elections during the winter of 1945-1946. Coalition Leftist governments that included Communists came to power in France, Italy, Belgium and the Netherlands. The strong showing made by the Communists raised the possibility that they might muster enough strength to achieve power in open elections.

Among the smaller nations, predictions of a Communist takeover soon proved to be exaggerated. Despite spectacular gains, the Communists of Scandinavia and the Low Countries remained minority parties—and relatively peaceful. In Belgium there had been a momentary scare in November 1944 when the government in newly liberated Brussels ordered all Resistance forces to disarm and disband. A Communist mob besieged Parliament—dispersing only after a clash with police during which several people were wounded. But Communist leaders told their followers to surrender their arms, and fears of an uprising subsided.

The situation in France and Italy was far more dangerous. These two pivotal countries were by far the most divided of the European democracies—and hence the most susceptible to Communist domination. In both countries the War had left deep animosities and political and social divisions that widened when the fighting stopped.

France's economy was in a perilous state. Its output of coal was down to one fifth and electricity to one half the prewar level. Prices were 14 times higher than in 1938, and government studies showed that 75 per cent of the urban population was undernourished. There were food riots in Paris, and near Lille, 1,200 people swarmed into a coal mine and carted off 150 tons of coal. Wartime bombings and ground fighting had destroyed not only factories but railroads, roads, bridges—including all of those on the Seine between Paris and the sea—and much shipping and rolling stock. The industrial plants that had survived the War were mostly small, inefficient, family-run affairs.

A half million Frenchmen had lost their lives in one way or another during the War. In Normandy, along the route of the Allied invasion, whole towns had been leveled and several hundred thousand people were homeless. In many areas of rural France, partisan leaders for a time constituted the only effective government. The public complained bitterly that punishment for *l'indignité nationale*—wartime collaboration with the Germans—was unevenly administered and that former Vichy officials with sufficient influence not only escaped punishment but sometimes remained in the posts they had held during the Occupation. The desire for vengeance was fed by a national sense of guilt that led thousands of citizens to claim a role in the Resistance they had never earned. The typical Frenchman of the period, according to one popular story, was the plump bourgeois who six months after the liberation told his wife and children, "I have just joined the Resistance."

In this divisive atmosphere, the Communists quickly drew new support and emerged as the best-organized party in France, with 900,000 dues-paying members and an even larger army of sympathizers. Their main source of strength was the French trade-union movement, which historically had opposed virtually any government in power. As major opponents of the wartime Vichy government, the Communists had a natural appeal to the union rank and file. Communists were elected to key posts in many unions, and they eventually took over the leadership of the giant Confédération Générale du Travail (CGT). Thus the Communists could count on massive support in any labor dispute—with the CGT's six million workers joined by additional millions of Socialist sympathizers and a large portion of France's Catholic labor movement.

Pending elections, France was ruled by the Provisional Government that the Free French had declared in Algiers in May of 1944 and transferred to Paris after its liberation that August. At the head of this caretaker government, by virtue of his commanding role in the Free French movement, was General de Gaulle.

A resolute nationalist, de Gaulle was in some ways an anachronism in the egalitarian France that was emerging from the War. Critics insisted that he was living in the wrong century—he confused himself, they said, with Joan of Arc—and that he was out of touch with the aspirations of most of his countrymen. But no other Frenchman had de Gaulle's immense moral authority—or his almost mystic conviction that he had a historical mission to save France. He was, wrote his friend the novelist François Mauriac, "the last Frenchman who made his countrymen believe they were still a great nation."

De Gaulle's chief concern in the turbulent months just after the liberation was to see that the extreme Left did not become entrenched as a kind of de facto government in large areas of rural France. To establish the Provisional Government as the sole governing authority, he began touring the country almost immediately after his return—assuring people everywhere that he was the legal heir of the prewar Third Republic and that the regional Resistance organizations, with their armed "patriotic militias," were no longer needed. Two months after the liberation of Paris he abruptly disbanded the militias without even bothering to consult Resistance leaders.

At the same time, he made two shrewd moves to conciliate the Communists. One was to invite Communist officials to join the Cabinet as the heads of two comparatively minor ministries. He thus partially satisfied the Communists' desire for legitimacy—and saddled them with shared responsibility for whatever decisions the government might make.

In a related move, de Gaulle extended amnesty to Communist leader Maurice Thorez. This robust former coal miner, the leading Communist in France, had deserted the French Army in 1939 because he did not want to fight against a Germany that was then allied with the Soviet Union. On his return to France from Moscow, where he had sat out the War, Thorez dutifully pursued the policy of conciliation with the West then being promoted by the Russians. His avowed aim was to "reconcile the tricolor of our fathers with the red flag of our aspirations." He boasted that with the new Cabinet appointments, "we have sent two of our best men into the government of the Republic." To doubters who wondered if French Communism could free itself of the police-state mentality of its Russian model, Thorez replied: "Different countries, different methods."

In France's first postwar elections, held in October of 1945, the Communists became for the first time an important force in the French government—capturing nearly a third of the seats in the legislature. They thus received five Cabinet posts, including the important Ministry of Defense. De Gaulle was returned as head of government, but shortly afterward he resigned in a bitter dispute over the relative power of the legislature and the executive in the new government. De Gaulle was succeeded by a Socialist, Felix Gouin, at the head of a coalition of three parties of the Left—Socialists, Communists and the Catholic-oriented Popular Republicans (MPR).

With the Communist position enhanced, Maurice Thorez had dreams of becoming the Premier of France. "Thorez to power!" became a popular slogan of the party. The Communist leader talked to journalists of "a new people's democracy," and insisted he was free from Soviet control. But to get the votes he needed, he required substantial support from either the Socialists or the MPR, and this he could not get. Throughout 1946, therefore, the Communists worked within the Leftist coalition in support of expanded social security and nationalization of industry designed to shift power away from the prewar privileged class.

By 1947, however, Moscow's priorities for Western Europe were changing. The major aim now was neither to assume elective office nor to seize power by force. Instead, national Communist leaders were exhorted to wage war against the Marshall Plan by disrupting the economies of the "bourgeois democracies" by any means possible. Accordingly, the French Communists exchanged their policy of accommodation for a campaign of increasingly violent action.

One of the immediate consequences of the shift was that the Communists lost their place in government. In the spring of 1947, some 20,000 Renault workers went out on a wildcat strike in defiance of Socialist Premier Paul Ramadier's enforcement of frozen prices and wages. The Communists, who until then had supported the government's policy, decided to back the Renault strikers. Ramadier confronted the Communist ministers in his Cabinet, and with the words "Let us separate," he dismissed them. For a few anxious hours, police reinforcements patrolled central Paris. But the Communists accepted their dismissal from government with only token protests—content with the greater freedom of action they enjoyed in opposition.

To strike was the Communists' greatest weapon, and they now began to use it. In the fall of 1947, after an uncoordinated series of walkouts that included dock and rail workers and, very briefly, the Paris police, Thorez issued a call for a revolutionary general strike designed to paralyze all major industries and communications networks. In Marseilles, exuberant strikers hoisted the red flag over the Palais de Justice and heard Communist leaders declare their support for the "working and democratic population of Marseilles.'' Factories and public buildings—including the central post office in Nice—were seized and occupied by militant workers.

Across the country, some two million men and women were idle. Coal was not mined, transport was disrupted, food was in short supply. The directors of the CGT adopted a resolution condemning Marshall Plan aid. One Communist leader even called for the French Army to mutiny.

In the National Assembly, Communist deputies contributed to the insurrection by shouting insults and beating on the lids of their desks, making orderly debate all but impossible. Jacques Duclos, leader of the Communist delegation, denounced the current Premier, Robert Schuman, as a ''boche,'' or German—a slang reference to Schuman's birth in the often-disputed territory of Lorraine, on the German border. Minister of the Interior Jules Moch, whose police daily battled the Communists in the streets, was greeted in the Assembly with Communist cries of ''Heil Hitler!'' During one frenzied demonstration the Communists seized the speaker's lectern and held it overnight. They eventually had to be expelled from the Assembly by guards.

Acts of industrial sabotage were commonplace. Throughout the length of France's troubled rail system, as many as five trains were derailed in a single day. In one planned accident that shocked the public, the Paris-to-Tourcoing express went off the rails near Arras, killing 16 people and injuring 40 others.

As industrial turmoil increased and rumors of a coup d'état spread, so did verbal abuse and physical violence. French intellectuals, among them the philosopher Jean-Paul Sartre, fought violent pro- and anti-Marxist battles in print, nearly coming to blows over provocations like Sartre's assertion that the French Communist Party must be judged not by its actions but by its prospects.

The mood of France became increasingly ugly. In Marseilles, the moderate mayor, Michel Carlini, was hauled out of his office by a Communist mob protesting a streetcar-fare increase; he was so badly beaten and kicked that he would not have survived had he not been rescued by a detachment of riot police. The crowd was yelling ''à mort, à mort, à mort!'' the mayor recalled after he was released from the hospital. The next day 13,000 troops had to move in to restore order to the rioting city.

All over France, pitched battles were being fought in the streets. In the Place de l'Étoile in Paris, refugees from Eastern Europe scheduled a rally to protest Soviet domination of their home countries. The Communist paper L'Humanité summoned the rank and file to break up the meeting: ''Silence to the insulters of the Soviet Union!'' In the Place and on the broad avenues surrounding it, 3,000 heavily armed police clashed with 8,000 demonstrators in a battle that sent scores of people to hospitals and left railings uprooted and paving stones torn from the curbs. The press asked whether the country was sliding into civil war.

In the ornate chamber he occupied as Vice Premier of France, Maurice Thorez (right) talks with an aide in December 1946. Thorez, who had spent the War years in Moscow, became one of five Communists named to the Cabinet in postwar France.

Yet even as the raging violence seemed out of control, forces were at work that soon would contain it. The first tangible sign was Premier Schuman's decision to ask the National Assembly for emergency powers. "A state of insurrection exists in France," he said, and "as long as I head a French government, force will be on the side of the law." Despite a sit-down strike by Communist deputies, Schuman got the powers he wanted. He immediately called up 80,000 troops and sent them to replace striking workers and to patrol the troubled streets, with orders to fire if necessary.

In a parallel move, the government warned strikers that they risked losing their social-security benefits. It was a serious threat, for the unions lacked the cash resources to compensate workers for such a loss. Individually at first and then in groups, workers returned to their jobs, breaking the ranks of the solidly disciplined CGT for the first time since the Communist take-over. When elements of the 600,000-member Transport Workers' Union began straggling back, a Paris Métro strike collapsed and had to be abandoned.

As a result of this wavering of discipline, the more moderate wing of the CGT decided to break away and form an independent union. The CGT thus lost a third of its membership and its stranglehold on French labor.

At the same time, the Communists found their public support dwindling rapidly. The general strike had made it clear that the French Communist Party was serving Russian interests rather than those of France. Nobody had failed to note that at the height of the strike Thorez went to Moscow—presumably to receive instructions. He was later quoted as saying that French Communists would not resist a Soviet army if it crossed the French frontier.

One measure of how disenchanted the public had become with the Communists was the immense success of the Rassemblement du Peuple Français (RPF), a new political party launched by General de Gaulle. Running on a platform of extreme anti-Communism, the RPF won an overwhelming victory in the municipal elections of October 1947, just four months after its creation.

Perhaps most important of all, by the autumn of 1947 American aid money was flowing into France, stabilizing the franc and the national economy. The general strike had lasted 28 days, costing the government an estimated $16 million a day. Yet the economy sustained the loss and even began to gather momentum. With Marshall Plan aid, French industrial output in 1948 almost reached prewar levels. Having failed to come to power by the vote—and having failed equally to cripple the economy—the French Communist Party now began to decline in membership and influence. It would, however, remain an important minority voice in France.

In turbulent postwar Italy, the Communist Party underwent much the same transformation. As in France, the Italian Communists had fertile ground to cultivate at the end of the

Carried aloft by his admirers, General Charles de Gaulle leads a rally outside Paris on May 1, 1948. While de Gaulle addressed this anti-Communist crowd in the suburbs, French Communists celebrated May Day with a parade through downtown Paris.

War. The economy had been severely damaged—with industrial production down to one fifth of what it had been in 1938 and agricultural production down by nearly half. Most of the inland transportation system had been destroyed, along with much of the Navy and merchant marine. The amount of money in circulation was 20 times as great as in 1938, and as a result inflation was out of control. More than three million Italians were homeless, two million were unemployed, and uncounted millions were underfed.

Traveling across the ravaged country in those first months after the War, historian Nino Arena was struck by his nation's mood of both exhilaration and uncertainty. Free at last of a dictatorship that had shaped their lives for more than two decades, Italians were groping toward a future they found hard to envision. For all Italians of whatever conviction, recalled Arena, "it was year zero."

In the prevailing atmosphere of anarchy, banditry flourished and random separatist movements sprang up to proclaim spurious governments representing visionary ideals. Areas of Sicily were forcibly occupied and governed by members of the Sicilian Independence Movement, whose aim was to sever all ties with Italy. The movement was suppressed after a number of pitched battles with police in which scores of people were killed or injured. Similarly, a group of Communist mayors in the southern province of Reggio di Calabria took advantage of the absence of any visible central authority to proclaim the "Republic of Caulonia," which was to be ruled according to Soviet principles. The founding fathers of this ragtag republic blew up a bridge connecting the state highway to the Caulonia area and fought the local *carabinieri* (national military police) before being forced to surrender.

In the months immediately following its liberation, Italy was ruled by an interim government formed under Allied auspices from six underground organizations that had resisted the occupying Germans. Pending national elections, they ruled as a true coalition government that eventually coalesced around three parties—the Socialists under Pietro Nenni, the Communists under Palmiro Togliatti, and the Christian Democrats under Alcide de Gasperi. Togliatti and de Gasperi soon became the two dominant figures in Italian politics—and the symbols of much that postwar Italy both hoped for and feared.

Togliatti had spent 18 years in Moscow, returning to Italy in March of 1944 in a conciliatory mood that reflected Moscow's early desire for postwar collaboration. He was ready, said Togliatti, "to participate in government even with the King." No Communist leader was more adaptable, and very few were as intelligent. Son of a Genoa bookkeeper, Togliatti was a well-educated man—a law graduate of the University of Turin—whose political speeches were sprinkled with Latin maxims and quotations from Dante, Lincoln and the Bible. Yet he understood the popular mood as well as any politician in Italy: He sensed as soon as he returned from the Soviet Union that the time was right for a *partito nuovo*—a more broadly based Communist organization that would include the middle class.

To casual observers, Togliatti's chief rival had none of the charisma of a great political leader. Alcide de Gasperi was unimpressive personally and boring as a speaker. Professorial in appearance and manner, he sometimes appeared abstracted and was known as "The Priest." But in fact he was a shrewd and tough politician who in the months after Italy's liberation forged an improbable coalition of interests into the most successful political party in Western Europe.

De Gasperi drew on long experience in political maneuvering: As a young Christian Democrat in his native Trentino, he had displayed great skill mediating between Austrian and Italian interests when the region was under Austrian rule. The techniques he learned then served him well as he strove to bring landowners and peasants, industrialists and Catholic workers, and a broad range of the middle class under the umbrella of the Christian Democratic Party. Aside from their aversion to Communism, these uneasy bedfellows had almost nothing in common except their loyalty to the Catholic Church. Even de Gasperi was unable to define the coalition he presided over—although he once vaguely described it as a Center party moving to the left. In fact, the Left Wing of the party—associated with the Catholic trade unions—was the dominant political faction immediately after the War, when no party without a strongly Leftist orientation had a chance at the polls. But after 1945, the party developed an extreme Right Wing—made up in part of former Fascists—that had an increasingly important voice in Christian Democratic policy.

De Gasperi made this unruly coalition work by playing

Parisian Leftists hurl café chairs at retreating police during an Armistice Day riot on the 11th of November, 1948. The violence began when Left-Wing veterans' and Resistance groups, who had decided to boycott the official celebration, attacked police lines along the Champs-Élysées.

on its fear of Communism, and by bending now in one direction and now in another. He came to power as Premier in the coalition government granted civil jurisdiction by the Allies in 1945, and he remained in office, almost without interruption, for more than seven years.

In June 1946, Italy held its first free elections since 1921. The Christian Democrats got 35 per cent of the vote, as compared to 21 per cent for the Socialists and 19 per cent for the Communists. Although it seemed that the Christian Democrats' lead over the Communists was insurmountable, de Gasperi and his advisers were uneasy. For one thing, the Communist Party was growing more rapidly than the other two parties and was recruiting vigorously. For another, the Socialists under Pietro Nenni were siding more and more frequently with the Communists; it was feared that the two parties would soon form a voting bloc under the domination of Togliatti. Most important of all, the Italian Communists—like their counterparts in France—had a strong hold on the nation's workers through their control of Italy's federation of trade unions, the six-million-member Confederazione Generale del Lavoro Italiano (CGIL). The Communists thus possessed a veto power over governmental policies that was far greater than their voting strength.

Much of the political struggle in postwar Italy, in fact, was carried out not at the polls but in the streets. The Italian Communists, like their French counterparts, resorted to strikes only sparingly until 1947. In January of that year a splinter group of Socialists, unhappy about Nenni's increasing subservience to the Communists, broke away to form their own autonomous organization. Encouraged by this erosion of Communist voting strength, de Gasperi dismissed his Cabinet and formed a new one leaving out the Communists entirely. Togliatti stopped talking about collaboration and started speaking of a "decisive democratic battle" and "eruptions of revolutionary character."

Soon the eruptions were shaking the whole political structure of Italy as Moscow called for an all-out war against the Marshall Plan. Italy's Communist workers responded by occupying factories, wrecking offices of "the fascist press," and battling the police. "The workers do not want civil war," labor leader Nazzareno Buschi had told a rally, "but the government must be warned."

Suddenly weapons appeared everywhere—most of them from caches hidden by partisan forces at War's end. Communist and fascist "action" squads battled one another, and a gang of Communist gunmen known as the *volante rossa* (Red flying squad) spread terror with a series of assassinations of prominent anti-Communists. Exhorted by Communist labor leaders to "collectively occupy the land of those who have too much," several thousand peasants around Rome marched on the great farms of the region, marked out subdivisions with stakes and divided the land among themselves. In the Italian Assembly, nearly 200 Communist and Rightist deputies hurled inkwells and exchanged blows on the chamber floor.

The Parliamentary election of April 1948 was the most bitterly contested in Italy's history. The Communists seemed to be in a strong position, for they had finally formed a popular democratic front with Nenni's Socialists. At a meeting in Rome in January 1948, Communist and Socialist leaders spoke of "the great popular masses united" in a crusade

against the forces of fascism. "When we face fascist rifle fire, shall the Communists be in one square and the Socialists in another?" asked a Communist leader named Giuseppe Casadei. Between them, the two parties controlled 40 per cent of the popular vote—a considerably greater percentage than any single party, even the Christian Democrats, could muster against them.

"All reliable indications have pointed to success for the Communist-dominated popular front in Italy in the forthcoming elections," wrote U.S. diplomat Henry Tasca to an inquiring U.S. congressman in the winter of 1948. Tasca was reflecting a view that was widely held in both the diplomatic corps and the U.S. government. Concern in Washington was heightened by the fact that a Communist congress in Milan in January had declared that the party would seize power by force if it lost the election. Indeed, as the election approached, President Truman and the men around him became alarmed that a Communist government might soon rule Italy and thus felt justified in launching a campaign of undisguised interference in the affairs of a sovereign state.

U.S. Secretary of State Marshall bluntly announced that all economic aid to Italy would stop if the Communists came to power. U.S. Ambassador James C. Dunn toured the Italian peninsula, reminding audiences of the "great national effort made by the American people to save Italy from starvation, chaos and possible domination from outside." Dunn became such a familiar figure that Communists at one particularly stormy political meeting shouted the line,

"Your speech was written with Dunn's fountain pen."

Americans of Italian origin were urged to write their relatives in Italy and tell them to vote against the Communists. American Catholic priests reminded their Italian-American parishioners of the evils a Communist regime would visit upon Italy. Aware that Moscow was reputed to have given $15 million to the popular front, the U.S. government quietly funneled several million dollars in campaign funds to the Christian Democrats.

In Italy itself, some of the most vigorous campaigning against the Communists was done by the Catholic Church, which in February 1948 created an anti-Communist lobbying group known as the National Civic Committee, half of whose funding was said to come from the United States. The committee not only helped the Christian Democrats choose their candidates but converted parish-church meeting rooms into local political headquarters. A priest in Rome called Padre Lombardi became widely known as "God's Microphone" because of his fire-and-brimstone denunciations of the Communists. In a voice that was described as "hoarse and apocalyptic," Lombardi would ask his audiences, "Who are they that carry within themselves this cosmic sin, this sacrilege, this damnation? They are, brothers, the Communists and the Communist Party!"

Some cardinals and bishops ordered their priests not to administer the sacraments to anyone voting for the Communists. The National Civic Committee flooded the country with posters *(pages 141-143)* depicting alleged Russian and

other Communist atrocities. In response, Togliatti was goaded into an attack on the Pope and the Catholic Church—he called them proimperialist. Such public criticism was unprecedented in the history of Italian politics and probably cost the Communists votes.

In the prevailing atmosphere of fear and hatred, the real economic and social problems facing Italy were largely ignored in favor of hysterical accusations and calculated deceptions. One trick favored by the Christian Democrats was to undermine faith in Soviet promises by alerting people in port cities to expect the imminent arrival of food supplies from Russia—in ships that of course never appeared. The Communists, for their part, warned of American plans to manipulate Italy's future as the price for Marshall Plan aid.

All over the country, strikes and political violence flared. A Communist trade-union leader in Camporeale, Sicily, was ambushed and machine-gunned to death. Near the southern Italian city of Lecce, bombs were thrown into a Communist crowd, killing two and wounding 20. In Milan, a Rightist candidate was shot dead in his home. One killing that for many people symbolized most poignantly the senseless violence of the campaign involved a Christian Democratic youth named Gervasio Federici, who was stabbed by a band of young Communists when he refused to shout "Long live Communism!" More than 100,000 Italians, including de Gasperi and other government leaders, attended Federici's funeral in Rome.

The election itself came almost as an anticlimax. Drawing support from various moderate and Right-Wing splinter groups and from Socialists who deserted the popular front, the Christian Democrats won a landslide victory with 48.5 per cent of the popular vote—as against 31 per cent for the Communists and their Socialist allies—and became an absolute majority in the Chamber of Deputies. Church pressure on Catholic voters and fear of a Communist coup d'état undoubtedly helped the Christian Democrats, as did Marshall Plan aid, which by now was pouring into Italy.

The election of 1948 ended the Communists' hope of coming to power by the vote, but it did not cool the passions they had aroused. Political violence reached a peak in July, with an attempt on Togliatti's life. His assailant was a violently anti-Communist Sicilian law student named Antonio

Pallante who said later he could not bear the thought that Togliatti, an Italian, attended meetings of the Cominform. Pallante ambushed the Communist leader as he was leaving a Parliamentary session in Rome and shot him three times.

Although police who arrested Pallante on the scene insisted that he had acted independently, Communists were convinced that the shooting was part of a plot by the triumphant Christian Democrats to annihilate the Communist Party. As Togliatti underwent an operation in a Rome hospital, workers walked out of their factories and took to the streets. The 48 hours of violent demonstrations that followed in cities throughout northern Italy had the look of a planned insurrection.

Communist senators were seen leading the demonstrations in Turin, and the Communist mayor of Genoa personally directed rioters attempting to occupy the city's police barracks. Interior Minister Mario Scelba charged in a speech before the National Assembly that the Communists were trying "to replace the popular vote with violence in the piazza." As he spoke, Christian Democrats and Communists hurled pencils and pens and shouted curses at each other.

For a brief time, it seemed that Italy had plunged into civil war. Newspaper and political offices were set afire, shops were looted, police were attacked and beaten, railroad bridges were blown up. In Livorno, a mob looted the armory for weapons; in Milan, workers seized the large Motta baking company and the Bezzi mechanical-equipment factory. Workers who took over the Fiat auto factory in Turin held the management hostage and defended their prize by mounting machine guns on the roof. Trains and buses were halted by mobs, and their passengers were forced to abandon them. In Tuscany, two regiments of artillery had to be called in to repulse an attack on the nation's main telephone center. At Pisa, a young man in a horse-drawn carriage fired on a Communist protest meeting and was pursued and beaten to death by the crowd.

All told, 16 people died and 600 were injured. But then the violence died away almost as quickly as it had flared, and in two days an exhausted quiet settled over Italy. A general strike called by the CGIL abruptly collapsed as well. Far from being a planned insurrection, the rioting was plainly an embarrassment to the Communist leadership. When he woke from anesthesia and was declared out of danger,

Italy's postwar political rivals—Christian Democrat Alcide de Gasperi (rear left), Socialist Pietro Nenni (third from left) and Communist Palmiro Togliatti (right)—sit together at a Cabinet meeting in Rome in December 1945. Along with other leaders from the wartime underground, the three men cooperated in an interim government that ruled with Allied backing until the first Italian elections in the spring of 1946.

Togliatti bid his followers to "be calm—don't do foolish things." The Soviet Union restricted its comment to a mild rebuke of the Italian Communists for not taking better care of their leader.

In the aftermath of the riots, a number of union groups broke away from the CGIL to form independent labor federations. The Communists thus lost about a third of their trade-union support. Communist political strength was further eroded by revelations of the party's close ties with Moscow. Like Thorez in France, Togliatti made no secret of his expectation that in the event of a Soviet invasion, the Italian Communists "would have the evident duty of helping the Soviet Army." As distrust of the Communists grew, the improving economy made many of their claims against the de Gasperi government obsolete. As in France, the party would remain an important force in Italian politics, but its immediate postwar drive for power was over.

Across the Ionian Sea from Italy's toe, Communism was waging a different kind of war, on a battleground where it seemed for a time that it could not possibly lose. Greece had suffered more grievously under the German occupation than perhaps any country except the Soviet Union. Seven per cent of its prewar population of 7.5 million had died, and 1,700 villages had been destroyed. With agricultural production reduced to a third of the prewar level, much of the population was close to starvation. The drachma was worth so little that wads of freshly printed notes could be seen discarded in the gutters of Athens.

In this volatile situation, the Communists enjoyed the advantage of a formidably strong army that had been waging civil war in the mountains since before the German surrender. More important, they had the sympathy of large segments of a population that before the War had viewed the Communists as dangerous outsiders in a society devoted to family and church. Unlike their counterparts in Italy and France, the prewar Greek Communist Party (KKE) was never able to appeal to a specific segment of the society, such as the urban working class. Instead, the party drew most of its membership from aggrieved minorities of various kinds— Jews, Turks, gypsies, Slavic ethnic groups in Greek Macedonia. At the outbreak of war they were isolated sociologically and banned politically—a "minority of minorities" within the Greek state.

When the Germans occupied Greece in April 1941, the Communists were the first of the prewar political factions to organize armed resistance. There were two Greek governments in existence at the time—one set up by the Germans in Athens and a government-in-exile established under British auspices in Cairo. Though they were banned by both these governments, the Communists clandestinely began recruiting new members in rural Greece. To widen their appeal, they set up a succession of front organizations—the most important being the so-called National Liberation Front (EAM), which many Resistance fighters joined without realizing that it was Communist-controlled. The military arm of EAM, known as the National Popular Liberation Army (ELAS), soon became the dominant force in the Greek Resistance movement.

By 1943, the Communist leadership realized that the Germans were likely to lose the war; they began preparing to seize power when peace came. In 1944, proclaiming a

A club-swinging Italian policeman charges a Communist demonstrator in Rome during the 1948 election campaign. About 50,000 jeering Communists had gathered to disrupt a rally of the Rightist Italian Social Movement.

CAMPAIGN ART ROOTED IN FEAR

"A rash of posters now defaces almost every wall and ancient column in Rome," wrote one observer of the preliminaries leading up to Italy's pivotal postwar election in 1948. And indeed the virtual papering of Rome was testimony to the intensity and bitterness of the battle between Left and Right for control of the nation.

The most prolific user of poster art was the National Civic Committee, a Vatican-supported political-action group that distributed more than 300 different posters and placards in the months leading up to the April vote. Though the committee did not support specific candidates, it sought to rally Italians against the Communist-Socialist popular front by instilling the fear of Soviet rule should the far Left win.

The poster at right subtly portrayed Moscow's unseen influence on Italian Communism. But most of the art was anything but subtle, depicting an Italy subjected to brutal Communist assault or about to explode in revolution *(following pages).*

A few posters illustrated specific issues. In one an Italian soldier, one of thousands still held in the Soviet Union, pleaded with his mother to "vote for me, too." In another, the Russian veto that had kept Italy out of the United Nations was contrasted with the Italian *voto*—vote—that could keep the Communists out of Italy. A pro-American poster showed a roll broken unequally, with the legend: "The bread we eat is 40 per cent Italian flour and 60 per cent American flour sent to us free."

Italy's children figured prominently in many posters. One showed a little girl about to be crushed by a Red Army tank. In an even more chilling example, a boy pointing a finger said: "I accuse my parents!" The moral was explicit: "This could be your son if the Communists win."

FRO. DE. POP.

W il fronte democratico?

capovolgi e vedrai la frode

An anti-Communist poster distributed during the 1948 election campaign in Italy features a sketch of the noted 19th Century patriot Giuseppe Garibaldi, whom the Communists and Socialists used as their symbol. Turned upside down, the face becomes that of Josef Stalin.

LA TAGLIOLA

Dripping blood, the Italian boot is fettered by a hammer and sickle in a poster that warns of the "trap" of Soviet domination in case of a Communist election victory.

salvati!

VOTA

In a poster designed to get out the anti-Communist vote, a ballot falls like a sharp wedge, chopping off the burning fuse of a Communist revolution before it destroys Italy. "Save yourself!" the legend reads; "Vote!"

"CIVILTÀ ITALICA"

ASCOLTATEMI!!

VOTATE ITALIA
E NON FRONTE POPOLARE

Fleeing from the horrors of imprisonment in Russia, a terror-stricken Italian POW calls out to Italians at home, "Listen to me! Vote for Italy, not the popular front."

A gleeful Russian with one foot bare strides across the Adriatic Sea in a poster warning against Soviet expansion. "Attention!" reads the legend. "Communism needs a boot."

Death appears in the guise of a Red Army soldier who stands guard over a Europe symbolically bleeding from the U.S.S.R. into Western Europe and Italy. The moral for Italians: "Vote or he will be your master."

A figure representing Italy lies martyred. "Prevent this crime," implores the poster for a Centrist coalition. "Vote national bloc —neither reactionary nor revolutionary."

"mountain government" as the only legitimate government of Greece, they stopped fighting Germans and turned to fighting their fellow Greeks in the non-Communist Resistance bands in the mountains. But they had struck too soon.

The British were deeply involved in the Greek Resistance movement, having sent in Commando units to work with the guerrillas as early as the autumn of 1942. Now the British cut off military aid to ELAS and threw their support to other Resistance groups. The Germans took advantage of the divisive situation to launch a devastating series of attacks in which 1,400 guerrillas were killed. Under this dual pressure from the Germans and the British, Communist leaders declared a truce and reluctantly agreed to become part of the Greek government-in-exile, which was now renamed the Government of National Unity.

On October 12, 1944, the Germans withdrew the last of their forces from Greece. The next day British paratroopers landed outside Athens. The immediate mission of the British command was to block a Communist take-over following the German withdrawal. Its longer-range goal was to protect British strategic trade routes to India and the Far East by seeing that a friendly government was in control in Athens. With that objective in mind, the British transferred Greece's Government of National Unity from Cairo to Athens without serious incident.

Two months later the Communists walked out of the government, and party leaders called on the membership to "plunge into the final battle." The issue this time was the government's attempt to disband the ELAS guerrillas. With an estimated 20,000 men in the Athens area and an underground force of close to 400,000 sympathizers, the Communists felt they were strong enough to challenge both the precarious Government of National Unity and the 6,000 British troops there to prop it up.

For four weeks fighting raged in the streets of Athens and in the countryside surrounding the city. A brigade of 2,000 guerrillas not only captured most of the police stations in Athens but came within a half mile of the government offices in the center of the city. In their first concerted attack on British forces in Greece, the guerrillas overran Royal Air Force headquarters outside Athens, killing 12 men and taking 500 prisoners.

In the face of this massive display of Communist strength,

the British rushed in two divisions from the Italian battle-front. With the aid of a Greek brigade and an additional 2,000 Greek troops from the Middle East, they gradually drove the guerrillas out of Athens and pursued them into the countryside. As the guerrillas fell back, they took with them 15,000 men, women and children as hostages, along with 1,000 British prisoners of war. Some they executed; others died of starvation or exposure during the long march into the wintry mountains.

Confronted with a full-scale British offensive, ELAS sued for peace. According to an agreement signed at a seaside villa in Varkiza, near Athens, in February 1945, the government legalized the Greek Communist Party, while the Communists demobilized ELAS. Although peace was thus restored, 12,000 guerrillas fled to the mountains rather than surrender their arms.

The Communists had "decisively lost the battle of Athens," a former Communist later acknowledged, "but the national government had not won the battle of Greece." In fact, the guerrillas still were able to move freely through much of northern Greece and the Peloponnesus—the peninsula forming the southern part of the Greek mainland.

On the other hand, the Communists were now suffering a severe loss of the public support they had enjoyed in the months just after the War. Survivors from areas briefly occupied by the guerrillas told of priests who had been crucified, of men, women and children who had been tortured and mutilated, of girls who had been raped and then killed. Not long after the Varkiza Agreement was signed, mass graves of ELAS victims began to be discovered all over Athens and in surrounding districts. It was estimated that some 4,000 hostages had died. Kenneth Matthews, a correspondent for the British Broadcasting Corporation, drove to one of the mass graves on a stony hillside outside Athens and watched the diggers lifting bodies out of trenches. For weeks afterward, he could not forget the mourning voices of the women who stood by the trenches greeting the appearance of each new victim with "a low wailing which rose from time to time to a blood-chilling shriek."

In the first postwar elections on March 31, 1946, a conservative coalition won a landslide victory, leaving Greek politics polarized between Right and Left. On the very eve of the elections, a guerrilla band of about 80 men swept down on the town of Litochoron, on the eastern slopes of Olympus. They burned many of the buildings to the ground, destroyed the police station, killed eight people and abducted seven more. The raid was the first of a series on isolated mountain towns that marked the start of the longest and bloodiest phase of the civil war.

The nature of the fighting was determined both by the Greek terrain and by Greece's geographic isolation at the tip of the Balkan Peninsula. On the crescent curve of Greece's northern frontiers were the Communist states of Albania, Yugoslavia and Bulgaria—all of which offered sanctuary and material support to the Greek guerrilla army. When pressed, the guerrillas had only to retreat through the northern mountain passes to the protection of their Communist neighbors.

Almost every night, truck and mule convoys crossed Greece's northern frontiers bearing food as well as medical and military supplies. The neighboring Communist states set up local Societies for Aid to the Greek People to collect funds for the guerrilla forces. In addition, eight training camps were established in Bulgaria, Yugoslavia and Albania. The most important of these was a Yugoslavian center named Bulkes, which was said to have graduated several hundred leaders of the guerrilla movement—although its role as a training facility was repeatedly denied by Yugoslavian officials. When BBC correspondent Matthews finally managed to visit Bulkes, he was astounded to find that it was not the shantytown he had expected to see but "an entire Greek town standing in acres of flat farmland," with street names neatly lettered in Greek.

Trained and supplied by the Communist states to the north, the guerrillas fought a war shaped by the mountain ranges that cover more than two thirds of the Greek peninsula. In the Grammos range along the Albanian and Yugoslavian frontiers, the guerrillas established permanent bases.

The mountains of northern Greece form a natural stronghold from which Red guerrillas could either retreat to the sanctuary of neighboring Communist nations or attack down the Pindus range, which, a correspondent wrote, extends "like a probing finger into the heart of Greece." American aid eventually enabled the Greek Army to clear the Peloponnesus, and then work northward to crush the Communists along the frontier.

From here they were able to penetrate by way of the Pindus mountains deep into southern Greece.

The guerrillas' tactics throughout 1946 and much of 1947 were to strike swiftly at isolated towns and garrisons and then to withdraw into the mountains before the government forces could react. A Communist military analyst writing in the party's underground newspaper in the spring of 1947 estimated that if a continuous line were drawn around the bases of the various intersecting mountain ranges being used by the guerrilla forces, it would constitute "a total front line of 3,000 kilometers." An adequate patrol of such a perimeter, he added dryly, presumed "huge forces on the part of the enemy."

The guerrillas were further favored by an interior road network that was primitive and totally unsuited to the passage of conventional forces. So difficult was it to move men and materials that the government was unable to exercise any effective control of the countryside even a few miles outside Athens. The guerrillas not only moved almost unimpeded across the plains and windswept highlands but virtually ruled the villages of gray, uncut stone that dominated the high passes. In tacit recognition of guerrilla sovereignty, journalists took to referring to the mountains as synonymous with the whole guerrilla movement: "The mountains," read a newspaper commentary at a time when the Communists were hinting they might negotiate, "have agreed, with certain reservations, to take part in an all-party government."

Throughout the spring of 1946, the guerrillas restricted themselves to occasional hit-and-run raids in the border areas, and the government deluded itself that the "bandits" could be restrained by police security forces. But through the summer and autumn the tempo and range of attacks increased, and it became obvious that a full-scale insurrection was under way. In August, the Communist leadership instructed a veteran commissar, 40-year-old Markos Vafiades, to leave for the mountains and set up the general headquarters of what was henceforth to be known as the Democratic Army of Greece. The new commander in chief was a tall, fiery man who had risen rapidly from the time he joined the Communists as a young tobacco worker in Kavalla. He called himself "General Markos" and began bringing under his command a large number of independent bands that had been fighting the government without previously allying themselves with the Communists.

By the end of 1946, guerrilla forces in the field numbered between 8,000 and 13,500 troops, of whom 20 per cent were women. There were another 12,000 in training camps outside Greece. Against the Communists, the government had 90,000 men of the Greek National Army and 30,000 of the gendarmery. But these forces were badly led and poorly equipped, and they had no experience in antiguerrilla warfare. Moreover, the National Army was committed to a disastrous policy of "static defense" that was largely the result of political meddling. Because influential politicians in Athens insisted that the areas they represented had to be adequately protected at all times, troops were restricted to their assigned posts and were forbidden to rush to the assistance of a neighboring town even if it was falling before an attack by guerrillas.

As fearsome as the guerrilla forces in the field were the underground forces that served as informants and as terrorists charged with the murder of enemies. There were said to be some 50,000 of these secret Communists—a few of them at high levels of church and government—who were organized into so-called self-defense cells. Before the guerrillas launched an attack, they were provided by the self-defense forces with a plan of the town defenses, together with locations of the homes of progovernment sympathizers, utilities installations, military headquarters, factories

Greek soldiers in British-supplied uniforms rush to pull the driver from an Army truck that hit a guerrilla mine in Macedonia in July of 1947. The blast killed the officer lying at left and wounded nine other soldiers.

Spread out across a stony slope in the mountains of northwestern Greece, a National Army patrol sweeps toward the Albanian frontier in its search for Communist guerrillas in early 1948.

and shops worth looting. In addition, the attackers had a list of people thought to be recruitable. When the guerrillas withdrew, they left behind among the smoking ruins the bodies of whole families whose political sympathies had been denounced by the informers.

In the absence of any effective government restraint, killings on both sides became commonplace. In Sparta, a distinguished Leftist lawyer named Gramatikakis Panayolis was having a family dinner at home one night when a half dozen extreme Rightists walked in and opened fire, wounding Panayolis and killing his brother before they casually walked out again. Everywhere, violence fed on violence. After Communists killed eight policemen in a village in the Vale of Tempe, a band of Rightists intent on reprisal killed 16 of the town's reputed Communist sympathizers, only to be gunned down themselves in a Communist ambush as they were fleeing the scene.

So many guns were in so many hands that it was often impossible to know who was pulling the triggers. When American journalist George Polk, a correspondent for the Columbia Broadcasting System, was found floating with a bullet in his head in Salonika harbor, the government staged a show trial and pinned the crime on Communist assassins. In fact, many of Polk's colleagues were convinced that he had been killed by extreme Rightists who knew of his plan to interview General Markos.

The atmosphere of chaos and insensate violence intimidated and divided the coalition government in Athens. Security measures proposed by the conservatives so alienated the liberal minority that the two factions could not agree on a common national policy. Many on both sides doubted that the government could win the civil war; hedging their bets, they refused to vote an outright ban on the Communist Party. The Communists, for their part, decided on a campaign that would demoralize the population and the Army, undermine the economy and discredit the government. The Communists knew that they lacked the forces to seize power outright. They hoped, however, that Yugoslavia's Marshal Tito would support the insurgency when Greece became ungovernable, and would send in forces strong enough to topple the government.

The guerrillas struck almost nightly—sweeping in after sunset and stealing away before dawn. By the end of 1946, the Communist forces on and near Mount Grammos claimed control of more than 100 villages and guardposts, providing them with the infrastructure for the so-called Provisional Democratic Government of Free Greece they set up in late 1947 with General Markos as Premier.

The Communists established courts, collected taxes and even operated their own telephone service. Their advance southward in early 1947 carried them to the vicinity of Corinth, barely 60 miles from the capital. At Sparta they boldly attacked the town jail and released 200 prisoners. The situation in the Peloponnesus became so critical that people had to travel in convoys.

The elusive General Markos seemed to be everywhere. Although the guerrillas celebrated him in songs—"Markos, what mountain ridge are you treading now?"—he was no hero to the peasants whose villages he burned and whose livestock he slaughtered; 700,000 country folk fled to the big towns, where they lived in squalor in shanty camps. In the north, 40 per cent of the remaining population was homeless. Journalists who ventured beyond the cities were struck by the emptiness of a countryside from which most of the populace had gone. The guerrillas had abducted some 30,000 children of school age for "protection and education," and had stripped the fields of animals—making off with 1.3 million goats and sheep and more than 100,000 head of cattle and horses.

Around the Parnassus, the BBC's Matthews heard of the exploits of a renegade schoolmaster who called himself "The Diamond." In a raid on the village of Arachova, this freebooter burned 20 houses, seized the wives and daughters of rich olive growers for ransom, slaughtered the town's sheep and departed with all of the town's young men as conscripts for the guerrilla army.

Tactics such as these so demoralized the Greek Army that the chief of the General Staff had ceased talking of a quick

148

victory and was gloomily predicting a war that would last three more years. Sober politicians doubted that the government would survive even a fraction of that time. Yet forces were at work that would eventually turn the tide in the government's favor.

In the summer of 1947, Greece saw the first tangible results of the newly proclaimed Truman Doctrine, as ships loaded with American supplies arrived in the port of Piraeus. Emboldened by support from the United States, the government at last outlawed the Communist Party. Communist newspapers were shut down, and suspected terrorists were rounded up by the hundreds in nightly sweeps through the streets of the major cities. A reign of terror followed, in which executions following summary courts-martial became almost weekly events.

Working with American military advisers, the Greek General Staff began a total reorganization of the National Army. Abandoning its policy of "selective recruitment" of ideologically reliable youth, it began drafting even suspected Communist sympathizers and thus deprived them of the chance to go on with their subversive activities or flee to the guerrillas in the mountains. If the new recruits could not be "reeducated," they were assigned to nonsensitive posts. By employing this and other recruiting techniques, the National Army was able to double its forces, building to a maximum of 250,000 men. They were opposed by 28,000 guerrillas—a ratio of roughly 9 to 1.

At the same time, much of the Army underwent training in mountain fighting. Special commando units of 635 men each were organized to conduct quick sweep-and-destroy missions. These and conventional forces were equipped with American weapons—mortars, pack howitzers, rocket launchers, light machine guns and 75mm recoilless rifles —that gave them a great advantage in firepower over the guerrilla army.

Perhaps most important, the Greek National Army abandoned its policy of piecemeal defense of one town at a time in favor of a systematic widening of control over increasingly large expanses of territory. The key to the new policy was the establishment of a kind of no man's land, in which the populations of entire villages were removed and placed in evacuee camps. Having thus deprived the guerrillas of their underground intelligence network, the Army would launch a massive sweep of the territory to eliminate all guerrilla forces, and then move on to clear another tract of land. Left behind to defend their own villages were garrisons of armed civilians who were organized into a unit called the National Defense Corps.

Meanwhile, General Markos and the Communist command were experiencing mounting difficulties. In 1947, more than 7,000 guerrillas were killed and more than 5,000 taken prisoner. Another 5,000 deserted when the national government shrewdly made an offer of amnesty. Such enormous losses were impossible to make up by voluntary recruitment from a population that was becoming increasingly hostile. Repelled by guerrilla brutality, the country was experiencing a surge of nationalist feeling that made the Mediterranean Greek population suspicious of the very appearance of the guerrillas—many of whom were Slavs from Greek Macedonia. In this atmosphere of mutual distrust, the guerrillas could replace their losses only by forcible recruitment: From the middle of 1947, General Markos admitted, 90 per cent of his recruits were inducted into the guerrilla army against their will.

In the autumn of 1947, the Communist leaders made a disastrous miscalculation. They had concluded that their chances of bringing any of their Communist neighbors, particularly Yugoslavia, into the war on their side were decreasing and that the Greek government, propped up by American aid, was growing stronger. Hence their only hope for victory was to transform their guerrilla forces into a regu-

Greek women weep for their murdered men at a mass funeral in Naousa the day after Communist guerrillas raided the Macedonian town. Many of the dead, including young boys and their elderly schoolmaster, had been killed for talking to American military advisers who had visited the town a few days earlier.

The aircraft carrier U.S.S. Leyte, its flight deck crowded with Navy SB2C Helldivers, leads elements of a United States fleet northward from Crete to demonstrate American concern during the Greek civil war.

lar army and to destroy the Greek National Army in a conventional military campaign.

The new policy was vigorously supported by senior members of the Communist hierarchy—including Secretary-General Nikos Zakhariadis, who had fled to the mountains shortly before the party was outlawed. General Markos realized that he lacked the arms and men to win a conventional war without direct military intervention by Greece's Communist neighbors, and he argued bitterly against it. But he was overruled by Zakhariadis and eventually replaced. To conceal the fact that so popular a hero had fallen from favor, the Communist leadership announced that Markos was on sick leave in Yugoslavia.

Putting the new policy to its first test, the Communists broadcast to a startled nation on Christmas Eve, 1947, that the isolated hill town of Konitsa near the Albanian border would become the capital of their newly formed provisional government. Communist infantry backed by artillery struck Konitsa at 9:15 the next morning. Fighting against a garrison that had been weakened by numerous holiday leaves, the guerrillas quickly seized most of the heights above the town and seemed on the verge of victory. But the garrison fought a delaying action with the aid of supplies and ammunition dropped by British-built Dakotas, and soon government relief columns arrived. The guerrillas retreated, leaving behind more than 250 dead.

"The Army must strike, and its punches must be harder than those of the bandits," declared Greece's Premier Themistocles Sophoulis in March 1948. His statement signaled the beginning of an offensive designed to hunt down and destroy the guerrillas. The whole of the Peloponnesus was gradually secured, and slowly the population began to return to villages and farms they had fled. Sometimes they wreaked a terrible vengeance on the defeated guerrillas. In the town of Levidi a rebel chieftain named Kambelos, notorious as a murderer of civilians, was torn from his military guard by a mob of howling women and stoned to death in the main square. Afterward his body was tied to a horse and paraded through the streets.

In central and northern Greece, the guerrillas were defeated in battle after battle. In the Mornos River valley they lost virtually their entire committed force of 2,000 men, whose escape route was barred by the Gulf of Corinth. Reeling, the rebels fell back toward the frontiers. On their forced marches through the mountains, they came under continual harrying attack from the National Army and Air Force.

Standing above the rebel dead, Greek commanders and Lieut. General James A. Van Fleet (right), chief United States military representative in Greece, study the scene of a guerrilla defeat 20 miles from the border of Yugoslavia in May of 1949.

Many who survived the government pounding died of exposure or starvation.

In June the National Army launched its most ambitious offensive against the so-called State of Grammos—the Provisional Government enclave in the Grammos mountains that now included some 150 villages and the headquarters of the guerrilla command. To support the offensive, the Army blasted roads out of the mountain granite and brought up thousands of tons of supplies—by truck as far as the roads went, then on to forward positions by mule. In the fighting that followed, 2,500 guerrillas were killed and 2,000 were captured. The offensive was not the total disaster for the guerrillas it might have been—6,000 of them managed to slip with their heavy guns through a six-mile corridor into Albania. Yet it gravely weakened an army that was already bleeding away. By the end of 1948, guerrilla casualties were running at 1,500 a month—a loss that could no longer be made up by even the most ruthless recruiting methods.

What finally sealed the fate of the rebel army was its loss of international Communist support. On a visit to Moscow in February 1948, Yugoslavian official Milovan Djilas heard Stalin say that the Greek Communists should abandon their fight: With the United States lined up against them, said Stalin, "they have no prospect of success at all." Later in 1948, Yugoslavia's Tito had a dramatic falling out with Stalin. Anxious to improve his relations with the West and aware that the Greek Communists had almost no chance of victory, Tito gradually withdrew his endorsement of the guerrillas. On the 10th of July, 1949, he closed the Yugoslavian border with Greece. A month later the Greek National Army mounted a final drive.

The objective was the Grammos-Vitsi mountain area where the last of the guerrillas were pinned down. It was a region of pine, oak and chestnut forests beneath slopes of barren rock and icy peaks that rose 7,000 feet into the sky. Some 75,000 government troops faced 12,000 guerrillas, who were well dug in with concrete gun emplacements and machine-gun nests cunningly sited on the rugged slopes. Included in the government's arsenal were not only tanks, armored vehicles and massive artillery but also 51 Curtiss Helldivers, the latest ground-support dive bombers from the United States.

In the campaign that followed, the Greek government forces first feinted at Grammos, then launched a diversionary attack on Vitsi mountain, and finally unleashed a massive assault on the campaign's true target, the Tsarno Ridge, at the top of the Grammos range and serving as the backbone of the guerrilla defensive position. Pounded by artillery and by pinpoint air strikes, the guerrillas found their escape route blocked by the National Army's Ninth Division, which under cover of darkness had taken up positions behind them along the Albanian frontier. When the Tsarno Ridge fell to the Army's First Division after a day of brutal fighting, the civil war in Greece was virtually over. After another three days of localized operations, the Communist Democratic Army in effect ceased to exist.

Communist casualties at Grammos totaled 922 dead and 765 captured. Only 179 rebels surrendered. An estimated 3,000 to 4,000 of them fled and made their way by circuitous routes into Albania and Bulgaria. But they had lost practically all of their heavy equipment and had no way of replacing it. Denied further support by the Albanian and Bulgarian governments, as well as by Yugoslavia, Nikos Zakhariadis conceded defeat.

The war had exacted a terrible toll. Almost 160,000 people had died—50,000 civilians, 38,000 men in the guerrilla forces, 70,000 on the government side, including those in the militia. To the counterinsurgency experts who studied the war, the bitter experience of Greece—like the experiences of France and Italy—suggested that Communism could not come to power in a nation where it had not won the population to its cause. But for one whole section of Europe—those countries occupied by Soviet troops—that truth was irrelevant.

THE MIRACLE OF RECOVERY

Symbols of Europe's postwar recovery, ranks of newly manufactured motor scooters await shipment in 1950 from the Vespa Piaggio plant near Pisa, Italy.

EUROPE'S CLIMB UP A LIFELINE OF HOPE

"It was a life line to sinking men." So said British Foreign Minister Ernest Bevin of the massive European Recovery Program proposed by U.S. Secretary of State George C. Marshall in June 1947. And Bevin added: "We grabbed the life line with both hands." Bevin's simile was apt. To many Americans, Europe seemed a lost cause; its politics were in chaos, its economy moribund. The United States had given five billion dollars of aid, with little apparent effect.

But to Marshall it was inconceivable for the United States to turn its back on Europe. The old soldier and statesman assigned himself the task of persuading weary taxpayers and a skeptical Congress to invest additional billions. He explained the program to audiences everywhere and defended it before Congressional committees. By the end of 1947, polls showed that 2 out of 3 Americans understood the Marshall Plan and that 56 per cent of them supported it. In March 1948, in an overwhelming bipartisan vote, the Senate and House of Representatives approved the Plan.

Congress put strict limits on the program's dimensions: $17 billion to be spent over four years. They were unnecessary. In half the time and with half the sum proposed, the benefits Marshall had promised were evident in all 16 nations that subscribed to the Plan. The economics of capitalism, and the unprecedented willingness of Europeans to collaborate instead of compete, multiplied every Marshall Plan dollar into six dollars' worth of goods, services and capital equipment, from mules to motorbikes to gigantic dams. When the Marshall Plan formally ended in 1952, the U.S. contribution came to a little more than $13 billion.

By that time a new Europe more united and prosperous than the old was rising from the ashes of World War II— and Europeans knew whom to thank for it. Marshall's program, declared the Foreign Minister of France, "will be reckoned among the most decisive events in the history of the Western world." The London *Economist* broadened its thanks to include all Americans; the European Recovery Program, it said, was "the most straightforward, generous thing that any country has ever done for others."

U.S. Secretary of State George C. Marshall fields a question during Congressional hearings on the European Recovery Program in January 1948.

The Limberg dam, keystone of Austria's mammoth Kaprun hydroelectric power project, nears completion in 1950 after an infusion of Marshall Plan funds.

FEEDING THE CITIES, STOCKING THE FARMS

"The War," said Secretary Marshall in testimony before the Senate Foreign Relations Committee, "smashed the delicate mechanism by which European countries made their living." Simply rebuilding destroyed industrial plants would not be sufficient. "The worst of the many vicious cycles that beset the European peoples," he explained, is "the inability of the European workshop to get food and raw materials required to produce the exports necessary to get the purchasing power for food and raw materials."

The United States Economic Cooperation Administration, which presided over the Marshall Plan, attacked this cycle at two points simultaneously. It shipped food for hungry workers and sent livestock and fertilizer to increase the productivity of European farms—thus reducing the cost of agricultural products. In April of 1948, just 11 days after President Truman signed the Marshall Plan into law, 9,000 tons of wheat consigned to France left Galveston, Texas, aboard the freighter *John H. Quick*. As soon thereafter as possible, the ECA concentrated its agricultural investment on European self-help projects—such as Austria's effort to upgrade the quality of its beef cattle *(below)*.

Port workers in Marseilles stack sacks of American and North African grain rushed to France in 1948.

At Austria's Artificial Impregnation Institute, a prize bull parades past a structure built with U.S. aid.

Stevedores lead 900 American-bred mules ashore at Piraeus in August 1949, the first of 7,500 work animals sent to replace Greece's war-devastated stock.

TRANSFORMING RUINS INTO HOMES

Second only to food on the long list of postwar shortages was housing. Across the Continent, perhaps one person in four was without adequate shelter. A prime example was the Netherlands, which had been twice devastated by the Germans—first during their blitzkrieg invasion and then in their scorched-earth retreat. Yet a growth in population had left the Dutch with one million more people to house than they had before the War.

The main surge in home construction had to wait until Marshall Plan dollars had worked their way into such essential industries as steel and cement. Meanwhile, Europeans stretched available funds and materials to achieve some inspired makeshift solutions. The Dutch converted abandoned windmills into one-family dwellings, rebuilt burned-out masonry houses *(below)* and constructed new houses with walls made entirely of concrete blocks, which were cheaper and more easily obtained than imported lumber.

In Hamburg, where Allied bombs had destroyed 300,000 housing units and left 43 million tons of rubble, a minimum of American aid and a maximum of German industriousness and ingenuity combined to raise new apartment buildings from the ruins of the old. Rubble cleared by hand was fed into a specially designed crusher, mixed with U.S.-supplied cement, and poured into walls. The walls proved strong enough that expensive steel reinforcing rods were needed only at the corners.

The hulks of bombed-out row houses on a Dutch street (left) undergo a near-miraculous transformation (right) with the help of Marshall Plan assistance.

Hamburg apartments (left) are mere shells after 1943 Allied raids. By 1951, although some rubble remains, half the buildings have been replaced (right).

A Belgian worker guides a load of construction material to the top of a modern educational center being built with American money and technical advice.

PUTTING A CONTINENT ON WHEELS

Goaded by the postwar example of an American economic boom, Europeans set a higher goal for themselves than a mere return to their prewar standard of living. They recognized that European industrial production, in comparison with the United States and even with the Soviet Union, had been on the decline since before the First World War. With American aid they set out to match the United States in technology and to sell their products not just to one another but to the rest of the world.

Automobiles became a symbol of this new-found objective. Marshall Plan money helped to finance the retooling of automotive plants in France, England, Italy and West Germany; it paid for imports of such raw materials as copper for electrical wiring, nickel for hardening steel, zinc for die-casting and carbon black for strengthening tires. By 1952, Europe was producing nearly twice as many motor vehicles as it had before the War.

Most of the new cars were earmarked for export to bring in much-needed currency from abroad; in 1948, for example, Britain sold overseas 5 out of 6 cars it produced. As increased trade brought the promise of prosperity, however, new highways crisscrossed the Continent, and Europeans took to the road in numbers undreamed of before.

For those who could not yet afford a car, there was the postwar phenomenon of the motor scooter. The powered two-wheelers were relatively inexpensive to produce, buy and operate; the scooters carried Europeans back and forth to work and to the country on holidays—and gave them a sense of mobility that most of them had never experienced.

A French worker stacks tires made with rubber from Indochina and U.S.-financed hardening agents.

A highway-striping machine made in America marks a no-passing zone at a curve in rural Greece.

To speed up production lines—like this one of Alfa Romeo trucks—Marshall Plan officials arranged for advice from Detroit automakers.

160

London's Tower Bridge frames a car being hoisted onto a vessel for export. By 1949 British motor-vehicle production was 70 per cent higher than in 1938.

A NEW LIFE FOR ARTISANS

The effects of Marshall Plan aid extended even to the level of handcrafts, bringing to village and farm the means to buy and transport humble materials like silica sand and pottery clay. Once transportation had been restored, isolated artisans could ship their wares to distant markets—especially the United States, where postwar prosperity and a new global awareness had created an appetite for European products.

Italian potters shape their wares out of clay bought with American credits.

Austrians pack Christmas ornaments aglitter with American silver nitrate.

A jovial artisan hoists twin symbols of economic renewal, jugs of green glass

manufactured in Empoli after Marshall Plan aid helped to revive the Italian glass industry. Wrapped in woven straw, the jugs were used to export Chianti wine.

5

The making of a Communist Poland
Revolutionary cadres trained in Moscow
An election delayed to guarantee the result
A premier resigns by telephone
A short-lived alliance of King and Communist in Rumania
A stunning subversion in Czechoslovakia
"An iron curtain has descended"
An evolving policy of "vigilant containment"
Cold War crisis in Berlin
Soviet victories in a war of spies
A German intelligence team goes to work for the West
Kim Philby's years of betrayal
Stalin excommunicates a loyal satellite
The promise of stability and growth

"Communism does not fit the Poles," said Premier Josef Stalin in October of 1944. "They are too individualistic, too nationalistic."

To anyone familiar with Poland and its history, the truth of Stalin's statement seemed beyond dispute. Yet the Soviet dictator was the one man in all the world least willing to accept it. Stalin, by then rapidly becoming master of Eastern Europe, was determined to force the round Polish peg into the square hole of Communism—regardless of what that might do to his relations with the Western Allies.

An early sign of Stalin's purpose was his support of the so-called Lublin Committee, a Communist-dominated Polish resistance group established under Moscow's tutelage and named for one of the first large Polish cities liberated by the Soviets. As the Lublin group took root in Poland just behind the advancing Red Army, Stalin became increasingly abusive toward the Polish government-in-exile in London, which the West had supported as the country's legitimate government since the outbreak of the War. The conflict caused by Stalin's backing of the Lublin Communists was the first indication of serious strain in the wartime alliance, which until then had been a cooperative, if sometimes contentious, association.

Poland was not the only country whose future was at issue. In the course of pushing back the Germans on the Eastern Front during the last two years of the War, the Red Army had thrust into Rumania, Hungary, Bulgaria, Czechoslovakia, Finland and the eastern parts of Germany and Austria. Once the War ended, the Western Allies were anxious to see that these countries—whether they were the liberated victims of the Axis or its defeated partners—were left free to establish governments of their own choosing. Stalin, on the other hand, was equally committed to the Communization of his neighbors—both as a matter of defense and to advance the worldwide cause of Communism.

Publicly, Moscow had deemphasized its prewar policy of fostering global revolution; in 1943, for example, it had abolished the Communist International, or Comintern. The Soviets, however, had never abandoned the idea of spreading their ideology—and with it their influence—wherever they could. Comintern or no, every country in Eastern Europe was represented in Moscow by a cadre of dedicated Communists, refugees from political persecution in their

AN IRON CURTAIN DESCENDS

homelands who had devoted many years to sharpening their revolutionary skills.

Even while German troops still occupied Russian soil, the Soviets began forming these cadres into political movements. As the Red Army drove westward, close on their heels came the cadres—embryonic governments ready to acquire power, sometimes in coalition with local Leftists of other parties, and usually with the backing of Soviet troops and political advisers.

The growing hostility between the Soviet Union and the Western Allies over the fate of Eastern Europe came as a shock to many people in the United States and Great Britain. Weary of conflict and at least partly conditioned by wartime propaganda to regard the Soviets as a peace-loving ally, they now had to become accustomed to the prospect of a new kind of war—a "Cold War," as the press soon termed it. And there was no guarantee that the Cold War might not suddenly turn hot.

In Poland, much had already happened by V-E Day to deliver the country into the Communist camp and to sour relations between the Western Allies and the U.S.S.R. But the issue that did most to set the two sides against each other was yet to come: Poland's first postwar elections.

Despite the often vague and ambiguous agreements that emerged from the wartime summit conferences, the Americans and British felt sure of one thing—all parties, the Russians included, had agreed that Soviet-occupied Poland would be permitted to conduct free and fair elections at the earliest possible date. For Western leaders, fulfillment of that agreement was to be a test of Soviet designs.

Those designs soon became clear. By intimidating, jailing and even executing non-Communist Poles, especially the leaders of the wartime anti-Nazi underground, the Russians poisoned the atmosphere for democratic politics in Poland. They delayed the election interminably, allowing themselves time to guarantee a favorable vote for a Communist-dominated coalition.

When election day finally came, in January of 1947, many of the candidates of the Peasant Party—led by Stanislaw Mikolajczyk, head of the London faction of the provisional government—were in prison. Mikolajczyk later asserted that 100,000 rank-and-file members of his party were also behind bars that day. The Communist-controlled election commission disqualified lists of Peasant Party candidates in 10 of the country's 52 voting districts, containing one fourth of the population. Office and factory workers in many cities were marched in formation to polling places and voted for the Communist coalition in what was termed "voluntary open voting."

The official count gave the coalition 394 seats, the Peasant Party 28 and other parties 22. Mikolajczyk and two Peasant Party ministers resigned from the Cabinet the day after the election. He told the new Parliament, "If by some odd chance one of our members was elected to that body, we would be placed in a position of accepting the fraud on which this gathering bases its presence here."

A new Polish government was formed under Józef Cyrankiewicz, one of eight Socialists serving in the 24-member Cabinet. Only five portfolios went to Communists—the vice premiership and the Ministries of Foreign Affairs, Security, Industry and Education—but they enabled the party to strengthen its domination of the country.

Mikolajczyk continued to defy the Communists in blunt language, but he was warned in October of 1947 that his parliamentary immunity was about to be removed, which would expose him to arrest. He fled Warsaw and was pursued. There followed a week-long melodrama of high-speed car chases, of nights holed up in a barn and of a chilling escape from a house full of partying Russian and Polish soldiers. Professional smugglers escorted him through eastern Germany and he reached safe haven in the British zone. Behind him, Mikolajczyk left a Poland slipping rapidly under total Communist control.

The Polish election evoked official protests from the U.S. and British governments, but the language of their notes revealed the limits of their willingness or capacity to influence the situation. The United States declared itself "especially perturbed" and threatened "to approach the Polish government with a reminder of its obligations." Not surprisingly, the protests changed nothing.

Meanwhile, other neighbors of the Soviet Union were experiencing variations on the Polish theme. In Hungary, the process had begun in the autumn of 1944 when the Hungarian First Army, hitherto an Axis force, went over to the Soviet side as the Red Army approached. General Béla Miklos, the First Army's commander, offered to form a government that would sue for peace. Elections were duly held in the liberated parts of the country, and on December 21 a coalition of four parties, including the Communists, formed a provisional government under Red Army control at the town of Debrecen.

The new Hungarian regime signed an armistice in Moscow on January 20, 1945. Budapest was soon liberated by the Soviets and the government moved into the capital in April. Under the guidance of Soviet commissars, a series of "people's courts" across the country began the process of eliminating influential Hungarians who were likely to oppose a Communist regime.

Despite the house cleaning of anti-Communist elements, however, the Communist Party received only 17 per cent of the vote in Hungary's first postwar election in November of 1945. The Smallholders, a Centrist peasant party, received 57 per cent and formed a coalition government. Backed by a threat of Soviet intervention, the Communists demanded and got control of the key Interior Ministry—which included the police—in the new government.

Throughout 1946, the Communists tightened their control of the police and in early 1947 they charged the Smallholders with sheltering reactionaries and fascists. Leading Smallholders officials were rounded up one by one, and in May accusations of espionage were lodged against Premier Ferenc Nagy, who was then vacationing in Switzerland. In a bizarre deal that was consummated by long-distance telephone, Nagy resigned the premiership and the Communists agreed to allow his five-year-old son, Laczi, to leave the country.

Over the next two years a string of purges, government reorganizations and rigged elections solidified Communist control. In the election of 1947, the right to vote was withheld from people who at any time had been, in the words of the government, "condemned for crimes against democracy." In practice, this restriction applied not only to anyone who had ever been detained by the police but even to relatives living in the same house.

Members of one of the opposition groups, the Hungarian Freedom Party, were beaten and their campaign rallies were broken up by gangs of Communist toughs. When the party asked the Interior Ministry for protection, the Communist Minister, Lásló Rajk, replied that his police were not sure they could control "the just anger of the people against the enemies of democracy." The party disbanded rather than face further attacks.

Another major target for coercion was Hungary's educational system, which was largely in the hands of the Catholic Church. When the government moved to nationalize the schools, Josef Cardinal Mindszenty protested. Arrested and tried on charges of treason and black marketeering, he was sentenced to life imprisonment.

Almost as an afterthought, the Smallholders and all other non-Communist parties were dissolved one after another. By 1948, the only independents left were the Social Demo-

Poster portraits of leading Communist candidates—including President Boleslaw Bierut (second from right) and future Premier Ladislas Gomulka (right)—decorate party headquarters in Warsaw on the eve of Poland's national election in 1947. The banner at center salutes the second anniversary of Warsaw's liberation by the Red Army, and the one at bottom proclaims the party slogan: "Independence—Peace—Welfare."

crats; they had supported the Communists on all major issues, but in that year they came under heavy pressure to merge with the Communist Party. Those Social Democratic leaders who resisted were labeled Right Wingers and expelled. In June, the merger took place; all legal political opposition in Hungary had disappeared.

In November of 1947, Ana Pauker, a Moscow-trained Communist, took office as Foreign Minister of Rumania, swearing an oath of allegiance to Rumania's King Michael. It was probably the only time in history that a Communist minister came to power by pledging fealty to a monarch, although it was by no means the first time a Communist had made a tactical compromise to support the greater cause.

The unlikely alliance of King and Communist had its origins in the waning months of Nazi power in Eastern Europe. As the Red Army neared the Rumanian border in August of 1944, Michael took steps to rid his country of its pro-Nazi government. He dismissed Premier Ion Antonescu and ordered German troops to get out of Rumania. The Luftwaffe retaliated by bombing Bucharest, but even as the bombs were falling, a new military government under the leadership of General Constantin Sânâtescu took office in the capital and declared war on Germany. For his stand against the Germans, King Michael was awarded the Soviet Union's highest decoration, the Order of Victory.

Once the Red Army swept into Rumania, however, the new government came under Soviet pressure for reform and

was replaced in late 1944 by a Cabinet of civilians, including one Communist minister. The Rumanian Communist Party then set about organizing a National Democratic Front, a coalition dominated by the Communists and including a vaguely Leftist Plowman's Front Party and a few other Leftist groups.

In late February of 1945, just days after the Yalta agreement on free elections was announced, Soviet Deputy Foreign Minister Andrei Vyshinsky arrived in Bucharest and delivered an ultimatum to King Michael: Rumania would cease to exist as an independent state if a National Democratic Front government was not appointed immediately.

The King gave in, and Petru Groza, leader of the Plowman's Front, was named Premier of the new government in March. Vigorous British and American protests to this arbitrary shift in governments produced a pledge from Groza to hold early and free elections. But voter registration was restricted to Communists and their sympathizers, and when the elections were finally held in November of 1946 the National Democratic Front was declared to have received 80 per cent of the vote.

Throughout 1947, propaganda campaigns, arrests and show trials eliminated what remained of opposition to the Communist regime. Leaders of the National Peasant Party, the major group outside the National Democratic Front, were arrested on conspiracy charges in June, and the party was outlawed. Even the Social Democrats, the largest single party in the National Democratic Front, came under attack. Under Communist pressure for a merger of the two parties, the Social Democrats splintered. The majority voted in November of 1947 for fusion; a separate party formed by the dissident faction under the former Social Democratic leader, Titel Petrescu, was dissolved by the government shortly afterward and Petrescu was eventually arrested.

Ana Pauker and her fellow Communists moved into the Cabinet that November. The incongruity of a Communist-run monarchy was short-lived. On December 30, King Michael abdicated and went into exile. The transformation of Rumania into a People's Republic was formalized in the elections of March 1948.

The powerful presence of the Red Army was usually the chief means by which Moscow ensured the conversion of its neighbors to Communism. But as the War approached its

The presence of a Polish soldier, a submachine gun slung over his shoulder, ensures order as his countrymen line up to vote on the 19th of January, 1947, in a building still undergoing reconstruction. "It is all so painfully like Hitler's plebiscites," wrote U.S. Ambassador Arthur Bliss Lane, "even to the swaggering bands of the Citizens' Militia Reserve Corps, who revive memories of the Brown Shirts."

final phase, there were no Soviet troops in Bulgaria, nor was there any reason for their presence. Bulgaria was not and never had been at war with the Soviet Union.

Bulgaria had joined the Axis in March of 1941, but its chief wartime activity had been to occupy—and then annex—Yugoslavian and Greek territories overrun by the Germans. The Bulgarians had dutifully declared war against two distant enemies of the Axis, Great Britain and the United States, but they steadfastly maintained a neutral position toward their powerful neighbor, the Soviet Union.

As German strength waned in the late summer of 1944, a new anti-Axis Bulgarian government took power and put out peace feelers to the Western Allies through a mission to Cairo. Stalin found offense in the Bulgarians' failure to contact the nearest Allied outpost, the Soviet Embassy in Sofia. He believed Bulgarian affairs were of direct interest to the Soviet Union, and to make his point he abruptly declared war on Bulgaria.

On September 5, 1944, Soviet troops invaded the country, encountered no resistance and fanned out to occupy the Black Sea coast to the Turkish border. Four days later, while the Red Army was still far to the east of Sofia, an armed gang broke up a meeting of the Regency Council that was governing Bulgaria in the name of a moribund monarchy. A new council, peopled by a coalition of Leftists called the Fatherland Front, was installed and its leaders traveled to Moscow in October to sign an armistice.

Soon a familiar succession of events began to unfold. People's courts purged the nation of "war criminals"—a sweeping category that included not only Axis supporters but influential non-Communists. Elections were scheduled for August of 1945, but the British and Americans protested a Communist demand that all political parties in Bulgaria first join the Fatherland Front. The protest delayed the vote until November. By then the front's victory in the election surprised no one, and under the personal direction of Soviet emissary Vyshinsky a government was formed, made up entirely of members of the Fatherland Front.

There followed a government-sponsored campaign to discredit the already unpopular monarchy, and in September of 1946 a plebiscite brought down the royal house —whose tenant at that moment was King Simeon, the six-year-old grandson of another deposed monarch, Victor Em-

manuel III of Italy. A month later, with many opposition candidates and their campaign workers in prison, the Communists came out from behind the Fatherland Front and won 60 per cent of the seats in the country's newly established constituent assembly.

The Communists' election was the signal for the triumphant return, after more than 20 years in exile, of Georgi Dimitrov, the leading Bulgarian Communist. Dimitrov was a highly respected figure in the Communist world, having served as General Secretary of the Comintern before its dissolution. Now, installed as the Premier of Bulgaria, he ordered the elimination of the last vestiges of resistance to the new regime.

The process began with the trial of Nikola Petkov, leader of Bulgaria's Agrarian Party, who was convicted of treason and antigovernment conspiracy and was hanged in September of 1947. Shortly afterward, as a means of expressing disapproval of the government, Socialist Party chief Kosta Lulchev declared his opposition to a budget bill. Speaking openly in Parliament, Dimitrov replied, "In this assembly I many times warned Nikola Petkov's group, but they would not listen. They lost their heads, and their leader lies buried. Reflect on your own actions, lest you suffer the same fate." Lulchev persisted in his independent line, and Dimitrov made good his threat. The aged Socialist leader was arrested in November of 1948 and sentenced to 15 years in prison. By then, a large segment of his party had already merged with the Communists.

Bulgaria had adopted a new constitution modeled after that of the Soviet Union, and in December of 1947 the former kingdom had become the Bulgarian People's Republic. The few remaining non-Communist parties dissolved themselves, and Dimitrov in December of 1948 proclaimed to a Communist Party Congress that Bulgaria had become a dictatorship of the proletariat.

Of all the countries that fought alongside Germany, only Finland had entered the War not as an aggressor but as a victim—of a Soviet attack in 1939. For this reason, the doughty Finns avoided being lumped at War's end with the Nazis and fascists, even by the Russians.

After Finland detached itself from its German alliance and signed an armistice in Moscow in September of 1944,

DESPERATE FLIGHTS TO FREEDOM

Estonian refugees tie up at a Miami pier after a 5,000-mile crossing from Northern Europe.

The 11 Estonians had good reason to smile and wave from the deck of their broad-beamed, 40-foot sailing vessel. After 81 harrowing days at sea in flight from their Communist-absorbed homeland, they had reached safe harbor in Miami, Florida, on the 9th of September, 1946. The refugees had no visas, but President Truman bent the immigration laws and welcomed them to the United States.

The Estonians' flight to freedom was repeated thousands of times in as many guises during the immediate postwar years as people made brave by desperation fled homelands where Communist commissars had taken the place of Nazi *Gauleiters*. Most often their route was overland: By 1948, some 750,000 fugitives had filtered into the Western zones of Germany and Austria *(following pages)*.

From a concealed position (top), an American Army officer and a German border policeman watch two fugitives from Czechoslovakia cross the frontier along the rail line that connects Selb, Germany, and the Czech town of Asch. Challenged, the Czechs turned and made a run for it (center) but, burdened by their rucksacks, they were soon overtaken (bottom). After interrogation, the refugees were told they could remain in Germany.

At a checkpoint between British and Soviet zones in 1948, a German policeman helps two German women escape with their luggage to the West.

Roused at dawn by a policeman, refugees from eastern Germany huddle under blankets near Düsseldorf after crossing into the American zone.

events proceeded much as in the countries overrun by the Red Army—up to a point. But perhaps because Finnish valor had earned a special admiration in the West, and because the Finns might have proved as tough a nut for the Russians to crack in the aftermath as they had in 1939, Stalin repeatedly veered away from the final step of imposing a Communist regime on them.

The most dangerous moment for Finland came in February of 1948, when the Leftist Premier, Mauno Pekkala, was called to Moscow to execute a mutual assistance treaty. Although Pekkala's delegation submitted to the victors' demands—heavy reparations payments, loss of territory, punishment of fascists, a promise of friendly relations with the Soviet Union—they managed to preserve Finland's freedom of action in domestic affairs.

The take-over of Czechoslovakia by a Moscow-dominated Communist regime rattled the Western powers more than any European political event since the War. Western reaction to the ascendancy of Communism in other Eastern European countries had been tempered by the knowledge that democracy and independence had never been sturdy growths in the region, and that Rumania, Hungary and Bulgaria in particular had taken the Nazi side in the War. By contrast, Czechoslovakia had been a prosperous and sophisticated industrial state, one that seemed in many ways a happy synthesis of East and West. Its Slavic people shared feelings of ethnic solidarity with the Soviet Union while admiring and emulating Western society. The Czechs were predominantly Roman Catholic, their economy was part Socialist and part capitalist, and their political system was a Western-style parliamentary democracy.

The American and Soviet forces occupying Czechoslovakia withdrew in December of 1945. In a free election by secret ballot the following summer, the Communist Party won 38 per cent of the vote and the closely allied Social Democrats another 12.8 per cent. The Communists, pursuing Moscow's popular-front policy, formed a coalition government with other nonfascist parties. One of the heroes of post-World War I Czechoslovakian independence, Eduard Beneš, became President, and Communist leader Klement Gottwald became Premier. In addition to the premiership, the Communists and Social Democrats received 12 of the 26 posts in the Cabinet, including the all-important Interior and Information Ministries. The Czechs then settled into what appeared to be a return to their prewar democratic stability, enjoying good relations with the West and close, cordial ties to Moscow.

But as a generation of Soviet Communists had already learned, it was both difficult and dangerous to maintain close, cordial ties with the man in Moscow at the center of the Communist world. Josef Stalin had on more than one occasion developed a paranoid mistrust of party comrades, generals, scholars, artists, even ordinary Russian citizens. Some trifling act would simmer in his deeply suspicious mind, then boil over into a lethal charge of treason against the unsuspecting targets. In 1947 such a misfortune befell the entire nation of Czechoslovakia.

The trouble started when the Czech Cabinet, looking desperately for sources of economic aid, voted unanimously on the 7th of July, 1947, to accept the invitation of France and Britain to join other nations at a meeting in Paris. Its purpose was to discuss a coordinated European response to the proposed Marshall Plan. Czechoslovakian officials decided to attend the meeting without first consulting the Kremlin—and in the face of a Soviet denunciation of the Plan just a week earlier.

Premier Gottwald, who was in Moscow at the time, was summoned to meet with the Soviet leader and was subjected to a tirade for indulging in what the Russians considered an unfriendly act. "I have never seen Stalin so furious," Gottwald said later. Chastened, the Czechs withdrew their acceptance of the invitation to Paris. But the damage was done; Stalin's suspicions were sparked.

Trouble flared anew when the results of a secret opinion poll taken by the Czech Information Ministry indicated a sharp drop in support for the Communists, evidently triggered by food shortages and other economic hardships that were held to be the fault of various Communist-run ministries. It was projected that the Communists would lose 25 per cent of their voting strength in the national election scheduled for May of 1948—potentially enough to allow opposition parties to exclude them from a new government. Moscow feared that a non-Communist regime would sign up for Marshall Plan aid and integrate Czechoslovakia's economy with that of Western Europe.

Early in 1948 the Czech Interior Minister, Václav Nosek, began firing non-Communist police chiefs and replacing them with Communists. When, on February 12, he discharged eight senior officers of the Prague police force and installed his own men, 12 non-Communist Cabinet ministers resigned in protest, intending to force the naming of a new Cabinet. It was a fatal mistake. President Beneš delayed accepting the resignations in the hope of negotiating a compromise. But inexorable pressure built up: Armed Communist bands known as People's Militias staged demonstrations and riots throughout the country, raising the threat of a violent coup. And in the midst of the turmoil, a visitor arrived from the Soviet Union—former Russian Ambassador Valerian Zorin.

Zorin made clear to various leaders that although there were no Red Army units then in Czechoslovakia, that situation could quickly be changed, warning that "the Soviet Union might be forced to safeguard Czechoslovakia's independence." Zorin managed to be reassuring and ominous with the same words. "The Soviet Union," he told one Czech minister, "never deserts her friends."

Under the dual threat of a militia putsch and a Red Army invasion, Beneš gave in. On February 25, 1948, he accepted a new—predominantly Communist—Cabinet list that had been drawn up by Klement Gottwald with Zorin's approval. Jan Masaryk, a distinguished Czech patriot and son of the country's first President, chose to remain in the Cabinet as Foreign Minister. He hoped to preserve a vestige of democratic presence in the government, though he confided to friends that he was pessimistic about his chances. Two weeks after the coup, Masaryk's body was found in the courtyard of the Czernin Palace, site of his official residence. It was announced that he had committed suicide by jumping from a window of his apartment, several stories up. But whether Masaryk jumped, fell or was pushed has never been established.

With Masaryk's death, the last non-Communist of national standing had been removed from the new Gottwald government. Within a matter of days, Czechoslovakia had been converted from a parliamentary democracy to a government under firm Communist control. The array of satellite states buffering the Soviet Union from Western Europe was now complete. In the West, too—particularly in the United States—there was a closing of ranks, talk of rearmament, and the abandoning of the last shreds of the old wartime pro-Russian sentiment.

Harry Truman had come to the presidency of the United States on April 12, 1945, humble as any man might be who the day before was an inadequately informed, underemployed politician of high rank but modest reputation. He had no thought of undoing, at least for the moment, the policies of his predecessor—especially President Roosevelt's pragmatic attitude toward America's Soviet ally.

In 1941, before he dreamed of being in a position to speak for the entire nation, then-Senator Truman had expressed the sentiment that it would be a good thing if the Nazis and the Communists destroyed each other. Now, as President, he got his first look at secret documents that detailed the wartime alliance between the United States and the Soviet Union.

Truman learned of the years of careful diplomacy required to keep the relationship going, including the many times when Roosevelt bent over backward to placate Stalin. Truman also saw that Roosevelt, in the last months of his life, had become fed up with what he considered to be Soviet duplicity on the future of Eastern Europe.

Although Truman had no wish to provoke a split with Russia, he had come to power at a time when the United States—with the War almost over in Europe—was moving away from a policy of accommodation to one of insisting on more give and take. Truman told his aides that he would continue working with the Soviets as long as they were, by his lights, straightforward in their dealings with the United States. If not, said Truman, they could "go to hell."

Within a few days of taking office, Truman engaged in an act of conspicuous cooperation with Moscow. Truman wanted Soviet Foreign Minister Molotov to attend the organizational meeting of the United Nations in San Francisco as a signal of the Russians' commitment to the U.N.'s success. Stalin had been holding Molotov back, but when he was pressed on the matter by U.S. Ambassador Averell Harriman, he said he would send Molotov to the meeting if Truman publicly asked him to. The President responded with a formal request, giving Stalin the opportunity to accede to it, which he did.

When Molotov paid a call on Truman on April 24, however, the question of non-Communist representation in Poland's government inevitably came up. Truman saw the issue as one of adhering to the Yalta agreements; Molotov talked stubbornly of "difficulties." Truman's temper flared; he said bluntly that friendly relations with the Soviets could only continue if they were built on "mutual observation of agreements and not on the basis of a one-way street."

"I have never been talked to like that in my life," exclaimed Molotov, a man who had spent his career in the employ of Josef Stalin.

"Carry out your agreements and you won't get talked to like that," Truman shot back.

The angry exchange did nothing to advance the settlement of the Polish issue, and Molotov undoubtedly carried back to Stalin a sour report on the prospects for continued U.S.-Soviet accord.

Relations soon took another dip when Truman, on V-E Day, signed an order for a drastic cutback in Lend-Lease aid to U.S. allies. The stoppage came so abruptly that ships already on the high seas were ordered to turn back to American ports with their cargoes of food, clothing and arms. The cutoff had a dreadful effect on Britain, whose buying power was virtually nil, but the Russians protested bitterly that it was directed solely against them. Truman hastily rescinded the order, blaming overzealous bureaucrats for its severity, but Moscow's angry suspicions were not dispelled.

Nor was the Russians' increasing hostility restricted to the United States. Stalin accorded the British full partnership in what he saw as a growing conspiracy against the Soviet Union. Even the election of a Labor government in Britain in July 1945—and the fall of that dedicated imperialist, Winston Churchill—did not improve British-Soviet relations. Indeed, the Soviets were contemptuous of the Laborites and often were more vitriolic toward them than toward the Americans. At a foreign ministers' meeting, Britain's Ernest Bevin, an old-line Socialist and a former coal miner, was driven to his limits by Russian taunts. Enraged, he sprang toward Soviet Foreign Minister Molotov with his fists cocked, crying, "I've had enough of this, I have!" Security people moved in to prevent a personal escalation of the Cold War.

Relations between the former allies worsened throughout 1946 and 1947, the conflict fueled by the events in Eastern Europe and by the bellicose statements of American politicians and journalists. For example, James Burnham, a former Marxist who was then teaching philosophy at New York University, proposed in a 1947 issue of *Life* that the United States forcibly establish a "world empire" as a counterweight to the burgeoning Soviet empire. The resulting test of strength between the two superpowers would then have to be resolved. "This issue will be decided, and in our day," Burnham wrote. "In the course of the decision both of the present antagonists may, it is true, be destroyed. But one of them must be."

Such apocalyptic visions were much more common than the cool reason the situation called for, but exercises in reason were themselves likely to provoke hysterical reactions. The most famous such exercise was presented to an unprepared public in the city of Fulton, Missouri, on March 5, 1946. The occasion was an address by Winston Churchill at Westminster College. The speech, given in the presence of President Truman and apparently endorsed by him, was a landmark in the development of East-West relations in the aftermath of the War. It brought into plain view the existence of the Cold War, and it included a term that was to become a grim household expression throughout the West.

Churchill's speech shocked Americans by publicly naming the Russians, for the first time, as a dangerous, hostile adversary of the West. "A shadow has fallen upon the

Czechoslovakia's Communist Premier Klement Gottwald (left) and Defense Minister Ludvik Svoboda observe a minute of silence next to the empty Parliamentary seat of Foreign Minister Jan Masaryk. The staunch anti-Communist leaped or was pushed to his death on March 10, 1948, during the consolidation of Communist rule in Czechoslovakia.

Members of the Czech Workers' Militia—used to terrorize the non-Communist opposition—march through the Old Town Square of Prague in celebration of Czechoslovakia's new Communist government.

scenes so lately lighted by the Allied victory," he said. "Nobody knows what Soviet Russia and its Communist international organization intend to do in the immediate future, or what are the limits, if any, to their expansive and proselytizing tendencies. From Stettin in the Baltic to Trieste in the Adriatic," Churchill declared, "an iron curtain has descended across the Continent. Behind that line lie all the capitals of the ancient states of Central and Eastern Europe. Warsaw, Berlin, Prague, Vienna, Budapest, Belgrade, Bucharest and Sofia—all these famous cities and the populations around them lie in what I must call the Soviet sphere, and all are subject in one form or another not only to Soviet influence but to a very high and, in many cases, increasing measure of control from Moscow. Whatever conclusions may be drawn from these facts—and facts they are—this is certainly not the liberated Europe we fought to build up. Nor is it one which contains the essentials of permanent peace."

Churchill urged the West to meet Soviet force with superior force. "From what I have seen of our Russian friends and allies during the War," he said, "I am convinced that there is nothing they admire so much as strength, and there is nothing for which they have less respect than for weakness, especially military weakness." The once and future Prime Minister concluded by proposing a new military alliance of the United States and the British Empire against the expansion of the Soviet empire.

Truman commented that the speech was "admirable and would do nothing but good, though it would make a stir." It certainly did that. Much of the reaction to Churchill's words was negative. *The Chicago Sun* contended that "to follow the standard raised by this great but blinded aristocrat would be to march to the world's most ghastly war." In Russia the reaction to the speech was predictably violent. "Moscow received it hysterically," reported *The New York Times,* "as if the atomic bombs might start dropping before midnight." Stalin himself attacked Churchill bitterly. "Like Hitler," he said, "he also begins the work of unleashing a new war with a racist theory, asserting that only English-speaking nations are fully fledged nations who are called upon to decide the fortunes of the entire world."

The men formulating American foreign policy, on the other hand, strongly supported the Fulton declaration. At

the time Churchill spoke, the U.S. State Department was studying a 16-page report from George F. Kennan, the deputy chief of mission at the American Embassy in Moscow. Kennan, a 42-year-old, Princeton-educated Foreign Service officer, had held diplomatic posts throughout Eastern Europe. He had been part of the first U.S. mission to the Soviet Union in 1933 and was on his third tour of duty in Moscow. In his report he attempted to explain why the Russians behaved the way they did in international affairs and predicted how they might be expected to behave in the future. Kennan's analysis was to prove a turning point in American policy toward the Soviet Union.

To all intents and purposes, the U.S. government had been functioning in an intelligence vacuum as far as Russia was concerned. Aside from Kennan, there were almost no so-called Kremlin-watchers in the government, nor was there, as yet, a central intelligence service to collect and analyze information about the Soviet Union. Since the end of the War the government had been, as one official put it, "floundering about, looking for new intellectual moorings." Kennan's report provided what the State Department was looking for: a realistic appreciation of the Soviet situation that could become the basis for U.S. policy.

George Kennan presented a picture of a Soviet Union governed by a brutal and utterly unscrupulous regime that viewed the outside world with an immutable hostility. Marxism to such a regime was merely a "fig leaf of moral and intellectual respectability" that disguised repression at home and subversion abroad. The government of the Soviet Union, according to Kennan, saw itself as the victim of "capitalist encirclement" and was therefore determined to defend itself by undermining and destroying the capitalist world through a combination of overt official government activity and a "subterranean plan of actions undertaken by agencies for which the Soviet government does not admit responsibility."

Like Churchill, Kennan contended that the Moscow government was impervious to the logic of reason but was highly sensitive to the logic of force. He advocated a check to Soviet expansion by means of the very containment the Soviets seemed to fear. In a version of his report entitled "The Sources of Soviet Conduct," which appeared in the journal *Foreign Affairs* in July 1947 under the pseudonym X, Kennan wrote: "It is clear that the main element of any U.S. policy toward the Soviet Union must be that of a long-term, patient but firm and vigilant containment of Russian expansive tendencies. Soviet pressure against the free institutions of the Western world," he continued, "is something that can be contained by the adroit and vigilant application of a counterforce at a series of constantly shifting geographical

Separate but rigorously equal, the American and Soviet flags fly over Moscow airport in March of 1947. The ingenious Y-shaped flagpole was planted in the snow to welcome Secretary of State George C. Marshall to a four-power conference on the future status of Germany and Austria.

and political points, corresponding to the shifts and maneuvers of Soviet policy."

The problem inherent in conducting such a policy was that the Americans had no way of knowing exactly how Stalin's mind was working, no entrée to the inner councils of the Soviet government, no special intelligence source that could do for them in the Cold War what their intrepid codebreakers and agents had done in World War II. The premises on which the Truman Administration based its Soviet policy could only be drawn from surmise, hunch and inspired guesswork. But known facts about Soviet dispositions were open to more than one interpretation. Did their large standing army—smaller than on V-E Day but still several million strong—indicate offensive or defensive intent? Did it presage an invasion of Western Europe, or was it fully employed in occupying Eastern Europe?

In truth, the Soviet Union—with an appalling 20 million dead and much of the country in ruins—was in no mood and no condition to wage another war against powerful enemies, especially those armed with atomic bombs. In some respects it was weaker after the War than during it. In 1947, in rural Russia and even in the fertile Ukraine, people were still dying of starvation. On the other hand, Russia's seizure of political control over millions of people in at least six countries seemed proof of its long-term aggressive designs.

Ironically, the Truman Administration's first test of the new Kennan line toward the Soviet Union was in an area from which Moscow had kept itself studiously aloof—the Greek civil war. Stalin had not supported the Communist insurgency in Greece. He consistently was either indifferent or opposed to it, believing that Greece's strategic importance to the Mediterranean and the Middle East made it a vital interest of the United States and Britain, one he was loath to challenge. But the insurgents were receiving supplies and sanctuary from the new Communist governments in Bulgaria, Yugoslavia and Albania. It was the immediate threat of a Communist victory in Greece, as well as the increasing Soviet pressure being applied to neighboring Turkey, that spurred Truman to announce a doctrine of intervention. He declared in March of 1947 that the United States would give aid to any country in the world threatened by Communist subversion or invasion.

The Marshall Plan proposed that same year was similarly motivated, at least in part. Its primary aim was to undo the catastrophe of postwar European economic collapse; but the Americans also hoped that Europe's recovery would strengthen each country's ability to resist Communism. At the outset, the great threat to the Marshall Plan had been that it might be too successful in enlisting broad participation. Contrary to Washington's expectations, the Soviet Union showed early signs that it might accept the American invitation to participate in the Plan. The Soviets in fact had much to gain from joining. For one thing, they might have been able, in all apparent innocence, to wreck the whole project; the mere prospect of their participation might well have been enough to make an unfriendly U.S. Congress turn against the idea and kill it. Or if the Plan was funded they would receive a torrent of badly needed dollars.

But the risks were too great for Stalin. He could not accept the idea of American administrators roaming freely about Moscow and the provinces, gathering exact data on the weaknesses of Soviet industry and agriculture and contaminating the populace with Western political ideals.

Soviet Foreign Minister Molotov did go to Paris on June 27, 1947, with an impressive team of economic specialists to confer with French and British officials on preliminary planning for the European Recovery Program. But while he was there, Stalin apparently made up his mind to fight the Marshall Plan. On instructions from Moscow, Molotov abruptly lashed out at the Plan, saying it "may lead to renunciation of economic independence, which is incompatible with the preservation of national sovereignty." Europe, he predicted ominously, would become a vassal of American big business, and a revived Germany would become the dominant European nation.

After this brief flirtation with the idea of economic cooperation with the West, Stalin drew back and pulled the rest of Eastern Europe with him. The Iron Curtain clanged decisively shut. The Soviet Union returned to its prewar attitude of intense suspicion toward foreigners—particularly Westerners—and a near-hysterical fear of espionage and subversion within its borders. Many Soviet citizens who had been associated with foreigners during the War were arrested. This purge was the beginning of the so-called Little Terror, a replay of the great purge that had scarred the Soviet Union in the late 1930s. It darkened the years between 1948 and Stalin's death in 1953. Even loyal Communists from the satellite nations were distrusted as possible spies for the West.

At War's end, Stalin had hoped for a Germany unified on terms somehow favorable to the Soviet Union. When it proved impossible to get the Western Allies to agree to such terms, he became reconciled to the reality of a divided Germany. Using political manipulation backed by military force, he set about to Sovietize the Russian zone. The process intensified as the Cold War escalated, and as the Western Allies began to reevaluate their portion of Germany as a potential ally rather than a defeated enemy.

By 1946, Lieut. General Lucius Clay, military governor of the American zone, was advocating the merger of all three Western zones into a single economic unit. On December 2 of that year, an agreement was signed merging the British and American zones into what was called Bizonia, thus laying the groundwork for their economic and political stabilization; the French were unwilling to go along, dreading their neighbor and historic enemy Germany far more than they feared the distant Soviets.

The Russians viewed this merger with concern, fearing the rebirth of Germany as a European power and a bastion of anti-Soviet influence. At the same time they increasingly focused on the precarious Western position in Berlin as the most promising target for a countermove.

Of all the arenas of the Cold War, in only one—the divided city of Berlin—were Western and Soviet armed forces aligned face to face with a clear Soviet superiority. There, what had begun in May of 1945 as a joint Allied occupation of the defeated enemy's capital had turned into a battle of bureaucratic harassment and propaganda salvos; and the threat of naked force lay just beneath the surface.

The American, British and French Occupation forces had every legal right to be in Berlin. But the city was located deep within the Soviet zone, and in terms of power politics the Westerners were there on Soviet sufferance. By late 1947, the Soviets were showing signs that they put power before accepted rights.

Most of West Berlin's traffic in food, fuel and people moved in and out of the city by highway, rail and water routes that cut through the Soviet zone but were allotted to the Western powers. In December of 1947 the Russians began challenging the West's use of these routes—first by tightening restrictions on the movements of West Berliners who sought to get out of the city and relocate in the West. A month later Russian soldiers stopped an outbound British military train and detached two cars carrying German citizens. In February of 1948, about the time of the Communist coup d'état in Czechoslovakia, the pressure increased; going beyond harassment of German civilians, the Soviets delayed an American military train for several hours at a Russian checkpoint.

On March 5, General Clay sent a chilling message to Washington. "Although I have felt and held that war was unlikely for at least 10 years," Clay warned, "within the last few weeks I have felt a subtle change in the Soviet attitude which gives me a feeling that it may come with a dramatic suddenness." Neither Clay nor any other American knew the extent of the Soviet Union's unreadiness for war—Stalin had guarded that secret closely. Clay was reporting what he saw—a new attitude among Soviet officials in Germany, who were "faintly contemptuous, slightly arrogant and certainly assured." Such information was little enough to go on, but it led Secretary of State Marshall to describe the situation as "very, very serious."

On March 14, three days after Marshall's statement, Congress approved the Marshall Plan. Three days later, five nations—Britain, France, Belgium, the Netherlands and Luxembourg—signed the Treaty of Brussels, an agreement that provided for economic and social cooperation and for mutual defense. Ironically, the treaty had been conceived as protection against the revival of German militarism. By the time it was signed, however, most of the participating countries had the Soviet Union in mind.

Shortly afterward, the U.S. Joint Chiefs of Staff proposed that the Truman Administration strike a military alliance with the Brussels Treaty nations. A year later, the United States and the Brussels signatories would form the North Atlantic Treaty Organization—NATO for short—a mutual defense agency that featured a joint command and the standardization of arms and equipment. NATO's target was unambiguously the Soviet Union.

Into this ominous situation intruded the growing crisis in Berlin. As the Russians placed more obstructions in the way

Striking German workers, 30,000 strong, gather in Market Square, Nuremberg, in January of 1948 to protest against food shortages, black-market profiteering and partition. The placard displayed on the speaker's platform bears the legend: "We demand the unity of Germany."

of freight and passenger traffic in and out of Berlin, General Clay issued an order that within a few months was to have repercussions even he never imagined. Informed on April 1, 1948, that the Russians had turned back two incoming trainloads of supplies, he ordered the U.S. Air Force to fly 30 cargo flights the next day into Berlin's Tempelhof airfield. Although only 25 planes were available, the order was carried out to the letter, and the idea of bringing in supplies by air—if only during a brief period of crisis—took root.

Harassment by the Soviets intensified. Mail shipments were stopped, water supplies were cut off because of "technical difficulties," roads were closed for "repairs." Without notice or explanation, Soviet officials announced that this canal or that railway corridor would no longer be accessible to Western traffic.

On June 1, France joined with the United States, Britain and other West European countries in a plan to create a West German state that by 1949 would enjoy limited sovereignty. But there could be no independence or stability for West Germany without the revival of its economy, which

had been reduced to a predominantly black-market system. The first step had to be the destruction of the black market, and this could only be achieved by instituting a currency reform that would sweep away the much-abused and debased reichsmark, a carry-over from the Nazi regime, and substitute a new German currency with a stable and widely accepted value.

On June 18, 1948, a new currency, the West German mark, was announced. The number of new marks in circulation was carefully controlled, preventing inflation and giving the mark a strength its predecessor had long ago lost. That day marked the beginning of what became known as the German economic miracle. The black market's stranglehold on the economy began to weaken, and barons of this illicit trade were soon out of business. Cigarettes, which had been the basic unit of exchange, became valued only as something to smoke. Confidence in money was restored, and with it the incentive for merchants to abandon the cumbersome barter system and once again sell their wares for paper currency. Empty shops suddenly abounded with

foods and consumer goods the frustrated Germans had not seen on the legal market for years.

The Soviets reacted with alarm. Stalin's foreign policy had been based on a weakened Western Europe, a subordinate Eastern Europe, and a Germany that suffered from the disabilities of both. West Germany's first step toward independence and economic stability, coming on top of the Marshall Plan and the Treaty of Brussels, struck at the heart of that policy. Provoked into a countermove, Stalin decided to apply the full weight of Soviet pressure against the West's most vulnerable outpost, Berlin.

Currency reform in the Western zones provided the excuse. First, the military governor of the Soviet zone, Marshal Vasily Sokolovsky, denounced the new currency and retaliated on the 22nd of June by announcing a new currency for the Soviet zone, including all of Berlin. The French, British and Americans refused to allow money over which they had no control to circulate in their sectors of the city. Instead, they announced their intention to introduce the new mark into West Berlin.

The Soviet reply was sudden and direct. On the night of June 23, the Soviet-controlled East German news service disseminated the most important announcement in its brief existence: Stunned newsmen in West Berlin, drawn to the clattering teletype, read a dry, Soviet-style dispatch stating that all traffic in and out of West Berlin would be suspended indefinitely as of the next morning.

The message spelled it out: "Water traffic will be suspended. Coal shipments to Berlin from the Soviet zone are halted. The Soviet authorities have also ordered the central switching stations to stop the supply of electric power to the Western sectors. Shortage of coal to operate the plants is the reason."

The Russians had cut all of West Berlin's life lines, denying the more than two million inhabitants of that part of the city any recognized means of sustenance and supply. So began the Berlin blockade.

The Soviets had overwhelming forces in and around Berlin to back their move. The Western Allies had two alternatives. They could give up their occupation rights and abandon the city and its inhabitants. Or they could stick it out and risk a major confrontation or even war. To give way,

cautioned Churchill, would be to repeat the appeasement of Munich a decade earlier. General Clay warned of a domino effect. "We have lost Czechoslovakia," he told the Army Department. "Norway is threatened. When Berlin falls, West Germany will be next." And after Germany the rest of Europe would fall. West Berlin, Clay believed, had to be held in order to sustain the morale of all Western Europeans. Agreeing fully, President Truman declared: "We are going to stay, period."

For a brief time after the news of the Russian action was flashed to Washington, policy makers pondered a recommendation from Clay that the Americans take a "calculated risk" and force the blockade with an armored column. Clay believed the Russians were trying a bluff that should be called. Washington, however, deemed the risk too great, and Clay was informed that some other means of saving the situation would have to be found.

The idea of an airlift was proposed by Lieut. General Albert Wedemeyer, who happened to be visiting Clay when the crisis began. Wedemeyer, U.S. Army commander in China during the War, spoke from firsthand experience of being supplied by flights over "the Hump" from India. Clay accepted his suggestion on the spot and issued appropriate orders. The next day, cargo planes were winging into Berlin, and planning began for a huge effort of indefinite duration.

Air Force Major General William H. Tunner, the world's leading air-transport specialist and the man who had organized the airlift across the Himalayas for Wedemeyer, was called in to run the Berlin airlift. U.S. Air Force and British Royal Air Force transport planes—Skymasters, Globemasters, Yorks and Dakotas—were flown to West German airfields from all over the world and were integrated into a round-the-clock shuttle. At its peak, a plane was landing or taking off at one or another of West Berlin's three airfields every 30 seconds, day and night (pages 192-203).

It took several months to iron out the difficulties, but by the spring of 1949 the airlift was running smoothly, with more than 400 aircraft in service and daily cargo volume averaging 8,000 tons. Not even at the height of the War had air forces operated at such intensity over such a long period. Everyone in the airlift command was involved—cooks loaded coal, generals flew as copilots. The drone of aircraft engines in the sky over Berlin never ceased. One behind the other, planes came in low over the ruins and the crowded streets, a constant source of encouragement to the hard-pressed but defiant Berliners.

With the airlift making a mockery of their blockade, the Soviets finally conceded the failure of their plan to starve West Berlin into submission. On May 12, 1949, amid scenes of rejoicing by the city's inhabitants, they reopened road, rail and water communications with the West. The Berlin airlift had proved a triumph of technology and tenacity for the Western powers and for the West Berliners. It was also a severe moral defeat for the Russians. But the Cold War continued unabated, and on another of its shifting fronts—the shadow world of espionage and treachery—the West was struggling grimly to hold its own.

By the time of the Berlin blockade, the Cold War had ceased to be entirely a low-temperature affair. Both sides felt a rising sense of danger, and with it the urgent need to be informed of the capacity and intentions of the enemy. The Cold War, in short, was developing into a spy war.

The United States was slow to mobilize for this contest of espionage. President Truman in September of 1945 had disbanded the Office of Strategic Services, which had served as a wartime central intelligence organization. He believed that such an operation was inappropriate for a democracy in peacetime. The American attitude rapidly changed, however, as relations with the Soviets deteriorated, and with the revelation that for years the Soviet spy apparatus had been operating on a vast scale in North America.

The event that opened American eyes was the defection shortly after the War of Igor Gouzenko, a young cipher clerk in the Soviet Embassy in Ottawa. One evening early in September of 1945 Gouzenko left the Embassy with a selection of incriminating documents describing Soviet espionage activities. When he tried to turn himself and his evidence over to Canadian authorities the next day, no one took him seriously. That night four men from the Embassy broke down his door and ransacked his apartment, but Gouzenko, his wife and young son had found refuge down the hall with their Canadian neighbors. At last the police came and took the Gouzenkos into custody.

The defection by Gouzenko uncovered a Soviet military-intelligence spy ring in Canada. In due course it also ex-

A burned-out bus functions as a Red Army roadblock on the route leading to beleaguered Berlin, just east of Helmstedt on the border lying between the British and Soviet zones of Germany.

posed the operations of a number of traitors who had, during the War and afterward, delivered to the Soviets the essential details of the West's most closely guarded secret—the development of the atomic bomb.

The first major arrest made on the strength of Gouzenko's testimony came in London. Alan Nunn May, a British nuclear physicist, had been educated at Trinity College, Cambridge, where he acquired pro-Communist views. He went to Canada in 1943 as a senior member of a British nuclear-research team to cooperate in the atomic-bomb project already under way in the United States. May decided that nuclear knowledge should not be the monopoly of the Americans and the British but instead should be shared with the Russians, whom he saw as the hope of the postwar world. By the spring of 1945—prior to the explosion of the first atomic device—May had made contact with Russian military intelligence officials through the Soviet Embassy in Ottawa and passed them secret information on uranium and atomic-energy development.

When confronted by a Scotland Yard officer on March 4, 1946, May made no attempt to deny his guilt; in a statement to the police he said he had given atomic secrets to the Russians not for money but for idealistic reasons. "I felt," he declared, "that it was a contribution I could make to the safety of mankind."

In North America, the exposure of May and the rest of the spy ring aroused angry consternation. As Gouzenko put it, instead of expressing gratitude for the help rendered during the War, the Soviet government had developed an espionage force that was preparing to deliver "a stab in the back" to its former allies.

The anger would have been infinitely greater if it had been known that a spy network as yet undiscovered had penetrated to the very heart of the American atomic-bomb operation, the Manhattan Project. The key operative in this extraordinary treachery was a German-born, naturalized British scientist named Klaus Fuchs.

Fuchs, too, had become a Communist in his student days and had fled to England in 1933 during Hitler's rise to power. In 1941 he became a mathematics assistant to the British team working on the atomic project. At about this time he contacted Soviet intelligence and began work as a secret agent. In 1942 he became a British citizen, and the following year he was posted to the United States as a member of the British atomic team. From that sensitive position, Fuchs was able to give the Russians secrets so priceless that they could be said to have changed—or at least accelerated—the course of history. Fuchs's contact was Harry Gold, a Swiss-born American working for a spy ring that included an American couple, Julius and Ethel Rosenberg. Fuchs handed over to Gold vital information on the composition of the first uranium and plutonium bombs and thus ad-

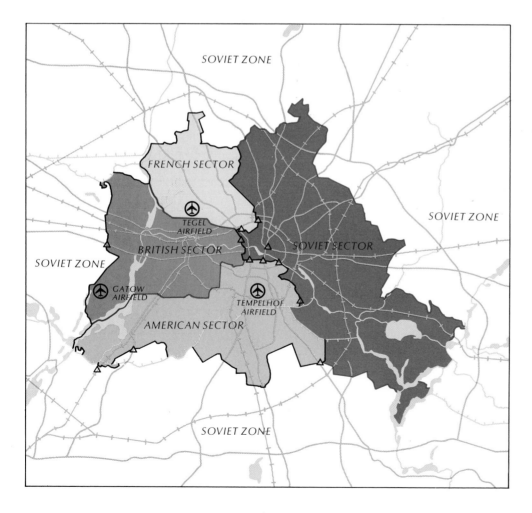

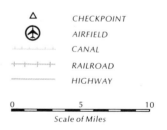

	CHECKPOINT
	AIRFIELD
	CANAL
	RAILROAD
	HIGHWAY

0   5   10
Scale of Miles

Like all Germany, the city of Berlin was divided into four sectors—one administered by each of the victorious Allies. But Berlin was surrounded by the Soviet zone of Germany, and as tensions between the four powers grew, the Soviets cut the city off from the West, closing canals, railroads and roadways; only the airfields kept the Western sectors supplied.

vanced the day when the Russians would have an atomic bomb of their own. Not until three years following his return to Britain in 1946 was any finger of suspicion pointed in Fuchs's direction.

Meanwhile, in the light of the Canadian spy scandal, it became apparent that a new permanent intelligence service was urgently needed to assist in the conduct of U.S. foreign policy. On President Truman's orders the Central Intelligence Group was set up in January of 1946; the group provided the President with a daily summary of information culled mainly from open sources. In 1947, under the newly enacted National Security Act, the Central Intelligence Group was superseded by the Central Intelligence Agency, a body that had been legally accorded much more authority and a far broader mandate.

Truman saw the CIA as primarily a national intelligence-coordinating organization. But that was not how professionals like OSS veterans William ''Wild Bill'' Donovan and Allen W. Dulles saw the CIA's role. They wanted an agency that was both covert and operational, like the old OSS.

In the end their view prevailed. A provision in the 1947 act allowed the CIA ''to perform such other functions and duties related to intelligence . . . as the National Security Council may from time to time direct.'' This vague clause furnished the CIA with what amounted to an open charter enabling it to engage in covert action and operate secretly in other nations.

In its early days the CIA was not particularly successful at collecting intelligence on America's new potential enemy, the Soviet Union. The agency found it difficult, if not impossible, to conduct operations inside a society as closed as that of the Soviet Union, and there seemed little prospect of penetrating the higher echelons of Soviet government. The agents the CIA did manage to slip into Russia—in most cases Soviet citizens who had fled to the West—were usually apprehended in short order. Stymied for a time, the CIA got help from an unexpected quarter—Major General Reinhard Gehlen, a former Nazi secret-intelligence chief.

From 1942 until shortly before the end of the War, Gehlen had been head of a section of the German General Staff that handled intelligence about the Soviet Union and Eastern Europe. He had concluded that Germany could not win the War and that there would come a day when the Western powers would need the help of the Germans to defend themselves against the Soviets. His unit's vast collection of information could guarantee his future.

In the early spring of 1945 Gehlen prepared to defect to the Western Allies. During April, copies of his unit's archives were packed into about 50 steel cases and dispatched to hiding places in the Bavarian Alps, followed later in the month by Gehlen himself and members of his staff.

High atop the shell-pocked Brandenburg Gate, a lone civilian rips down the red flag during an anti-Soviet demonstration by 300,000 Berliners on September 9, 1948, in the third month of the West Berlin blockade.

Two weeks after the hostilities ended, Gehlen came down from the mountains and surrendered to the Americans.

After several false starts, Gehlen convinced the U.S. Army of the worth of the information he was offering. In September 1945, the Army flew him to Washington. There, for the best part of a year, he was pumped for what he already knew about the Soviets, though little interest was shown in his capacity to find out more. However, in June 1946 Washington approved the formation of a West German secret service, under the direction of Gehlen. A contract was drawn up between the U.S. government and the Gehlen organization, which was also known as "the Org."

The Org opened for business in January of 1947 at a few unpretentious dwellings nestled in the Taunus mountains of western Germany. It soon suffered a major setback—the discovery that Gehlen's wartime network of agents in Russia had by now cut themselves out. Having decided that there was no point in risking their lives further for the sake of the defeated Germans, they had buried their radios in the woods or dropped them in lakes.

Although Gehlen had no active agents left inside the Soviet Union, he did have more than three million of his German countrymen—primarily prisoners of war—scattered in camps or working in factories, collective farms, forests, mines and docks, and along roads and railways throughout the length and breadth of Russia. Many had learned to speak Russian and had found out far more about the Soviet Union than their keepers suspected.

In the summer of 1947 Gehlen launched Operation *Hermes* in an effort to gather their accumulated knowledge. Whenever German prisoners were repatriated, members of the Gehlen organization were there to meet the convoys and debrief each prisoner, often in highly detailed interrogations over a long period of time. Gradually thousands upon thousands of debriefing reports were collected at the Org's headquarters. They provided an astonishingly detailed picture of the Soviet scene, including word of a renewed build-up of the Red Army after an initial demobilization, and an increase in the Soviet production of planes and tanks. All this information was duly passed on to the Americans. In a very short time the Gehlen organization had become the most important and successful intelligence-collecting organization in the West.

The Central Intelligence Agency, although it could not match the Org in gathering intelligence about Soviet Russia, thought that it could manage covert operations well enough inside the other Iron Curtain countries. In the late 1940s, when complete Communist rule in the Soviet bloc had been in place only a short time, the Americans (and to some extent the British) believed it was still possible to roll back the Iron Curtain by means of civil insurrection. They theorized that Eastern European émigrés could be armed and trained to carry out subversion and sabotage and to organize civil rebellion in their homelands. But attempts to implement this theory proved difficult in the extreme.

Major British and American efforts to infiltrate guerrilla groups into Albania and the Ukraine met with utter failure. Subsequent attempts by the CIA to slip agents into Poland to gather intelligence and to foment rebellion proved to be equally disastrous.

In addition to these doomed incursions behind Communist lines, the CIA provided lavish backing for indirect anti-Soviet activities in Europe—subsidizing non-Communist parties in Western Europe, aiding anti-Communist émigré political organizations, founding its own propaganda radio stations. But the intelligence community's dream of liberating Eastern Europe from Bolshevism slowly began to fade. The biggest single factor in bringing about this loss of hope was the unaccountable failure of the so-called Albanian subversion, a series of operations run initially by the British Secret Intelligence Service (SIS), and later jointly by the SIS and the CIA, to overthrow the new and still insecure Communist regime in Albania.

On the face of it, the times seemed propitious for such an operation. The Balkans were proving the weakest sector of the Russian sphere of influence. Stalin's supremacy was being challenged in Yugoslavia. The Communist rebels in Greece were in a state of collapse. In Albania itself the regime was wobbly enough to require Soviet advisers at every important level of the government.

The Albanian subversion came under the control of a senior SIS officer, Harold A. R. "Kim" Philby, who had been head of the counter-Soviet section of SIS during the War. The SIS conduct of the project was low-keyed and inconclusive until 1949, when the CIA joined in. From then on, the project

PRIZES IN THE "BATTLE FOR THE BRAINS"

Unlike many nations, the United States did not demand material reparations from defeated Germany. But it was assiduous in collecting spoils of another sort: the scientists who had made Germany superior to the Allies in rocket-powered missiles.

Intelligence teams were assigned to the advancing U.S. armies expressly to fight this "battle for the brains." Their job was made easier by the scientists themselves, hundreds of whom, led by 33-year-old physicist Wernher von Braun, had fled from their Baltic base at Peenemünde to find the Americans. The scientists wanted to avoid capture by the Russians, or by the British, whose cities had been terrorized by V-1 flying bombs and V-2 rockets.

In early May 1945, at Oberammergau in southern Germany, the scientists turned themselves over to the Americans, who recruited the best of them to work in the United States. Braun and the first contingent came in September; by 1946 more than 100 German scientists were interned at Fort Bliss, Texas, and other U.S. military posts. There they evaluated captured documents, answered questions from American experts and began refining the missiles they had designed for Germany.

At first strict security was imposed on the Germans. They could go nowhere unless accompanied by U.S. Army guards. Braun sardonically referred to himself as a POP—a "prisoner of peace."

In time the restrictions were relaxed. The Germans learned English, started social clubs and won the right to roam beyond their compound. The first of their families joined them for Christmas 1946. Most of them became American citizens and in the ensuing decades contributed mightily to the U.S. missile program—and to building the powerful engines that lifted American astronauts into space.

With his arm in a cast—it was broken as he fled from the Russians—Wernher von Braun stands at top with other German missile experts after surrendering to the U.S. Seventh Army on May 3, 1945. At right, 18 months later, a shirt-sleeved Braun is framed by the tail assembly of an American rocket at White Sands Proving Ground in New Mexico.

gained momentum, progressing to the point where it was time to begin operations inside the target country.

A first batch of six Albanian émigré agents was ferried across to Albania from the Greek island of Corfu in the spring of 1950. A second group followed a few days later. Their assignment was to recruit other disaffected Albanians and form the nucleus of a rebellion. For almost a month there was silence. Then the British military mission in Athens began to pick up rumors that groups of agents landing on the Albanian coast had been captured or wiped out by Albanian patrols within minutes of coming ashore.

The only explanation that made any sense to the SIS and CIA was that the radio operator in the first group ashore had been caught and broken or turned to reveal the radio codes and the prearranged signal that would let headquarters know he was transmitting under duress. If this purely isolated cause was the true explanation—and there seemed to be no other—then there could be no objection to trying again. Over the next two years, small groups were dispatched at irregular intervals. But it became depressingly clear that no matter when or where the SIS and CIA agents entered the country, the police were always waiting for them.

Finally, after a particularly bloody failure ending in a show trial in the Albanian capital of Tirana in 1952, a per-manent halt was called to the operation. By now the idea of attempting such incursions behind the Iron Curtain had been totally discredited in Britain, and its validity was seriously questioned in the United States. Although the CIA was still training bands of Eastern European volunteers for paramilitary forays into their homelands as late as 1956, insurgency operations against Communist governments were gradually abandoned. The much more feasible task of intelligence gathering became the agency's top priority.

As for why the Albanian subversion had failed, the Americans became convinced that only treachery could explain it. What few clues existed seemed to implicate the former joint controller of the operation, Kim Philby. But at the time that seemed an absurd explanation.

Philby, the popular and respected SIS liaison officer to the CIA in Washington, seemed to personify the best type of English public servant. Born in British India, he had been brought up in the Middle East and educated in England. But like many young English intellectuals of the early 1930s, he was dismayed by the rise of fascism and the terrible social and economic conditions in Britain during the Depression. While at Cambridge, he secretly embraced Communism.

Philby went a step further than most of his contemporaries. He had come to the attention of a small cell of Commu-

Soviet "moles" Donald Maclean (left), Guy Burgess (center) and Harold "Kim" Philby burrowed into the heart of the British intelligence establishment—exposing hundreds of Western agents, transmitting atomic secrets and poisoning British-American relations. All three made a clean escape behind the Iron Curtain.

nist conspirators led by two fellow students, Guy Burgess and Anthony Blunt, who were in contact with the resident director of the Soviet secret-intelligence service in Britain. The Russians were looking for able, middle-class dissidents who might become "moles," burrowing upward through the power structure of the English Establishment. Philby, along with a student named Donald Maclean and several others, was recruited for Soviet intelligence.

On the orders of their Russian control, the Cambridge conspirators fabricated new Right-Wing, even profascist, political personas and took Establishment jobs. Maclean entered the Foreign Office, where he was soon marked as a rising star. Burgess, dazzlingly witty but wildly drunken and dissolute, joined the BBC and later the Foreign Office. Philby went to work for *The Times of London* as a correspondent reporting the Franco side of the Spanish Civil War. To further his profascist image, he went so far as to file a story downplaying the infamous German air raid on Guernica in 1937 and blaming the destruction on bombs planted by Basque *agents provocateurs*.

When World War II began, Philby was recruited into the SIS, which was signing up likely amateurs as part of its wartime expansion. By 1941 Philby's superiors were sufficiently impressed with his ability to give him a key job in Section V (counterespionage), and he was soon put in charge of the Iberian subsection. This was a crucial penetration: Philby had reached the inner sanctum of Britain's secret operations. Making full use of his privileged position, he passed on to his Soviet masters vital information from the central archives of the SIS.

In 1944 Philby was promoted again—to head a new department charged with carrying out espionage operations against the Russians. The department's mission was both defensive and offensive: to penetrate the Soviets' worldwide espionage network and to establish anti-Soviet spy networks in Eastern Europe. Philby's new job put him in a position to intercept a Soviet agent who was trying to defect to the Western side. Alexander Rado, the chief of Russia's so-called Lucy network in Switzerland, was considered the most successful Soviet spymaster in Europe. When he attempted to double-deal by contacting a British field agent, the agent's cabled request for instructions came to Philby.

Both to serve the Soviets and to save himself from exposure, Philby arranged to have Rado whisked back to Moscow and prison before he could tell the British what he knew.

Philby's position was doubly powerful, for the FBI and OSS were working closely with British intelligence, and he was accorded almost as free an entrée into the American secret world as he was into the British.

When the War ended, Philby settled down in London to his secret purpose of destroying the Western intelligence effort. Almost immediately he was confronted with a crisis. A certain Konstantin Volkov, an intelligence agent at the Soviet consulate in Istanbul, was seeking asylum in Britain in return for important secret information. Volkov offered to reveal the names of three British officials who were working for the Russians—two in the Foreign Office (Burgess and Maclean) and one in British counterintelligence (Philby).

Philby saw that it was either Volkov's head or his own. Through his Soviet controller in London he warned Moscow of Volkov's intent. Then he stalled for time. When Philby turned up in Turkey, ostensibly to take charge of the Volkov affair, the unfortunate Russian had been spirited home to his doom. Once more, Philby had saved his own neck. But among a few of his British colleagues the first inklings of suspicion were aroused concerning his competence, if not his loyalty. Philby's superiors continued to regard him with confidence, however, even after it was learned that Philby's estranged first wife had become a Soviet agent in East Berlin.

In October 1949, Philby achieved the greatest coup of his career as a double agent—he was sent to Washington as the SIS liaison to the CIA in the Albanian subversion, using as cover the important post of First Secretary in the British Embassy. Philby found himself at the heart of the Western intelligence war against the Soviets. His access to secret information was almost without limit. He often was briefed on policy by General Walter Bedell Smith, chief of the Central Intelligence Agency, and was given priceless information about the agency's planning and what it knew about Soviet intelligence operations. Everything that Philby heard he promptly relayed to Moscow. The CIA, unknowingly, had been critically compromised.

Philby was at the height of his effectiveness. But the days of the British traitors were numbered. Even while he was be-

BELEAGUERED BRITAIN'S SHINING SUMMER

From May through September 1951, Britons put aside their nagging postwar woes and threw a nationwide party called the Festival of Britain. Its purpose: to celebrate the triumph of British spirit over a decade doubly cursed with suffering in war and austerity in peace.

The main exhibits, built on 27 bomb-devastated acres along the Thames, included a great Dome of Discovery that offered a capsule history of British civilization. For pure fun, the nearby Pleasure Gardens offered celebrants fireworks and follies, carnival rides, cafés and a children's zoo.

Some 1,600 other events and exhibits throughout the nation hailed Britain's achievements in everything from agronomy to Welsh music, town planning and nuclear physics. The festival drew millions of visitors—more than eight million to London alone, among them many thousands of free-spending tourists. It was, as one visitor put it, "a kind of Cloud-Cuckoo-Land—colorful, joyous and temporary."

Pyramid fountains, a mock-Gothic tower and whimsical bamboo figures enliven the sparkling Main Vista of the London Pleasure Gardens.

traying the Albanian operation from Washington's Embassy Row, Philby picked up disturbing information. A security leak had been discovered in the British Embassy, and the available evidence pointed tenuously toward Donald Maclean as the culprit.

Ever since his arrival in Washington in 1944 as head of chancery at the British Embassy, Maclean had been passing top-secret political intelligence of the highest quality to the Soviet Union. His information had a direct influence on the various shifts that took place in Soviet foreign policy. At the end of the War, Maclean was moved to an even more sensitive post—as joint secretary of the Western Allies' new combined policy committee on atomic development. He passed to the Kremlin—through the Soviet consulate in New York—a wealth of highly detailed secret information on Allied nuclear policy, planning and stockpiling.

The sheer volume of material Maclean passed along during the first summer after the War was to prove his—and eventually Philby's—undoing. American radio-interception and code-breaking teams noticed an unusual increase in the volume of Moscow-bound radio traffic emanating from the New York consulate. Systematically they began trying to decipher the intercepted signals. Many months later came a break. One of the Soviet cipher clerks inadvertently began to encipher messages in an out-of-date code already known to the American cryptanalysts. They decoded enough of the intercepts to conclude that the Russians had an agent operating inside the British Embassy in Washington. The Americans informed the British, and the FBI put a watch on Maclean, among others.

Independently, the U.S. Atomic Energy Commission had by 1948 belatedly become aware of a disturbing fact: A foreigner possessed a permanent pass to the commission's headquarters that allowed him to move about unaccompanied whenever he was in the building. Records showed, furthermore, that the person was a frequent visitor in the evenings, after normal work hours. (When the story came out, FBI Director J. Edgar Hoover grumbled, "I was always required to have an escort.") The night-prowling foreigner proved to be Donald Maclean.

Evidence continued to accumulate against Maclean, but so secure was his position within Britain's hierarchy that he was promoted twice more during the next few years. At his newest post in London, he gained access to a briefing summary of British and American political strategy on such matters as the Korean War, Middle East oil and NATO that had been prepared for a Washington summit conference in December of 1950 between President Truman and Prime Minister Clement Attlee.

But the noose was tightening at last around Maclean's neck. In February of 1951, Kim Philby—still based in Washington and still systematically betraying the CIA and the SIS—felt so alarmed about the Maclean investigation that he warned Guy Burgess of the danger. Burgess had come to Washington the previous August as Second Secretary in the Embassy and was living with Philby and his family. With Moscow's approval, Philby assigned Burgess the job of trying to rescue Maclean.

Burgess' first task—one for which he was eminently qualified—was to get himself shipped back to England in disgrace for outrageous conduct unbefitting a diplomat. After creating drunken scenes at several parties and in a posh Washington restaurant, he topped off his campaign by being stopped for speeding in nearby Virginia three times in one day and arrogantly demanding diplomatic immunity. He was ordered home at the end of April. Then, on the morning of Friday, May 25, Burgess learned that Maclean's interrogation by the British Security Service (MI-5) was scheduled for the following Monday. There was no time to lose. That Friday evening, Burgess drove Maclean to the Southampton docks. It was intended that only Maclean should flee. But at the last moment Burgess, though not under immediate suspicion, decided he would make the channel crossing as well. The two spies hurried on board the night ferry to France.

The pair had the full weekend to make a getaway eastward before the alarm was raised on Monday afternoon. By June 6—nine days after their absence was discovered—they had reached Prague, safely behind the Iron Curtain. The next day the news of their sensational defection was made public—to the glee of Moscow, the dismay of Washington and the mortification of London. The unexpected flight of Burgess, however, left Philby high and dry in Washington. His close relationship with the newly revealed traitor, who had lived in his house and was identified with him both professionally and personally, put Philby under suspicion too obvious to ignore. Rattled, he buried his camera and other incriminating equipment in some woods outside Washington and awaited the worst.

The American intelligence services were beside themselves with fury. British and American cooperation sank to a low ebb. At the FBI, Hoover regarded the flight of Burgess and Maclean as confirmation of his belief that British security had rotted from within. At the CIA, Smith washed his hands of Philby and asked the SIS to recall him to London as *persona non grata*. That summer the SIS requested Philby to leave the service. Beginning in November, MI-5 subjected him to a prolonged and rigorous interrogation that culminated the following summer in what amounted to a secret trial. Through it all, Philby did not break down, and in the end no evidence of treason was produced that could have brought about a conviction in court. Philby emerged legally unscathed, but unemployed, and was abandoned by his Soviet control.

Not until the early 1960s, after his guilt was affirmed by a Russian defector, did the SIS conclude beyond doubt that Philby had been a Soviet agent. With British justice apparently closing in on him at last, the Russians made arrangements for him to escape to Moscow, and on the evening of January 23, 1963, Kim Philby quietly slipped out of Beirut, Lebanon, where he had been working since 1956. Six months later the Supreme Soviet announced it had granted Philby political asylum and had conferred Soviet citizenship on him. Eventually Philby became a general in the Soviet secret service.

In one of its most important arenas, the early rounds of the Cold War had been won hands down by the Soviets. Their prewar investment in the loyalties of certain young English gentlemen had earned them handsome dividends in the ungentlemanly postwar world.

Philby and his fellow turncoats made a shambles of the Western intelligence establishment. Just how many CIA and SIS agents lost their lives because of Philby's betrayals alone is not known. A total of three dozen has been suggested for the period 1945-1947, and many more after that date. In the worst case, the Albanian subversion, 300 agents were believed to have been killed as a direct result of his treachery.

A usually close-mouthed CIA official later summed up the effect of the Philby years: "When you look at the whole period from 1944 to 1951, the entire Western intelligence effort was what you might call a minus advantage. We'd have been better off doing nothing."

While some of Stalin's agents were scoring devastating successes in the Western world, others farther east were contributing to his greatest failure. Soviet advisers had come to Yugoslavia with the Red Army, just as they had to the other countries of Eastern Europe. As elsewhere, the fledgling Communist government of Marshal Tito paid the salaries and living costs of Russians stationed on Yugoslavian soil.

Tito was an ardent Communist and a devoted follower of Stalin. But he was also an independent-minded nationalist, and even before the end of the War he had grown restive over certain aspects of Soviet-Yugoslavian relations. Paying the wages of Soviet advisers was especially rankling when they spent their time spying on him and trying to undercut his leadership.

Stalin apparently felt that Tito, the resistance hero, was too much the master in his own house. He sought to rein him in by going over his head to line up allies among other top Yugoslavian Communists. The ploy backfired, and Tito in 1946 asked Moscow to recall most of its advisers, pleading economic straits. Relations between the two governments went downhill from there.

By 1948 the Russians had lost patience with the impudent Yugoslavs. Stalin fired a series of brutally arrogant notes at Tito, accusing him of a "hostile attitude" and of exercising "secret supervision over Soviet representatives." To each message the Yugoslavs gave a conciliating and humble answer, but to no avail. Tito was driven to say, "No matter how much each of us loves the land of Socialism, the

U.S.S.R., he can in no case love his own country less." Russian recrimination alternated with explanations from Tito throughout the spring of 1948, until on June 28, Stalin finally ordered the Yugoslavs booted out of the family of Communist nations.

If, as seemed likely, Stalin expected the Yugoslavian Communists to overthrow Tito and come crawling to the Soviet bloc to seek reinstatement, he was sorely disappointed. Despite economic and political isolation, Yugoslavia stuck to its course of independent Communism and made it work. Before the decade was out, the Yugoslavs began the first tentative softening of their attitude toward the Western powers, leading ultimately to cooperative relations.

If 1948 was a year of instability and crisis in Europe—with gains and losses for the West and the Soviet Union alike—1949 was a year of stabilization. Although the passions of the Cold War did not diminish in the least, and the West continued, all unsuspecting, to suffer espionage defeats, the year proved a watershed.

Most of Europe's political and military divisions were solidified in 1949. On the 23rd of May, eleven days after the lifting of the Berlin blockade, the Federal Republic of Germany was created from the West German zones. Several weeks earlier, the United States, Canada and most of Europe's non-Communist countries had signed the North Atlantic Treaty, which subsequently took shape as NATO, and thereby pledged themselves to mutual assistance in case of foreign aggression. The Soviet Union had already begun rearming its satellites and had signed bilateral defense treaties with each of them, although a formal Communist counterpart to NATO, the Warsaw Pact, would not be created until 1955. On the 23rd of September, 1949, President Truman announced that the Russians had successfully exploded their first atomic bomb, putting an end to the West's monopoly of this fearsome weapon. And on October 5, the German Democratic Republic was formally created from the Russian zone of Germany.

Although crises would erupt periodically in East-West relations after 1949—especially over Berlin—the Cold War in Europe had reached an equilibrium of sorts. Center stage in the conflict between democracy and Communism was about to shift elsewhere, and on June 25, 1950, the attention of the world moved from the European Cold War to a hot war in Korea.

Above all else, the aftermath of World War II in Europe made a mockery of the aims of Adolf Hitler. One of Hitler's purposes had been to bring all Germans within the borders of the Reich—by expanding those borders. In an outcome he never dreamed of, that purpose was accomplished when millions of ethnic Germans in the lands east and south were driven out of their ancestral homes and back into Germany. Another of Hitler's goals had been to wrest living space from the Slavs; in the aftermath, it was the Slavs who took German land. Nazism was supposed to crush Bolshevism, but now it was the Communists who ruled half of Europe. Even Hitler's war against the Jews, for all its ferocious efficiency, contributed eventually to the success of Jewish nationalism in Israel.

Europeans who had survived Hitler's cataclysm—at least those outside the Iron Curtain—might take a measure of comfort from the shape of things at the close of the aftermath period. Europe in 1950 was stable. The formerly restive Balkan States were functioning obediently under Communist domination. Germany, widely believed to have started both World Wars, was split in two—perhaps forever—and was thus unlikely ever to start a third war.

In fact, Europe in 1950 was entering a period of peace and prosperity unequaled in its tumultuous history. Improbably, after its worst orgy of slaughter and destruction, Europe had found the path to its greatest era of growth in population, in living standards and in political continuity. In only one way had Europe lost ground—it no longer dominated the world. And perhaps in that fact lay the seeds of its miraculous rebirth.

THE BERLIN AIRLIFT

Trucks deliver coal to U.S. Air Force C-54s waiting at Frankfurt am Main to fly the fuel to West Berlin after the Soviet Union blockaded the city in 1948.

AN AIRBORNE ARMADA TO RESCUE A CITY

On June 24, 1948, teleprinters in Berlin newspaper offices clattered out a terse declaration from the Russian zone of the occupied city: "The Soviet administration is compelled to halt all passenger and freight traffic to and from West Berlin for technical reasons." The Russians had cut all roads to West Berlin from West Germany, 100 miles away. Their obvious intent was to starve the city into submission and drive out its U.S., French and British protectors. But the three Western powers refused to knuckle under. The next day, American C-47 transports flew in 80 tons of goods from West Germany, and the Berlin Airlift—the greatest supply operation in aviation history—was under way.

By July, Allied planes were carrying 1,500 tons of food and fuel a day—a huge amount, but far short of the 4,500 tons that the city needed to survive. Clearly the airlift's capacity—for coal in particular—had to be improved before winter. In response, the U.S. Air Force brought in 180 C-54s, big, four-engined craft whose cargo capacity of nine tons was three times that of the twin-engined C-47s. And Major General William Tunner, who during the War had masterminded the massive Allied air-supply operation over "the Hump," was named to command the airlift.

For speed, Tunner ordered aircrews to stay in their planes between landing and takeoff, both at Berlin and while loading at West German airfields. Food was sent out to the fliers, and weathermen came on board to brief them. Mechanics serviced the planes while cargoes were being stowed. Tunner's methods and the additional aircraft paid off: By October, the average turnaround time had been cut to 30 minutes and one million sacks of coal had been delivered.

The airlift flew in everything Berliners asked for, from Volkswagens for the police to two million seedlings to replace trees cut for fuel. When Tempelhof field in the U.S. sector and Gatow in the British zone became too crowded, the planes flew in machinery to build a third field, Tegel, in the French zone. On return trips, the planes carried exports stamped "Made in Blockaded Berlin"—proof of the airlift's effectiveness and of West Berlin's will to survive.

Workers stencil Berlin's bear symbol on a case of export goods. Radios, optical goods and textiles were produced throughout the blockade.

Citizens of rubble-strewn West Berlin watch a supply-laden C-47 land. "The sound of the engines," wrote one man, "is beautiful music to our ears."

A MARATHON OF FAST TURNAROUNDS

Every three minutes, 24 hours a day, an American transport plane filled with supplies landed at West Berlin's sprawling Tempelhof field. Most crews made two or three trips a day from such bases in West Germany as Frankfurt, Wiesbaden, Fassberg and Lubeck. Their marathon effort became a test of endurance as the blockade continued into the winter of 1949.

Life photographer Walter Sanders joined the crew of one C-54, code-named *Big Willy 2719*, on a typical day's work, a tedious but vital routine that General Tunner himself called "about as glamorous as drops of water on a stone."

At 3:20 a.m., *Big Willy* took off from Frankfurt. One hour and 40 minutes later, the plane touched down at Tempelhof and a ground crew hustled to unload its nine-ton cargo of coal. After 84 minutes on the ground—a slow turnaround by Tunner's standards—*Big Willy* took off for Frankfurt carrying 31 displaced persons. "Twice on the flight, Yak fighters cruised dangerously close," Sanders reported, "but at 8:05 the plane reached Frankfurt without mishap." There, the tempo of *Big Willy's* routine barely slowed: By 8:15 the 31 passengers had deplaned, trucks were refueling the C-54 and a ground crew had begun manhandling sacks of precious coal aboard for another run to West Berlin.

On the curving apron of Tempelhof field, U.S. transports await clearance for the 275-mile return flight to Frankfurt. To fly the three 20-mile-wide corridors over

A radar operator scans his screen in the darkened Air Traffic Control Center in Berlin. The Russians had access to the center—set up jointly by the four occupying powers—but did not interfere with its operation.

Soviet-occupied Germany, the U.S. Air Force trained 100 crews per month at a base in Montana, where duplicates of the approach patterns had been set up.

TWO-WAY TRAFFIC IN GOODS AND PEOPLE

To keep an average of 5,000 tons of supplies a day flowing smoothly into West Berlin, British and American quartermasters became experts in the art of loading and unloading literally thousands of different items. Because almost all such work had to be done by hand, most packages were limited to two cubic feet in size. And valuable cargo space was saved by dehydrating fruits and vegetables; whole potatoes, for instance, took up 80 per cent less space when dried.

Occasionally, American aircrews found time in the grueling schedule for an unorthodox treat. The crews fashioned miniature parachutes to drop a rain of candy on the city, prompting the children below to dub the planes "chocolate bombers."

The big planes rarely returned home empty. Besides carrying out export goods, they ferried sick, elderly and very young Berliners who authorities feared would not otherwise survive the winter. By the following spring, more than 50,000 people had flown the airlift to West Germany.

German stevedores complete the transfer of 7,000 pounds of canned meat from an RAF Sunderland flying boat moored on the Havel River to a waiting barge. Several flying boats carried supplies every day from Hamburg to the broad river within Berlin's city limits.

A tractor eases from a rear-loading C-82 used to haul heavy equipment.

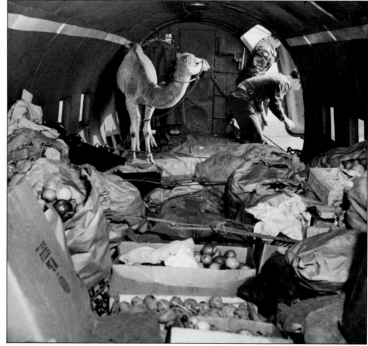

Clarence the camel, mascot of a U.S. food drive, arrives on a C-47.

198

Weary Polish Jews await takeoff from West Berlin in the cargo bay of a C-54. U.S. authorities evacuated 5,000 such refugees to ease the demand for food.

Smoke billows from the wreck of a C-54 that crashed in the wooded West Berlin suburb of Friedenau during the airlift's first month, killing its two-man crew.

A Berliner pauses to read a wreathed plaque honoring the airmen killed in the Friedenau crash. A German newspaper eulogized the crew for ''giving their lives for a free world'' and started a collection to aid their families.

CASUALTIES IN CROWDED SKIES

To avoid accidents in the suddenly crowded skies over Berlin, the airlift command instituted strict air traffic rules: If visibility was less than one mile, a pilot had to abort his landing. And a pilot who for any reason did not land on his first approach was forbidden to go around and slip into the pattern again; that maneuver was judged too complex, and he was sent home before trying again. All the while, the Soviet fighters buzzed the transports and held mock dogfights near the air lanes.

The 276,926 airlift flights resulted in 24 crashes and 48 deaths. ''We grieved about those men as if they were our own,'' said a Berliner. ''Nobody mentioned that perhaps the same boy had presented us with a different cargo a few years earlier.''

A VICTORY OF LOGISTICS AND WILL

In the spring of 1949, the airlift command decided to emphasize to the Soviets that their blockade was not working, and that West Berlin would remain an integral part of democratic West Germany. On April 16, the airlift flexed its muscles: 1,398 flights brought an astonishing 12,994 tons of supplies to West Berlin in a single day. Four weeks later, on May 12, the Russians agreed to reopen roads and rail lines into the besieged city.

All over West Berlin, Germans, Americans, Britons and Frenchmen celebrated the end of the blockade and the accomplishment of a staggering logistical feat: In 11 months, 1,592,287 tons of supplies had been delivered by air to keep the city alive. West Berliners in particular celebrated what they recognized as the end of a Soviet threat and the beginning of their readmission to the world community. The airlift, said one housewife, was "the intermediary between us and the rest of the Western world."

General Clay, the U.S. commander in Europe, later underscored that thought. "I saw the spirit and soul of a people reborn," Clay said in a report to the American Congress on May 17, 1949. "This time the people of Berlin cast their lot with those who love freedom."

A crew of West German airlift mechanics salutes the end of the Soviet Union's blockade of West Berlin with cheers and a homemade sign that declares, "Hurrah, we're still alive."

203

BIBLIOGRAPHY

"Airlift to Berlin." *The National Geographic*, May 1949.

"Along Hunger's Highway." *Consumer's Guide*, December 1946.

Ambrose, Stephen E., *Rise to Globalism*. London: Allen Lane The Penguin Press, 1971.

Andrus, Burton C., *I Was the Nuremberg Jailer*. Coward-McCann, 1969.

Arendt, Hannah, *Eichmann in Jerusalem*. Penguin Books, 1964.

Arnold-Forster, Mark, *The Siege of Berlin*. London: Collins, 1979.

Bailey, George, *Germans: Biography of an Obsession*. Avon Books, 1972.

Balfour, Michael, *Four-Power Control in Germany and Austria, 1945-1946*, Vol. 1, *Germany*. Oxford University Press, 1956.

Bell, J. Bowyer, *The Long War: Israel and the Arabs since 1946*. Prentice-Hall, 1969.

Bennett, Lowell, *Berlin Bastion*. Frankfurt am Main: Fred Rudl, 1951.

"The Berlin Airlift." *Fortune*, November 1948.

Bethell, Nicholas, *The Last Secret*. Basic Books, 1974.

Blum, Jerome, Rondo Cameron and Thomas G. Barnes, *The European World*. Little, Brown, 1966.

Bohlen, Charles E.:
The Transformation of American Foreign Policy. W. W. Norton, 1969.
Witness to History: 1929-1969. W. W. Norton, 1973.

Boyle, Andrew, *The Climate of Treason: Five Who Spied for Russia*. London: Hutchinson, 1979.

Brewer, Sam Pope, "Jerusalem Torn by Rioting; Arabs Use Knives, Set Fire; Jews Reply, Haganah in Open." *The New York Times*, December 3, 1947.

"Berlin in Crisis." *Life*, April 28, 1947.

"Britain in Crisis." *Life*, April 28, 1947.

Butcher, Harry C., *My Three Years with Eisenhower*. Simon and Schuster, 1946.

Byford-Jones, W., *Berlin Twilight*. London: Hutchinson, 1955.

Byrnes, James F., *Speaking Frankly*. Harper & Brothers, 1947.

Calvocoressi, Peter, and Guy Wint, *Total War*. London: Allen Lane The Penguin Press, 1972.

Chambers, Frank P., *This Age of Conflict*. Harcourt, Brace & World, 1962.

Churchill, Winston S.:
The Grand Alliance. Houghton Mifflin, 1950.
Triumph and Tragedy. Houghton Mifflin, 1953.

Ciborowski, Adolf, and Stanislaw Jankowski, *Warsaw Rebuilt*. Warsaw: Polonia, 1962.

Clay, Lucius D., *Decision in Germany*. Doubleday, 1950.

Clough, Shepard B., ed., *A History of the Western World*. D. C. Heath, 1964.

Collins, Larry, and Dominique Lapierre, *O Jerusalem!* Simon and Schuster, 1972.

Courlander, Harold, *Shaping Our Times*. Oceana Publications, 1960.

Currivan, Gene:
"3 Slain on Zionist Vessel as Refugees Fight Britain." *The New York Times*, July 19, 1947.
"Incensed Britons Kill 5 in Tel Aviv to Avenge Hanging." *The New York Times*, August 1, 1947.

Daniel, Clifton, "Palestine Hangs Three Terrorists; Hostages in Peril." *The New York Times*, July 29, 1947.

Davidson, Eugene:
The Death and Life of Germany. Alfred A. Knopf, 1959.
The Trial of the Germans. Macmillan, 1966.

Davis, Franklin M., Jr., *Come as a Conqueror*. Macmillan, 1967.

Davison, W. Phillips, *The Berlin Blockade*. Princeton University Press, 1958.

Deane, John R., *The Strange Alliance*. Viking, 1946.

De Gaulle, Charles, *The Complete War Memoirs*. Simon and Schuster, 1955.

De Zayas, Alfred M., *Nemesis at Potsdam*. London: Routledge & Kegan Paul, 1979.

"Displaced Germans." *Life*, October 15, 1945.

Djilas, Milovan:
Conversations with Stalin. Harcourt, Brace & World, 1962.
Wartime. Harcourt Brace Jovanovich, 1977.

Donnison, F. S. V., *Civil Affairs and Military Government North-West Europe: 1944-1946*. London: Her Majesty's Stationery Office, 1961.

Donovan, Robert J., *Conflict and Crisis: The Presidency of Harry S. Truman, 1945-1948*. W. W. Norton, 1977.

Dupuy, R. Ernest, *World War II: A Compact History*. Hawthorne Books, 1969.

Encyclopaedia Judaica. Jerusalem: Keter Publishing House, 1971.

Epstein, Julius, *Operation Keelhaul: The Story of Forced Repatriation from 1944 to the Present*. Devin-Adair, 1973.

Esposito, Vincent J., *A Concise History of World War II*. Frederick A. Praeger, 1964.

Eudes, Dominique, *The Kapetanios: Partisans and Civil War in Greece, 1943-1949*. Monthly Review Press, 1972.

"Europe's Hungry Winter." *Colliers*, December 8 and December 15, 1945.

"Exodus Refugees Begin Forced Trip to German Camps." *The New York Times*, August 23, 1947.

Feis, Herbert:
Between War and Peace. Princeton University Press, 1960.
Churchill, Roosevelt, Stalin. Princeton University Press, 1957.

Flanner, Janet (Genêt), *Paris Journal: 1944-1965*. Atheneum, 1965.

Fleming, D. F., *The Cold War and Its Origins: 1917-1960*. 2 vols. Doubleday, 1961.

Fontaine, André, *History of the Cold War*. Pantheon Books, 1968.

Franck, Dieter, *Jahre unseres Lebens: 1945-1949*. Munich: R. Piper, 1980.

Frederiksen, Oliver J., *The American Military Occupation of Germany: 1945-1953*. The Historical Division, Headquarters, United States Army Europe, 1953.

"Frenchmen Look West for Escape from Home." *Newsweek*, February 23, 1946.

Friedrich, Carl J., *American Experiences in Military Government in World War II*. Rinehart & Company, 1948.

Fritzsche, Hans, *The Sword in the Scales*. London: Allan Wingate, 1953.

Frostick, Michael, *The Jaguar Tradition*. London: Dalton Watson, 1973.

Gollancz, Victor, *In Darkest Germany*. Devin-Adair, 1947.

Gramont, Sanche de, *The Secret War*. G. P. Putnam's Sons, 1962.

"Grim Europe Faces Winter of Misery." *Life*, July 14, 1947.

Grosser, Alfred, *Germany in Our Time*. Praeger Publishers, 1971.

Grube, Frank, and Gerhard Richter, *Die Schwarzmarktzeit*. Hamburg: Hoffman und Campe, 1969.

Gruber, Ruth, *Destination Palestine*. A. A. Wyn, 1948.

Gunther, John, *Behind the Curtain*. Harper & Brothers, 1948.

Halasz, Nicholas, *In the Shadow of Russia*. Ronald Press, 1959.

Halle, Louis J., *The Cold War as History*. Harper & Row, 1967.

Harriman, W. Averell, and Elie Abel, *Special Envoy to Churchill and Stalin: 1941-1946*. Random House, 1975.

Herman, Stewart W., *The Rebirth of the German Church*. Harper & Brothers, 1946.

Höhne, Heinz, and Hermann Zolling, *The General Was a Spy*. Coward, McCann & Geoghegan, 1971.

Holly, David C., *Exodus: 1947*. Little, Brown, 1969.

"How the Air Lift Was Operated." *Picture Post*, London, July 17, 1948.

Hughes, H. Stuart, *The United States and Italy*. Harvard University Press, 1965.

Hulme, Kathryn, *The Wild Place*. Little, Brown, 1953.

Hurewitz, J. C., *The Struggle for Palestine*. Schocken Books, 1976.

Jankowski, Stanislaw, and Adolf Ciborowski, *Warsaw 1945: Today and Tomorrow*. Warsaw: Interpress, 1978.

Jones, Joseph Marion, *The Fifteen Weeks*. Harcourt, Brace & World, 1955.

Kennan, George F., *American Diplomacy: 1900-1950*. The University of Chicago Press, 1951.

Kennedy, Paul P., "Exodus Refugees Get Ultimatum." *The New York Times*, August 22, 1947.

Keyserlingk, Robert Wendelin, *Patriots of Peace*. Gerrards Cross: Colin Smythe, 1972.

Kimche, Jon and David, *A Clash of Destinies*. Frederick A. Praeger, 1960.

Knightley, Phillip, "The Man Who Was Q." *The Sunday Times*, London, November 4, 1973.

Kogan, Norman, *A Political History of Postwar Italy*. Frederick A. Praeger, 1966.

Kousoulas, D. G., "The Guerrilla War the Communists Lost." *Proceedings*, U.S. Naval Institute, May 1963.

Kramer, Jane, *Unsettling Europe*. Random House, 1972.

Kriegel, Annie, *The French Communists*. The University of Chicago Press, 1972.

Kulischer, Eugene M., *Europe on the Move*. Columbia University Press, 1948.

La Farge, Henry, *Lost Treasures of Europe*. Pantheon Books, 1946.

Lagoudakis, Charilaos G., "Greece." *Challenge and Response in Internal Conflict*. Department of the Army, 1955.

Lapica, R. L., ed., *Facts On File Yearbook 1946, 1947, 1948*. Person's Index, Facts On File, 1949.

Laqueur, Walter, *Europe since Hitler*. Penguin Books, 1972.

"Let the Echo Carry." *Time*, December 15, 1947.

Longmate, Norman, *When We Won the War*. London: Hutchinson, 1977.

Mallinson, Vernon, *Belgium*. Praeger Publishers, 1970.

Man, John, *Berlin Blockade*. Ballantine Books, 1973.

Marchetti, Victor, and John D. Marks, *The CIA and the Cult of Intelligence*. Alfred A. Knopf, 1980.

Martin, David C., *Wilderness of Mirrors*. Ballantine Books, 1980.

Maser, Werner, *Nuremberg: A Nation on Trial*. Charles Scribner's Sons, 1977.

Matthews, Kenneth, *Memories of a Mountain War, Greece: 1944-1949*. London: Longman, 1972.

Mayne, Richard, *The Recovery of Europe*. Harper & Row, 1970.

Mee, Charles L., Jr., *Meeting at Potsdam*. Dell, 1975.

Meigs, Cornelia, *The Great Design*. Little, Brown, 1964.

Memory Lane: A Photographic Album of Daily Life in Britain. London: J. M. Dent & Sons, 1980.

Mikolajczyk, Stanislaw, *The Rape of Poland*. Greenwood Press, 1948.

Mission Accomplished: Third United States Army Occupation of Germany, May 9, 1945-February 15, 1947. Department of the Army, no date.

Molotov, V. M., *Problems of Foreign Policy*. Moscow: Foreign Languages Publishing House, 1949.

Montagu of Beaulieu, Lord, *Jaguar*. Yeovil, Somerset, England: Haynes, 1975.

Moorehead, Alan, *The Traitors*. Harper & Row, 1952.

Morris, Eric, *Blockade*. London: Hamish Hamilton, 1973.

Murphy, Robert, *Diplomat among Warriors*. Pyramid Books, 1964.

Neave, Airey, *On Trial at Nuremberg*. Little, Brown, 1978.

Nettl, J. P., *The Eastern Zone and Soviet Policy in Germany: 1945-1950*. London: Oxford University Press, 1951.

"96 Days to Go." *Time*, February 16, 1948.

Page, Bruce, David Leitch and Phillip Knightley, *The Philby Conspiracy*. Ballantine Books, 1981.

"Palestine: Britain's Crown of Thorns." *The British Empire*, No. 18. London: Time-Life International, 1973.

"Palestine: Wanted, The Wisdom of Solomon." *Newsweek*, August 5, 1946.

Peterson, Edward N., *The American Occupation of Germany: Retreat to Victory*. Wayne State University Press, 1978.

Philby, Kim, *My Silent War*. Grove Press, 1968.

Pincher, Chapman, *Their Trade Is Treachery*. London: Sidgwick & Jackson, 1981.

Pogue, Forrest C., *George C. Marshall: Organizer of Victory*. Viking, 1973.

Price, Harry Bayard, *The Marshall Plan and Its Meaning.* Cornell University Press, 1955.

"The Promised Land." *Time*, August 26, 1946.

Proudfoot, Malcolm J., *European Refugees: 1939-1952.* Northwestern University Press, 1956.

"Reluctant Dragon." *Time*, May 24, 1948.

"Report on Chaos." *Picture Post*, London, September 8, 1945.

The Report of the Royal Commission. Ottawa: Edmond Cloutier, 1946.

Roberts, C. E. Bechhofer, *The Trial of William Joyce.* London: Jarrolds, 1946.

Rodrigo, Robert, *Berlin Airlift.* London: Cassell, 1960.

Rubin, Jacob A., *Pictorial History of the United Nations.* Thomas Yoseloff, 1962.

Seale, Patrick, and Maureen McConville, *Philby: The Long Road to Moscow.* Simon and Schuster, 1973.

Sereny, Gitta, *Into That Darkness.* McGraw-Hill, 1974.

Serfaty, Simon, and Lawrence Gray, eds., *The Italian Communist Party: Yesterday, Today and Tomorrow.* Greenwood Press, 1980.

Seton-Watson, Hugh, *The East European Revolution.* Frederick A. Praeger, 1951.

Smith, Bradley F., *Reaching Judgment at Nuremberg.* Basic Books, 1977.

"A Special Study of Operation 'Vittles.'" *Aviation Operations*, April 1949.

Speer, Albert, *Inside the Third Reich.* Macmillan, 1970.

Solzhenitsyn, Alexander I., *The Gulag Archipelago.* Harper & Row, 1973.

Stone, I. F., *Underground to Palestine.* Pantheon Books, 1978.

Szulc, Tad, *Czechoslovakia since World War II.* Viking, 1971.

Taylor, A. J. P., *The Second World War: An Illustrated History.* G. P. Put-nam's Sons, 1975.

Togliatti, Palmiro, *On Gramsci and Other Writings.* London: Lawrence and Wishart, 1979.

Townsend, Peter, *The Last Emperor.* Simon and Schuster, 1976.

Truman, Harry S., *Memoirs:*
Vol. 1, *Year of Decisions.* Signet Books, 1955.
Vol. 2, *Years of Trial and Hope.* Signet Books, 1956.

Truman, Margaret, *Harry S. Truman.* Pocket Books, 1974.

Ulam, Adam B.:
Expansion and Coexistence. Frederick A. Praeger, 1968.
The Rivals. Viking, 1971.

Urwin, Derek W., *Western Europe since 1945.* London: Longman, 1972.

Voight, Fritz A., *The Greek Sedition.* London: Hollis & Carter, 1949.

Wechsberg, Joseph, ed., *The Murderers among Us: The Simon Wiesenthal Memoirs.* McGraw-Hill, 1967.

Welles, Sam, *Profile of Europe.* Harper & Brothers, 1948.

Werth, Alexander:
France: 1940-1955. Beacon Press, 1966.
Russia: The Post-War Years. Taplinger, 1971.

Woodhouse, C. M., *The Struggle for Greece: 1941-1949.* London: Hart-Davis, MacGibbon, 1976.

Ziemke, Earl F., *The U.S. Army in the Occupation of Germany: 1944-1946.* Center of Military History, United States Army, 1975.

Zink, Harold, *American Military Government in Germany.* Macmillan, 1947.

PICTURE CREDITS

Credits from left to right are separated by semicolons, from top to bottom by dashes.

COVER and page 1: Walter Sanders for *Life*. 2, 3: Map by Bill Hezlep.

THE PRICE OF WAR—8, 9: UPI. 10: Leonard McCombe. 11: Federico Patellani, Milan. 12: BBC Hulton Picture Library, London. 13: Artkino Pictures, Inc. 14, 15: Toni Frissell, courtesy Frissell Collection, Library of Congress; Ernst Haas from Magnum, from *Ende und Anfang*, by Zsolnay Verlag, Vienna. 16, 17: UPI; Imperial War Museum, London. 18, 19: Press Association, London.

NEW RIVALRIES AMID THE ASHES—22: Archives Tallandier, Paris, courtesy Centre Jean Moulin, Bordeaux. 24, 25: Staatliche Landesbildstelle, Hamburg. 26: Sud-deutscher Verlag, Bilderdienst, Munich; UPI. 28: Hans Wild for *Life*. 29: David E. Scherman for *Life*. 30: Saidman from Black Star. 31: *Resistance*, Paris. 33: Mark Kauffman for *Life*—courtesy Time Inc. Picture Collection. 34: Wide World.

GERMANY'S BITTER HARVEST—38: Gehard Gronefeld, Munich. 41: British Official Photo. 42: U.S. Army. 43: Map by Bill Hezlep. 44: Bundesarchiv, Koblenz. 45: U.S. Army. 46: From *The Murderers Among Us*, edited by Joseph Wechsberg, published by McGraw-Hill Book Company, © 1967 by Opéra Mundi, Paris. 47: Private Collection, Karlsruhe. 48: Der Polizeipraesident, Berlin (West). 49: UPI. 50: William Vandivert for *Life*. 53: Toni Schneiders, Lindau, Gesellschaft Erben Otto Dix, Hemmenhofen, courtesy Galerie der Stadt Stuttgart. 54, 55: Toni Schneiders, Lindau, Gesellschaft Erben Otto Dix, Hemmenhofen. 56: Ralph Morse for *Life*. 58: Edward Vebell. 60: BBC Hulton Picture Library, London. 62: Popperfoto, London—Ernst Haas from Magnum, from *Ende und Anfang*, Zsolnay Verlag, Vienna—William Vandivert for *Life*.

JUSTICE AT NUREMBERG—64, 65: Courtesy Time Inc. Picture Collection. 66: Painting by Dame Laura Knight, courtesy Imperial War Museum, London. 67: Walter Sanders for *Life*. 68: U.S. Army, except bottom right UPI. 69-71: U.S. Army. 72, 73: Wide World; Archives Tallandier, Paris—U.S. Army. 74, 75: Wide World. 76: UPI. 77-79: U.S. Army.

ARMIES OF WANDERERS—82: Edward Clark International. 83: Leonard McCombe. 84: National Archives (No. 208-AA-215A-1). 85: BBC Hulton Picture Library, London. 86: U.S. Army. 89, 92: UPI. 94: I. F. Stone. 96: Keystone Press Agency, London. 97: UPI. 98: Keystone Press Agency, London.

VOYAGE INTO ADVERSITY—100, 101: Wide World. 102: Map by Bill Hezlep. 103: Popperfoto, London. 104: Ruth Gruber—Archives Tallandier, Paris. 105: Wide World. 106, 107: Ruth Gruber; *The Times*, London. 108, 109: Photoworld; *The Times*, London. 110, 111: *The Times*, London; Archives of YIVO Institute for Jewish Research.

A NATION BORN IN VIOLENCE—112, 113: National Archives (No. 306-NT-1187-13A). 114: UPI. 115: The Illustrated London News Picture Library, London. 116, 117: Keystone Press Agency, London. 118, 119: Wide World. 120: David Douglas Duncan for *Life*. 121: Keystone Press Agency, London—David Douglas Duncan for *Life*. 122, 123: Wide World. 124, 125: UPI. 126, 127: Frank Scherschel for *Life*, inset UPI.

POLITICS OF CONFRONTATION—130: International Communications Agency. 134: Nick de Margoli for *Life*. 135: UPI. 137: Interpress, Paris. 138: Farabola, Milan. 140: Wide World. 141: Salmi, Milan. 142: Rizzoli, Milan, except bottom left Museo Civico "L. Bailo," Treviso, Italy. 143: Aldo Durazzi, courtesy Comitato Civico Nazionale, Rome; Rizzoli, Milan—Salmi, Milan. 144: Map by Bill Hezlep. 146: Wide World. 147: Dmitri Kessel for *Life*. 148: David Douglas Duncan for *Life*. 149: Anthony Linck for *Life*. 150: David Douglas Duncan for *Life*.

THE MIRACLE OF RECOVERY—152, 153: ECA, courtesy George C. Marshall Research Foundation. 154: Francis Miller for *Life*. 155: U.S. International Communications Agency. 156, 157: Ernst Haas from Magnum, courtesy George C. Marshall Research Foundation—National Archives (2) (Nos. 286-MP-AUS-428; 286-MP-GREE-329). 158: U.S. International Communications Agency, courtesy George C. Marshall Research Foundation; ECA, courtesy George C. Marshall Foundation —National Archives (2) (Nos. 286-MP-GER-914, 286-MP-GER-915). 159: Agency for International Development, courtesy George C. Marshall Research Foundation. 160: U.S. Information Agency Photo; Dmitri Kessel for *Life*—National Archives (No. 286-MP-GREE-1124). 161: National Archives (No. 286-MP-UK-1325). 162, 163: National Archives (Nos. 286-MP-ITA-735—286-MP-AUS-799; 286-MP-ITA-751).

AN IRON CURTAIN DESCENDS—166, 167: Anthony Linck for *Life*. 169: UPI. 170: Walter Sanders for *Life*. 171: UPI—BBC Hulton Picture Library, London. 174: Black Star. 175: Walter Sanders for *Life*. 176: Thomas D. McAvoy for *Life*. 179: Wide World. 180: Keystone, Hamburg. 182: Map by Bill Hezlep. 183: Wide World. 185: U.S. Army—Thomas McAvoy for *Life*. 186: Keystone Press Agency, Ltd., London (2); UPI. 188: Popperfoto, London.

THE BERLIN AIRLIFT—192, 193: Walter Sanders for *Life*. 194: Landesbildstelle, Berlin (West). 195: Walter Sanders for *Life*. 196, 197: AAF, inset National Archives (No. 342-G-93030). 198: Popperfoto, London—National Archives (No. 342-G-71696AC); H. G. Walker for *Life*. 199: Walter Sanders for *Life*. 200, 201: Landesbildstelle, Berlin (West). 202, 203: Ullstein Bilderdienst, Berlin (West).

ACKNOWLEDGMENTS

The editors wish to thank Nino Arena, Rome; Mimi Bloxam, George C. Marshall Research Foundation, Lexington, Va.; Ugo Casiraghi, Milan; Jeannette Chalufour, Archives Tallandier, Paris; Cécile Coutin, Curator, Musée des Deux Guerres Mondiales, Paris; Volker Dünnhaupt, Rheinisches Landesmuseum, Bonn; The Dutch State Institute for War Documentation, Amsterdam; Paul E. Foster, Springfield, Va.; Luigi Gedda, Comitato Civico Nazionale, Rome; Jürgen Grothe, Landesbildstelle, Berlin (West); Hermann Gutermuth, Munich; Edward Hine, Imperial War Museum, London; Marcellin Hodeir, S.H.A.A., Vincennes, France; Alfredo Hummel, Milan; Heidi Klein, Bildarchiv Preussischer Kulturbesitz, Berlin (West); Roland Klemig, Bildarchiv Preussischer Kulturbesitz, Berlin (West); Claude Lévy, Institut d'Histoire du Temps Présent, Paris; Royster Lyle, George C. Marshall Research Foundation, Lexington, Va.; Erika Mayer-Kaupp, Otto Dix Archiv, Hemmenhofen, Germany; Linda McGreevy, Old Dominion University, Norfolk, Va.; Françoise Mercier, Institut d'Histoire du Temps Présent, Paris; the Reverend Lucio Migliaccio, Comitato Civico Nazionale, Rome; Catarina Minet, Rome; Tim Mulligan, National Archives, Washington, D.C.; Maurizio Pagliano, Milan; Hannes Quaschinsky, ADN-Zentralbild, Berlin, DDR; Georges Roland, E.C.P. Armées, Ivry-sur-Seine, France; Eberhard Roters, Gisela-Ingeborg Bolduan Berlinische Galerie, Berlin (West); Wolfgang Streubel, Ullstein Bilderdienst, Berlin (West); Marjorie Willis, BBC Hulton Picture Library, London. Certain passages from *Underground to Palestine* by I. F. Stone, copyright © 1978 by I. F. Stone, reprinted by permission of Pantheon Books, a Division of Random House, Inc. Excerpts from *Decision in Germany* by Lucius D. Clay, copyright 1950 by Lucius D. Clay, reprinted by permission of Doubleday & Company, Inc. The index was prepared by Nicholas J. Anthony.

INDEX

Numerals in italics indicate an illustration of the subject mentioned.

A

Acheson, Dean, 128-129
Albania: Communist control of, 2, 26; and Greek civil war, 145, 151, 177; subversion attempts in, 184, 186-187, 190
Alexander, Harold, 87
Allied Control Council, 36-38, 41, 43-44, 48, 61-63. *See also* Germany, Occupation policies
Allied nations: rivalries among, 20-21, 37; war casualties, 22
Alsace-Lorraine, 25
Amery, John, 23
Angel, Zuleta, 28
Antonescu, Ion, 167
Antwerp, 31
Arabs, and Palestine, *122-125*
Arena, Nino, 136
Athens, 140, 144
Atomic Energy Commission, 189
Attlee, Clement, 30, 41, *42*
Austria: and displaced persons, 96, 98; economic recovery, 155, *156*, 162; Nazis tried by, 23; occupation policies in, 26; war casualties and damage, 22
Axmann, Arthur, 48

B

Baden-Baden, 50, 59
Bamberg, *84*
Baumgard, Victor, 99
Bebler, Aleš, 32
Begin, Menachem, 114
Belgium: black market in, 31; collaborators tried by, 23; Communist pressure in, 26-27, 131-132; economic recovery, 31, *159*; war damage, 22, 31
Belgrade, 22, 31, 130
Beneš, Eduard, 81, 172-173
Bergen-Belsen concentration camp, *41*, 52, 56
Berlin, 83; black market in, *58*, 60-61; blockade and airlift, 178-181, *192-203*; commodities shortages, 52, *62*; displaced persons in, 82; Occupation zones, 36, *map* 43, *map* 182; in prisoners' repatriation, *10, 12*; rehabilitation program, *130*; surrender ceremony, 21, 36; war damage, 37, 51
Bevin, Ernest, 42, 154, 174
Bierut, Boleslaw, *166*
Black market, 30-31, 57, *58*, 59, *60*, 61, 179
Blunt, Anthony, 187
Bohlen, Charles E., 129
Bormann, Martin, 48, *49*, 68
Braun, Wernher von, *185*
Breslau, 82
Brno, 81
Brunoy, *31*
Brussels, 26-27, 132
Brussels, Treaty of, 178
Bucharest, 167
Buchenwald concentration camp, 56
Budapest, 22, 166
Bulgaria: Allied policy on, 168; Communist control of, 168; and Greek civil war, 145, 151, 177; Soviet domination, 26, 168; territorial gains, 25
Burgess, Guy, *186*, 187, 189
Burnham, James, 174
Buschi, Nazzareno, 137
Byrnes, James F., *28*, 40, 42-43, *45*, 61-63

C

Canada, 22, 182-183
Carlini, Michel, 134
Casadei, Giuseppe, 138
Cecchi, Mario, 131
Central Intelligence Agency, 183-184, 186-187
China, and United Nations, 28
Churchill, Winston: and Berlin blockade, 181; and displaced persons, 81; electoral defeat, 27, 41-42, 174; on European devastation, 23, 40-41; and Hitler defeat, 20-21, 41; Iron Curtain speech, 174-175; Occupation policies, 39-42; and Poland boundaries, 39, 81; at Potsdam Conference, 41, 81; and prisoners, repatriation of, 84-86; on Soviet threat, 174-175; Stalin, relations with, 175; and United Nations, 28. *See also* United Kingdom
Clark, Norman, 82
Clay, Lucius D., *44*; and Berlin airlift, 63, 179, 181, 202; and food shortage, 52; and German economic recovery, 61-62; and German self-government, 63; and Occupation policies, 36-38, 40, 43, 178; on Soviet hostility, 178
Collaborators, trials of, 23, 47-48, 132
Cologne, *1*, 51
Connally, Tom, *28, 63*
Cossacks, 87
Currency manipulation and control, 59-61, 179-180
Cyrankiewicz, Jósef, 165
Czechoslovakia: British policy on, 172; Communist control of, 172, *175*; displaced persons from, 91, 95-96, *170-171*; France, relations with, 172; and Germans, mistreatment in, 81; Soviet occupation, 25-26, 172-173; territorial gains, 25

D

Dachau concentration camp, 45, 78
Danzig, 81
De Gasperi, Alcide, 136-137, *138*, 139
De Gaulle, Charles, 43, 131-133, *135*. *See also* France
De Lattre de Tassigny, Jean, 36
De-Nazification program, 23, 36-39, 43, 45-46, *47*, 48, 59, 76
Dimitrov, Georgi, 168
Displaced persons, 10, 17, 21, 51-52, 82-83, *84-86*, 87-93, 95-96, 98, 160, *169-171*, 199
Dix, Otto, *53-55*
Djilas, Milovan, *150*
Dobruja region, 25
Dönitz, Karl, 21, 68, *72*, 76
Donovan, William "Wild Bill," 183
Dos Passos, John, 68
Dresden, 23, *38*
Duclos, Jacques, 134
Dulles, Allen W., 183
Dunn, James C., *138*
Düsseldorf, 51, *171*

E

East Prussia, partition of, 2, 25, 39, 42, 81
Economic Cooperation Administration, 156
Eden, Anthony, 84-86
Eichmann, Adolf, 46-47
Eisenhower, Dwight D.: and German economy, 51-52; and nonfraternization policy, 56-57; and Occupation policies, 37, 39-40; and surrender ceremony, 36
Empoli, *162-163*
England. *See* United Kingdom
Estonia, 2, 25, 88, *169*
Europe: commodities shortages, 21, 23-25, 160; Communist expansion in, *map* 2-3, 26-27, 131; construction program, 158, 160;

displaced persons in, 10, 17, 21, 51-52, 82-83, *84-86*, 87-93, 95-96, 98, 160, *169-171*, 199; economic decline and recovery, 128-131, 154, *155-163*, 177-178, 191; political philosophy changes, 131-132; political structure changes, *map* 2-3, 25-27; Soviet policy in, 129, 164-165, 180; transportation shortage, 10, 21; war casualties and damage, 21-23. *See also individual countries*
Exodus 1947 (ship), *100-101*, 102, *103-105*

F

Federici, Gervasio, 139
Finland: Communists in, 32, 168, 172; reparations to U.S.S.R., 31-32, *33*; Soviet policy on, 168, 172; territorial losses, 25, 31
Forrestal, James V., 85
France: Austria, occupation of, 26; and Berlin airlift, 192, 200; black market in, 30; collaborators tried by, 23, 132; commodities shortages, 10, 30-31; Communist expansion and pressures in, 26-27, 129, 131-134, *135*, *137*; and currency control, 60-61, 179-180; and Czechoslovakia, 172; and displaced persons, 31, 82-84, 98; economic decline and recovery, 30-31, 132, 135, *156*, 160; industrial sabotage in, 134; Jews, emigration from, 98-99, 102, *106-107*; and Marshall Plan, 134; and Occupation policies, 39, 43, 49-50, 173; Occupation zones, 25-27, *map* 43, *map* 182; political unrest in, *34*, 133-135, *137*; and reparations, 39, 42; territorial gains, 25; transportation shortage, 30; and United Nations, 28; war brides, *31*; war casualties and damage, 22-23, *193*; and war criminals, trials of, 66; and West Germany sovereignty, 179. *See also* De Gaulle, Charles
Frank, Anne, 46
Frank, Hans, 66, 68, *69, 77*
Frankfurt am Main, *12*, 51, *192-193*, 196
Frick, Wilhelm, 69
Friedenau, *200-201*
Fritzsche, Hans, 44, 69, 76
Fuchs, Klaus, 182-183
Funk, Walter, 69, 76

G

Garibaldi, Giuseppe, *141*
Gehlen, Reinhard, 183-184
Germany: art control by, 53; atrocities by, 22, *40*, 45-46; black market in, 57-59, *60*, 61, 179; cigarettes, role in economy, 59-61, 179; civilian death rate, 52; commodities shortages, 10, *16*, 37, 51-52, *62*, 83, *179*; communications damage, 51; construction program, *38, 158*; cultural objects destroyed by, 22-23; currency manipulation and control in, 59, 61, 179-180; de-Nazification program, 23, 36-39, 43, 45-46, *47*, 48, 59, 76; displaced persons in, 10, 17, 21, 51-52, 83, *84-86*, 87-93, 95-96, 169, *170-171*, 199; economic aid to, 59, 63, *130*; economic recovery, 61-63, 160, 179-180, 191; housing shortage, *16-17*, *24-25*, 51, 83, 158; Jews, emigration from, *94*, 102; Jews interned in, 102, 107, *108-111*; Jews mistreated by, 40, 45-46; living conditions in, *1*, 10, *40*; military government in, 48-50; military philosophy of, 23-25; morals, standards of, 57, 59; nonfraternization policy in, 39, 56, 57; Occupation policies, 25-27, 36-44, 48-50, 59, 61-63, 178; Occupation zones, *map* 2-3, 25-27, *map* 43, *map* 182; partition into East and West, 2, 44, 178-179, 191; Poles, mistreatment of, *82-83*; prisoners, repatriation of, *10, 13*, 184; public health in, 52; relief agencies in, 83; reparations from,

39, 42, 62-63, 83, 185; self-government restored, 61-63; surrender ceremony and terms, 21, 36; territorial losses, 2, 25, 39, 42, 81; transportation shortage, 12, 51, 58-59; unemployment in, 26, 83, 91; war brides from, 31; war casualties and damage, 37, 50-51; war criminals, escapes by, 46-48; war criminals, trials and executions, 37, 43-45, 64-65, 66, 68-79
Goebbels, Joseph, 44, 66
Gold, Harry, 182-183
Gollancz, Victor, 51-52
Gomulka, Ladislas, 166
Göring, Hermann: art appropriated by, 50; trial and suicide, 66, 67-68, 70, 72, 74-75, 78-79
Gottwald, Klement, 172-173, 174
Gouin, Felix, 133
Gouzenko, Igor, 181-182
Grammos mountains, 145-147, 151
Greece, map 145; assassinations and terrorism in, 144-145, 147-148; commodities shortages, 140; Communist insurgency in, 27, 128-129, 140, 145, 146-148, 149, 150, 151, 184; construction program, 160; economic and military aid to, 128-129, 144, 149, 151, 156; Soviet policy on, 151, 177; war casualties and damage, 140, 144; Yugoslav policy on, 145, 147, 149-151, 177
Grew, Joseph C., 85
Groza, Petru, 167
Gypsies, casualties among, 21-22, 45

H

Haganah, 93-96, 102, 110, 114, 116, 124
Haganah (ship), 98-99
Haifa, 97-98, 99, 100-105
Hamburg: in Berlin airlift, 196; construction program, 158; housing shortage, 16-17, 24-25; Jews interned in, 102, 109; public health in, 52
Harriman, Averell, 173
Havel River, 198
Henderson, Loy, 128
Hess, Rudolf, 68, 70, 72, 75, 76
Himmler, Heinrich, 66
Hitler, Adolf: atrocities by, 44, 191; and German expansion, 191; and Lidice destruction, 22; suicide, 66; and Warsaw destruction, 33
Hoover, J. Edgar, 189-190
Hulme, Kathryn, 89-93
Hungary, 22, 25-26, 165-167

I

International Red Cross, 82-83, 91
Inverchapel, Lord, 128-129
Irgun, 114, 118
Israel, sovereignty proclaimed, 93, 114, 127, 191
Italy: Catholic Church influence in, 138-139, 141; coalition government, 136-137, 138; commodities shortages, 11, 14, 136; Communist expansion and pressures in, 26-27, 129, 131-132, 135-139, 140; and displaced persons, 47, 90, 98-99; economic decline and recovery, 135-136, 138-139, 152-153, 160, 162-163; Fascists tried by, 23; housing shortage, 136; political unrest in, 136-139, 140; propaganda in, 138-139, 141-143; territorial gains and losses, 25; United Nations, entry into, 42; United States policy on, 138; war casualties and damage, 22-23

J

Jackson, Robert H., 44, 64-65, 66, 73
Jaffa, 114
Jerusalem, 115, 121-127
Jews: casualties among, 21-22; emigration by,

92, 94, 95, 98, 99, 100-101, 102, 106-107, 109, 113, 114, 116, 124, 199; mistreatment of, 92, 95
Jodl, Alfred, 69, 70, 76, 77
Joint Chiefs of Staff, 39-40, 43, 49, 56, 178
Joyce, William (Lord Haw-Haw), 23

K

Kaltenbrunner, Ernst, 47, 68, 69, 72, 77
Kaprun power plant, 155
Karelia, 31
Keitel, Wilhelm, 69, 72-73, 76, 77
Kennan, George F., 176
Kielce, 92

L

Lane, Arthur Bliss, 167
Latvia, 2, 25, 88
Laval, Pierre, 23
Lawrence, Geoffrey, 44, 66
League of Nations, 28, 93
Lebanon, 28, 124
Lend-Lease, reductions in, 174
Leningrad, 34
Ley, Robert, 68, 70
Lidice, 22
Limberg dam, 155
Lithuania, 2, 25, 88
Lombardi, Padre, 138
London, 22, 29, 161, 188
Lord Haw-Haw (William Joyce), 23
Lulchev, Kosta, 168

M

Macedonia, 146, 148
Maclean, Donald, 186, 187, 189
Markos, General, 146-147, 149-150
Marseilles, 23, 133-134, 156
Marshall, George C., 154, 176; European Recovery Plan, 128-131, 154, 155-163, 177-178; and Italy, economic aid to, 138; on Soviet hostility, 178
Martin, Clifford, 118-119
Masaryk, Jan, 173-174
Matthews, Kenneth, 144
Mauriac, François, 132
May, Alan Nunn, 182
Michael, King of Rumania, 167
Mihailovich, Drazha, 23
Miklos, Béla, 165-166
Mikolajczyk, Stanislaw, 165
Mindszenty, Josef Cardinal, 166
Moch, Jules, 134
Molotov, Vyacheslav M., 45; and German economic recovery, 61-63; and Marshall Plan, 177; and Occupation policies, 42; and prisoners, repatriation of, 85; and United Kingdom, 174; and United Nations, 173-174; and Yugoslav peace treaty, 32. See also Soviet Union
Montand, Yves, 131
Montgomery, Bernard Law, 36
Morgenthau, Henry, Jr., 39-40, 61-63
Mornos River valley, 150-151
Mulde River, 86
Müller, Heinrich, 47
Murmansk, 86
Murphy, Robert D., 37-38, 40, 42
Musson, Geoffrey, 87

N

Nagy, Ferenc, 166
National Security Act (1947), 183
Neisse River, 25, 39, 81
Nenni, Pietro, 136-137, 138
Netherlands, 23, 131-132, 158
Neurath, Constantin von, 68, 69, 76
North Atlantic Treaty Organization, 178, 191

Norway, 23
Nosek, Václav, 173
Nuremberg: food shortage, 16, 179; war criminals, trials of, 37, 43-45, 64-65, 66, 68-79; war damage, 51

O

Oder River, 25, 39, 81
Office of Strategic Services, 181

P

Paice, Mervin, 118-119
Palermo, 11
Palestine: hostilities in, 114-127; Jews, immigration into, 80, 93-95, 96-98, 99, 100-101, 103-127, 191; partitioning of, 28, 114, 123; United Nations policy on, 28, 114, 123
Pallante, Antonio, 139
Panayolis, Gramatikakis, 147
Pannwitz, Hellmuth von, 87
Papen, Franz von, 68, 76
Paris, 10, 26-27, 34, 137
Pauker, Ana, 167
Pekkala, Mauno, 172
Peloponnesus, 144, 145, 148, 150
Pétain, Henri Philippe, 23
Petkov, Nikola, 168
Petrescu, Titel, 167
Petsamo, 31
Philby, Harold A. R. "Kim," 184-185, 186, 187-190
Pickman, David, 99
Pindus mountains, 145, 146
Piraeus, 149, 156-157
Pokrovsky, Y. V., 73
Poland: Allied policy on, 165-166; Communist control of, 26, 32-33, 164-165, 166-167; displaced persons from, 90-91, 93; Germans, mistreatment of, 82-83; Jews, emigration from, 92, 95, 98, 102, 199; Jews, mistreatment of, 92, 95; reconstruction program, 33-34; territorial gains and losses, 2, 25, 39, 42, 81, 174; war casualties and damage, 8-9, 21-23, 33
Polk, George, 147
Pomerania, 42, 81
Potsdam Conference, 38-41, 42, 43, 61, 83, 85, 88
Pound, Ezra, 23
Prague, 175
Prisoners of war: atrocities against, 45; repatriation of, 10, 13, 84-88, 89, 184
Proudfoot, Malcolm, 82

Q

Quisling, Vidkun, 23

R

Rado, Alexander, 187
Raeder, Erich, 69, 72, 76
Rajk, Lásló, 166
Ramadier, Paul, 133
Rhineland, 39, 42
Ribbentrop, Joachim von, 66, 68, 69, 70, 72, 76, 77
Richter, Hans Werner, 49
Roman Catholic Church, and Communism, 138
Rome, 14, 26-27, 137, 140
Roosevelt, Eleanor, 28
Roosevelt, Franklin D.: death of, 39, 42; Occupation policies, 38-39; and Poland boundaries, 39, 81; and prisoners, repatriation of, 85; and Soviet Union, 173; and United Nations, 28
Rosenberg, Alfred, 69, 77
Rosenberg, Julius and Ethel, 182-183
Royal Air Force, 144, 192, 198, 200
Royal Navy, 96, 102

Ruhr region, 42
Rumania, 25-26, 167
Russell, Bertrand, 82

S

Saar region, 39, 42
Sânâtescu, Constantin, 167
Sanders, Walter, 196
Sartre, Jean-Paul, 134
Sauckel, Fritz, *69, 72, 77*
Scelba, Mario, 139
Schacht, Hjalmar, *68, 70,* 76
Schirach, Baldur von, 68, *69, 72,* 76
Schleswig-Holstein, 52, 83
Schuman, Robert, 30-31, 134-135
Selborne, Lord, 84
Seyss-Inquart, Arthur, *69, 77*
Shawcross, Hartley, 44
Sicily, separatist movement in, 136
Silesia, 39, 42, 81
Simeon, King of Bulgaria, 168
Smith, Walter Bedell, 21, 187, 190
Sokolovsky, Vasily, 43, 180
Solzhenitsyn, Alexander, 20
Sophoulis, Themistocles, 150
Soviet Union: atomic-bomb development, 191; Austria, occupation of, 26; Berlin blockade by, 178-179, *180,* 181-182, *183;* and Berlin Occupation, 37; Bulgaria, occupation of, 26, 167-168; currency manipulation by, 60-61; Czechoslovakia, policy on, 25-26, 172-173; demobilization and rearmament, 35, 184; and displaced persons, 82-86, 88-89; and East Prussia partition, 2, 25, 42, 81; Eastern Europe, control of, 164-165, 177; emergence as superpower, 26; espionage by, 181-190; Finland, policy on, 168, 172; Finland, reparations from, 31-32, *33;* food shortage, 27, 35, 52, 177; and German economy, 34-35, 61-63; and Greek civil war, 141, 177; housing shortage, 34-35; Hungary, occupation of, 26; and Italy, entry into United Nations, 42; Italy, pressure in, 138, 140; and Jews, emigration of, 95; living conditions in, 34-35; and Marshall Plan, 129-130, 133, 137, 172, 177; Occupation policies, 39, 43-44, 49-50, 178; Occupation zones, 25-27, *map* 43, *map* 182; and peace negotiations, 21; Poland, domination of, 26, 33; political prisoners in, 20; political purges in, 177-178; and prisoners, repatriation of, 84-88, *89;* reconstruction program, 34-35; reparations demanded by, 31-32, *33,* 62-63, 83; Rumania, occupation of, 26, 167; and surrender ceremony, 21; territorial gains, *map* 2-3, 20, 25-26, 31, 81, 88; Turkey, pressure on, 130; United Kingdom, relations with, 28, 174, 190-191; and United Nations, 28, 173-174; United States, relations with, 173-178; war casualties and damage, 21, 23, 34, 177; and war criminals, trials of, 44-45, 66; and Warsaw Pact, 191; Yugoslavia, relations with, 32. *See also* Molotov, Vyacheslav M.; Stalin, Josef
Sparta, 147-148
Speer, Albert, *69,* 70, *72,* 76, 78
Stalin, Josef, *141;* Allies, relations with, 35; and Bulgaria, 168; Churchill, relations with, 175; and Czechoslovakia, 172; and displaced persons, 84-86; distrust of associates, 172; and Eastern Europe control, 164-165; European policy, 129, 180; and Finland, 168, 172; and German reparations, 39; and Germany partition, 178; and Greek civil war, 151, 177; and Marshall Plan, 177; Occupation policies, 41-42; and Poland boundaries, 39, 42, 81; and Polish Communism, 164; political purges by, 27; at

Potsdam Conference, 41, 42, 81; and prisoners, repatriation of, 85-86; and surrender ceremony, 21; Tito, relations with, 151, 190-191; and United Kingdom, 174, 190-191; and United Nations, 173; victory announcement, 20; and Yugoslavia, 32. *See also* Soviet Union
Stalin, Yakov, 86
Stalingrad, 34-35, 39, 87
Stangl, Franz, 47
Stanislas II Augustus, King of Poland, 33
Stars and Stripes, 56
Stern Gang, 114, 118
Stettinius, Edward, *28*
Stimson, Henry, 40
Stone, I. F., *94,* 95-96, 98-99
Streicher, Julius, 68, 69, 70, 76, *77,* 94
Stumpfegger, Ludwig, 48
Stuttgart, 63
Sudetenland, refugees from, 10
Svoboda, Ludvik, *174*
Sweden, 88
Switzerland, 10
Syria, 28, 124

T

Tasca, Henry, 138
Tel Aviv, *116,* 119
Thirkell, Angela, 10
Thorez, Maurice, 133, *134,* 135
Tito, Marshal, 32, 87, 147, 151, 190-191. *See also* Yugoslavia
Togliatti, Palmiro, 131, 136-137, *138,* 139-140
Treblinka concentration camp, 47
Trieste, 25
Truman, Harry S.: and Berlin airlift, 181; and Communism containment doctrine, 129-130, 138, 149, 177; and displaced persons, 83, 169; and intelligence agency, 181, 183; and Lend-Lease cuts, 174; Occupation policies, 39-42; and Poland, 81, 174; at Potsdam Conference, 40-41, *42,* 81; on Soviet atomic bomb, 191; and Soviet Union, 173-175, 177; and United Nations, 28. *See also* United States
Tunner, William H., 181, 194, 196
Turkey, 128-130

U

United Kingdom: and Austria occupation, 26; and Berlin airlift, 192, *198,* 200; black market in, 30; Bulgaria, policy on, 168; collaborators tried by, 23; commodities shortages, 10, *18-19,* 27, 30, 52; and Communist pressures, 128; and currency control, 179-180; Czechoslovakia, policy on, 172; and displaced persons, 82-86, 88-89, 92; economic decline and recovery, *26, 27,* 160, *161,* 188; Festival of Britain, *188;* and Greek civil war, 144, 150; housing shortage, 27; industry nationalized, 27; and Jews, emigration of, 95, 99, *100-101, 103-113,* 114, 116, 124; labor unrest in, 27-30; and Lend-Lease cuts, 174; and nonfraternization policy, 57; Occupation policies, 49-50, 178; Occupation zones, 25-27, 39, *map* 43, *map* 182; and Palestine, 93-94, *114-127;* Poland, policy on, 165-166; and prisoners, repatriation of, 85-87; Rumania, policy on, 167; Soviet espionage in, 184-190; Soviet Union, relations with, 28, 174, 190-191; and surrender ceremony, 36; tax programs, 27; transportation shortage, 19; war brides from, *30;* war casualties and damage, 22-23, 26; and war criminals, trials of, 66; welfare programs, 27; and West Germany sovereignty, 179. *See also* Attlee, Clement; Churchill, Winston

United Nations Organization, *28, 29,* 59, 89-93
United States: Albania, subversion attempts in, 184, 186-187, 190; and Austria occupation, 26; Berlin airlift by, 178-181, *192-203;* and black market, 57-61; and Bulgaria, 168; collaborators tried by, 23; and currency manipulation and control, 179-180; demobilization by, *34;* de-Nazification program, 47-48; and displaced persons, 82-86, 88, 92-93, 96, *169;* and Economic Cooperation Administration, 156; economic status, 26; emergence as superpower, 26; and German economy, 61-63; and German scientists, *185;* and German self-government, 61-63; Greece, military aid to, *148-149,* 151; intelligence operations, 181-190; Italy, policy on, 138; nonfraternization policy, 39, *56,* 57; Occupation policies, 25-27, 37, 39-42, 61-63, 178; Occupation zones, *map* 2-3, 25-27, *map* 43, *map* 182; Poland, policy on, 39, 81, 165-166, 174; and prisoners, repatriation of, 85, 87; and reparations, 185; Rumania, policy on, 167; Soviet espionage in, 182-183, 187, 190; Soviet Union, relations with, 173-178; and surrender ceremony, 21, 36; and United Nations, 28; war casualties, 22, 26; and war criminals, trials of, 45, 66; and West Germany sovereignty, 179. *See also* Clay, Lucius D.; Marshall, George C.; Truman, Harry S.
United States Air Force. *See* Berlin, blockade and airlift

V

Vafiades, Markos (General Markos), 146-147, 149-150
Van Fleet, James A., *150*
Vandenberg, Arthur, 63
Varkiza Agreement, 144
Venezia Giulia, 25
Vienna, *15,* 22, 96, 98
Vitsi mountains, 151
Volkov, Konstantin, 187
Vyshinsky, Andrei, *37,* 167-168

W

War brides, *30*
War criminals, trials and executions of, 37, 43-45, *64-65,* 66, 68-79
Warsaw, *8-9,* 10, 22-23, 33-34
Warsaw Pact, 191
Wedemeyer, Albert, 181
West, Rebecca, 68
Wiener Neustadt, 22, 88
Wiesbaden, 196
Wiesenthal, Simon, *46,* 48
Wildflecken, 90-91
Women in Communist forces, 146
Woods, John C., *76*

Y

Yajur, *120*
Yalta Conference, 39, 41, 81, 85, 174
Yugoslavia: civil war in, 32; collaborators tried by, 23; Communist control of, 2, 26, 32, 130; displaced persons from, 91; economic conditions, 32; and Greek civil war, 145, 147, 149-151, 177; morale in, 32; Soviet Union, relations with, 32, 184, 190; territorial gains and losses, 25. *See also* Tito, Marshal

Z

Zakhariadis, Nikos, 150-151
Zhukov, Georgy K., 36-37
Zorin, Valerian, 173